I.B.TAURIS SHORT HISTORIES

I.B.Tauris Short Histories is an authoritative and elegantly written new series which puts a fresh perspective on the way history is taught and understood in the twenty-first century. Designed to have strong appeal to university students and their teachers, as well as to general readers and history enthusiasts, *I.B.Tauris Short Histories* comprises a novel attempt to bring informed interpretation, as well as factual reportage, to historical debate. Addressing key subjects and topics in the fields of history, the history of ideas, religion, classical studies, politics, philosophy and Middle East studies, the series seeks intentionally to move beyond the bland, neutral 'introduction' that so often serves as the primary undergraduate teaching tool. While always providing students and generalists with the core facts that they need to get to grips with the essentials of any particular subject, *I.B.Tauris Short Histories* goes further. It offers new insights into how a topic has been understood in the past, and what different social and cultural factors might have been at work. It brings original perspectives to bear on the manner of its current interpretation. It raises questions and – in its extensive bibliographies – points to further study, even as it suggests answers. Addressing a variety of subjects in a greater degree of depth than is often found in comparable series, yet at the same time in concise and compact handbook form, *I.B.Tauris Short Histories* aims to be 'introductions with an edge'. In combining questioning and searching analysis with informed history writing, it brings history up-to-date for an increasingly complex and globalized digital age.

www.short-histc

'This is an excellent contribution to an excellent series. Professor Swain's *A Short History of the Russian Revolution* is invaluable reading for those who seek to understand the Bolshevik seizure of power in October 1917. This brief, clearly argued and well-illustrated volume brings to bear decades of research of one of Britain's leading historians of the Russian Revolution.'

– James Harris, Senior Lecturer in Modern European History, University of Leeds

A Short History of . . .

A SHORT HISTORY OF THE RUSSIAN REVOLUTION

Geoffrey Swain

I.B. TAURIS

LONDON · NEW YORK

Published in 2017 by
I.B.Tauris & Co. Ltd
London • New York
www.ibtauris.com

ISBN: 978 1 78076 792 5 (HB)
ISBN: 978 1 78076 793 2 (PB)
eISBN: 978 1 78672 188 4
ePDF: 978 1 78673 188 3

A full CIP record for this book is available from the British Library
A full CIP record is available from the Library of Congress

Library of Congress Catalog Card Number: available

Typeset by Fakenham Prepress Solutions, Fakenham, Norfolk NR21 8NN
Printed and bound in Great Britain by T.J. International, Padstow, Cornwall

To Di

Contents

List of Illustrations

All images are public domain, unless stated otherwise.

Acknowledgements

This book is the product of many years' academic research and teaching. I would like to acknowledge the intellectual stimulation provided by teaching students at the universities of Cardiff, the West of England, and Glasgow, as well as the insights gained in discussions at conferences of the Study Group on the Russian Revolution.

Timeline

Note: until 1 February 1918 Russia used the old Julian Calendar, meaning that events took place 13 days before the date in those countries using the modern Gregorian Calendar. 1 February 1918 old style became 14 February 1918 new style.

1905

9 January	Bloody Sunday and the start of the 1905 Revolution.
16–17 February	Elected factory delegates debate their response to Bloody Sunday.
13–19 October	The general strike which forced the Tsar to issue his October Manifesto, promising to involve an elected assembly in future legislation.
13 October–3 December	The St Petersburg Soviet represents workers in discussions with the city authorities, before its Chairman Trotsky and other leaders are arrested.

1906

23 April	Reform of the Fundamental Law details the limited powers of the State Duma and formalises the undemocratic franchise for its election.
27 April–9 July	Sessions of the First State Duma. The Duma was

dissolved when it insisted on pushing ahead with land reform.

1907

20 February– 3 June	Sessions of the Second State Duma reveal that the Social Democrats found it easier to work with peasant representatives than liberal ones. The Duma was dissolved when it refused to pass the government's proposal for land reform.
15 November	Opening of Third State Duma on a revised and more restrictive franchise. The government's land reform was passed.

1908

10–16 December	Congress of Women's Organisations.

1909

1–6 April	Congress of Factory Panel Doctors – adopted Theses on Social Insurance.
28 December– 6 January 1910	Temperance Congress.

1911

15–29 January	Congress of Handicraft Trades.
February–March	The petition campaign highlights disagreements between reformist and revolutionary worker activists.

1912

4 April	Lena Gold Fields massacre.
3 June	Closure of the Third State Duma; one of its last acts was to pass a social insurance law.
1 November	Fourth State Duma opens.

1913

January	First elections to insurance councils; only eight factories involved.
September	Elections to insurance councils in St Petersburg; reformists defeated.

1914

March	Elections to St Petersburg city and provincial insurance boards; reformists defeated.

1915

27 September	Meeting of St Petersburg factory delegates to appoint representatives to War Industries' Committee. Reformists defeated; no support for war effort.
29 November	Rerun of these elections after Gvozdev's intervention. War effort supported.

1916

October	Elections to St Petersburg city and provincial insurance boards; reformists defeated.
1 November	Liberal leader Pavel Milyukov asks in Duma whether it is 'stupidity or treason' that guides the Tsar's poor handling of the war effort.

17 December	Murder of Rasputin held to be responsible for the Tsar's stubborn refusal to work with the Duma and liberal opinion in pursuing the war effort.

1917

26–27 January	Arrest of leading members of the Workers' Group on the War Industries' Committee, allegedly planning protests when the Duma session reconvened on 14 February.
22 February	As political turf wars caused the distribution of already limited food supplies to collapse, striking workers from the Putilov Works warn their representatives in the Duma that revolution is imminent.
23–28 February	Workers' demonstrations provoke the February Revolution and the overthrow of the Tsar. The key turning point came on 26–27 February when first one and then many military units refused to fire on the demonstrating workers.
27 February	Moves to re-establish the St Petersburg, now Petrograd, Soviet.
28 February	Duma commissioners take over the government ministries.
1 March	Petrograd Soviet extended to involve soldiers as well as workers. To reassure those soldiers who had mutinied by refusing to fire on workers, the Soviet passes Order No. 1, insisting that military orders stemming from the Provisional Government, still in the process of formation, had to be endorsed by the Soviet.
2 March	The membership of the First Provisional Government agreed: there will be no ministers representing the Soviet, but the Socialist Revolutionary and Duma deputy Kerensky will join the liberals as a lone socialist voice. The Tsar abdicates.

10 March	Soviet issues Declaration of the Rights of Soldiers, pre-empting the work of the government's commission on army reform.
10–11 March	Petrograd returns to work.
March	A series of liberal reforms establish Russia as a democratic state, freed of religious and social oppression.
14 March	Soviet resolution calls for a democratic peace.
24 March	Foreign Minister Milyukov tells press of Russia's need to acquire territory from Austria–Hungary and Turkey.
4 April	Lenin reads out his April Theses, having returned from exile the previous day. His journey from Switzerland, in a sealed train across Germany, caused much controversy.
19 April	Despite a common statement by the Soviet and Provisional Government on war aims being agreed on 27 March, Milyukov wrote to the Allies suggesting that obligations undertaken by the Tsar would be honoured; the Tsar had signed secret treaties on the acquisition of territory from Austria–Hungary and Turkey.
20–21 April	Demonstrations by soldiers and workers in protest at Milyukov's apparent determination that the Provisional Government to ignore the Soviet's call for a democratic peace. Soon afterwards, Milyukov resigned.
4–28 May	All-Russian Congress of Peasant Deputies.
5 May	Formation of the First Coalition Government. For the next two months, guided by Tsereteli, the Soviet Executive works to prove itself a loyal partner in government.
12 May	Kerensky commits the Russian Army to an offensive and starts a series of tours of the front.
23 May	The Bolshevik Military Organisation resolves to oppose any attempt to involve troops from the Petrograd garrison in the offensive.
27 May	The Conference of Petrograd People's Militias protests at Tsereteli's decision to wind up the

	negotiations, on 18 July, General Kornilov is appointed Supreme Commander.
17 July	Inter-district Conference of Soviets re-established and quickly falls under Bolshevik leadership.
7 August	Second Conference of Factory Committees, dominated by Bolsheviks.
10 August	Kornilov and Kerensky meet to discuss Kornilov's 'programme', which included the restoration of the death penalty and the establishment of military rule over the war economy.
12–15 August	The Moscow State Conference gives Kornilov a hero's welcome.
23 August	Ministry of Labour circular clarifying the limited powers of factory committees.
23–24 August	Talks between Kerensky's representative and Kornilov seem to go well: most of Kornilov's 'programme' would be introduced and any Bolshevik protest firmly resisted.
26–27 August	Kerensky warned that Kornilov is in fact preparing to stage a military coup. In response, he calls on the Soviet to defend the revolution.
1 September	Petrograd Soviet votes for a Soviet Government, a vote repeated on 9 September.
14–22 September	Democratic Conference backs the proposal for a third Coalition Government headed by Kerensky.
24 September	Bolsheviks vote not to participate in the Pre-parliament, to which the Third Coalition Government would have some responsibility.
25 September	Third Coalition Government formed.
6 October	Commander of the Petrograd Military District told to prepare to move garrison troops to the front.
7 October	The Bolsheviks walk out of the Pre-parliament.
10 October	Lenin attends a meeting of the Bolshevik Central Committee which puts an insurrection 'on the order of the day'.
12 October	Trotsky, now Soviet chairman, established the Soviet's Military Revolutionary Committee

	(MRC) to prevent garrison troops being redeployed.
16 October	The Bolshevik Central Committee again debates insurrection. The following day, Zinoviev and Kamenev make public their opposition to an insurrection.
17–22 October	First All-Russian Conference of Factory Committees.
18–21 October	Conference of the Petrograd Garrison.
21–23 October	MRC deploys commissars to all garrison units.
24 October	Kerensky closes the Bolshevik press and demands the arrest of the MRC commissars. Soldiers and Red Guards reopen the Bolshevik press and prevent the arrest of commissars. The cruiser *Aurora* supports the MRC. The Pre-parliament passes a vote of no confidence in Kerensky. Delegates to the Second Congress of Soviets vote to establish a Soviet Coalition Government. Lenin urges the Bolsheviks to seize power.
25 October	MRC takes control of strategic points of Petrograd. Troops loyal to Kerensky defend the Winter Palace, which surrenders only between 2 am and 3 am on 26 October. Second Congress of Soviets votes to establish a Soviet Government, but does not discuss its composition.
26 October	The newly formed Left SR (Socialist Revolutionary) party declines a Bolshevik invitation to join them in government. At 2.30 am on the morning of 27 October, the Bolsheviks announce the composition of their purely Bolshevik administration.
28 October	The Railway Workers' Union (Vikzhel) calls for the formation of a Soviet Coalition Government.
29 October	Officer cadets loyal to Kerensky try to overthrow the Bolsheviks. Talks brokered by Vikzhel begin with the aim of forming a Soviet Coalition Government.
30 October	A military advance by troops loyal to Kerensky

	is defeated on the outskirts of Petrograd by Red Guard units organised by the MRC and commanded by Lt.-Col. Muraviev.
31 October– 4 November	Talks on the formation of a Soviet Coalition Government continue. Agreement seems possible, but Lenin uses party discipline to prevent it.
4 November	Those Bolsheviks opposed to Lenin resign from his government in protest.
11 November	Extraordinary Congress of Peasant Soviets backs Left SRs.
12 November	Elections to Constituent Assembly begin.
14 November	Bolsheviks and Left SRs agree in principle to form a government. A Left SR appointed commissar of agriculture.
14–16 November	Contradictory instructions from the Bolshevik Government and the Fifth Congress of Petrograd Factory Committees on workers' rights.
20 November	Once the armies deployed in the North and West come out in support of the MRC, Lenin feels strong enough to arrest Kerensky's Supreme Army Commander and push ahead with armistice talks.
27 November	Second Congress of Peasant Soviets confirms backing for Left SRs.
2 December	Armistice agreed with Germany and Austria-Hungary.
9 December	Left SRs formally join government with four portfolios.
15 December	The Left SR commissar of justice achieves the release of political prisoners arrested by the MRC.

1918

4 January	After a trial of strength with the Bolsheviks, the Left SRs secure the right to be represented in the Cheka, the new secret police.
5 January	Constituent Assembly dissolved, after which

	the Third Congress of Soviets and the Third Congress of Peasant Soviets merge to form a new sovereign Soviet Executive.
7–14 January	First Trade Union Congress restricts the power of factory committees.
28 January	Peace talks at Brest-Litovsk break down and Trotsky announces a policy of 'no peace, no war'.
1/14 February	Russia moves from the Julian to the Gregorian calendar.
16 February	Germany announces it will resume fighting on 18 February, which it does.
18–19 February	Bolshevik and Left SR members of the government vote to seek new terms with Germany. When those terms are known, on 23 February, Lenin persuades the Bolsheviks to accept them, but the Left SRs will not.
3 March	Treaty of Brest-Litovsk signed, endorsed by the Fourth Congress of Soviets on 15 March. The Left SRs leave the government.
13 March	First meeting of the 'Workers' Conference of Factory Representatives', reflecting loss of Bolshevik support in factories.
15 May	Discussions begin with the German ambassador about a possible trade treaty. This marks the end of a period when Trotsky had suggested that the 'breathing space' offered by the Treaty of Brest-Litovsk might only last 'a couple of months' and contacts with Britain and France had continued.
8 June	Building on 'production brigades' established the previous month to extract grain from the peasantry by force, 'committees of the poor' are established by the Bolsheviks to support the expropriation of grain from 'kulaks' (rich peasants). On 11 June the Left SRs announce that the Peasant Section of the Soviet would resist this policy.
24 June	Left SRs call for an end to Lenin's 'breathing

space' and for terror to be used against 'representatives of German imperialism'.

6 July Left SRs assassinate the German ambassador. Bolshevik gerrymandering of the elections to the Fifth Congress of Soviets has convinced them there was no democratic way of preventing Lenin's Russia from becoming 'a colony of German imperialism'. The Left SR attempt to impose a new coalition of equal numbers of Left SRs and anti-Lenin Bolsheviks fails.

Introduction

It is no exaggeration to say that the events of 1917 in Russia set the political map for the rest of the twentieth century. The October Revolution of that year set in train the communist experiment, and the triumph of communism in the Soviet Union in the 1920s and 1930s prompted, as a reaction, the rise of fascism and Nazism in Europe and culminated in the barbaric horrors of World War II. Then, until the collapse of the Soviet Union in 1991, the obsession during the Cold War was the expansion of communism and its containment. Most of the history of the twentieth century can be traced back to the events of the night of 24–25 October 1917 when the street action which brought the Bolsheviks to power took place.[1] So how did Lenin and the Bolsheviks win and consolidate their power?

Writing history is all about editing the past to make sense of it. Writing a Short History of the complex events which occurred in Russia between February 1917 and July 1918 inevitably means that much has to be left out; however, even in a Short History there is a duty to suggest some interpretive guidelines through the maze of confusion that is the Russian Revolution. The interpretation offered here is simple and twofold. It is argued first, as Soviet scholars once argued, that the October Revolution represented the culmination of those revolutionary ambitions first articulated by Russia's masses during the failed 1905 Revolution; the essence of 'October' was a popular revolution against a discredited Provisional Government which restored the revolution to the path it had been on when the Tsar was overthrown in February. Second, however, and quite unlike

1

any Soviet scholarship, it is argued here that Bolshevik concepts of discipline and ideology meant that the party which had guided the masses to 'October' directed them in the months that followed along an unnecessary path which led to dictatorship and terror; enforcing an ideological view of history which insisted that only the working class could lead a socialist revolution led inexorably to one-party rule.

In terms of history writing, this Short History, written one hundred years after the events it describes, draws on two basic bodies of research: the social history mostly written in the 1970s and 1980s which did much to restore the idea of 'October' as a popular revolution, and more recent studies of the first year of Soviet rule in Russia, mostly written in the years after the collapse of the Soviet Union, which explored the formation of the Bolshevik dictatorship. On the 75th anniversary of 'October', the historian Richard Pipes, emphasising Lenin's role in the revolution, wrote, 'October was not a revolution but a classic coup d'état planned in the dead of night of October 10, and executed two weeks later, also at night [...] So surreptitious was the whole undertaking that the ever-cautious Lenin would not allow his plans to be committed to paper.'[2] Pipes went on to criticise those social historians who had asserted after reading 'mountains of innocuous [archive] papers documenting social matters' that the Bolsheviks rose to power in the wake of an explosion of popular anger. The work of Steve Smith and William Rosenberg on workers, Rex Wade on Red Guards, Alan Wildman on soldiers, Graham Gill on peasants, Moira Donald and, later, Sarah Badcock on women all showed rising impatience with Kerensky's Government as October and the Second Congress of Soviets approached.[3] This Short History will not consign such scholars to the dustbin of history.

The starting point for this Short History is to challenge ideas first developed 50 years ago in the West and still extremely popular in twenty-first-century Russia. In the 1960s the orthodox view, largely derived from the writings of Leonard Schapiro, was that, after the trauma of the 1905 Revolution, Imperial Russia entered a constitutional phase and the Russian labour movement settled into a tradition of reform rather than revolution. The Imperial State Duma, summoned for the first time in April 1906, was not a perfect form of parliamentary representation, but it marked a first step. Adapting to this reality, the labour movement moved away from a concern with revolutionary general strikes and towards German trade unionism. Schapiro looked at the development of a legal labour movement in Russia after 1905 and saw trade unions and other working-class organisations under moderate Menshevik leadership; at the same time he saw a weakened Bolshevik underground, betrayed left, right and centre by police agents. From this perspective, the Mensheviks emerged as the legitimate representatives of the working class, both during World War I, when they were willing to co-operate with liberal politicians both inside the State Duma and outside it, and in early 1917, when they supported the formation of a Provisional Government and eventually joined a Coalition Government. For Schapiro and others, the Mensheviks were the legitimate voice of the Russian worker and the Bolsheviks were the usurpers; the growth in support for the Bolsheviks by autumn 1917 was an ephemeral aberration, but an aberration that gave the Bolsheviks the opportunity to seize power.[4]

This Short History argues, on the contrary, that, from 1905 onwards, the Russian working class was consistently revolutionary rather than reformist in outlook, and that the aberration came in February 1917 when chance events put leading reformists in charge of the newly formed Soviet; by the end of June, if not earlier, the Bolsheviks had worked hard to help reassert the traditional revolutionary response of the working class. Winning over the soldiers took longer, but by September 1917 that too had been achieved, allowing the Bolsheviks to gain control of the Petrograd Soviet. Peasants were another matter. The Bolsheviks had little control over the peasants, but by autumn 1917 the only way to stop peasant disturbances was to grant the peasants what they and most Socialist Revolutionaries demanded: temporary control of the land they saw as theirs. One hundred years after the events of 1917 it is clear that the Bolsheviks were trying to give political form to an explosion of popular fury which was pushing towards a second revolution.

Yet the way that popular fury was channelled towards the political purposes of the Bolsheviks did involve elements of what Pipes called 'a classic coup d'état'. The Bolsheviks wanted to ensure that it was they who benefitted from the overthrow of Kerensky. Kerensky's Government was collapsing, the Second Congress of Soviets was going to establish a Soviet Government, and Lenin believed action was essential to ensure that it was the Bolsheviks who controlled that Soviet Government. The coup element to October 1917 was not to overthrow Kerensky but to prevent the other political parties in the Soviet, Mensheviks and Socialist Revolutionaries, from sharing political power with the Bolsheviks in a Soviet Government. It was also a coup against those members of the Bolshevik Party who were willing to work with other socialist political parties

The Bolshevik dictatorship did not begin in October 1917. Although Lenin had wanted the Bolsheviks to rule alone, the political realities of that autumn meant that the Bolsheviks could not avoid sharing power with the political representatives of the peasantry. For Lenin this was an unhappy alliance. Ideology told him that the construction of socialism in a backward peasant country like Russia was only possible with the support of the poor peasantry; an alliance with the peasantry at large was to risk being swamped by the country's peasant majority. So the Bolsheviks formed a coalition not with the Socialist Revolutionaries but with the left wing of that party, the Left Socialist Revolutionaries or Left SRs, the political voice of the poor peasant. When, however, the Left SRs seemed to be strong enough to vote the Bolsheviks out of power, the Bolsheviks adopted the classic tactic of authoritarian rule and rigged the elections to the Fifth Congress of Soviets in July 1918.

Speaking on British television on 3 November 1996, President Mikhail Gorbachev, the last leader of the Soviet Union, was asked by a member of the studio audience if there was any moment in history he would like to have changed. He answered, ignoring all the tempestuous developments during his own years in power, by turning to 1917. He said, to the obvious confusion of many of those present, that he would like to have seen 'the February Revolution continue its course', and added that if this had happened then there would have been no Stalin.[5] This Short History will explore when and how the processes set in train by the overthrow of the Tsar in February 1917 were derailed, and how Bolshevik theories of party discipline and an ideological conviction that the peasantry had to be led to socialism ended by creating a one-party dictatorship.

1

THE REVOLUTIONARY TRADITION OF RUSSIAN LABOUR

In 1917, Russia had been set on a course for revolution for over a decade. Since the 1905 Revolution, unrest which lasted in fact from the end of 1904 until the summer of 1907, the Tsar's control over the working masses of the population was tenuous and maintained by force. Pressurised by a revolutionary general strike to introduce a constitution of a sort, the Tsar reneged on his promise as soon as he could. The State Duma granted in 1906 had very limited powers to control legislation, and was based on an indirect electoral system which dramatically underrepresented the working-class and peasant population. When even this sham electoral system failed to produce a pliant assembly, the electoral system was adjusted on 3 June 1907, in a move technically illegal under the Tsar's own constitution; thereafter even fewer workers and peasants were elected to the Third State Duma, the only assembly to last a full term.

Throughout the 'constitutional' period of Russia's history, from 1906 to 1917, Russia's liberal politicians, led by the Constitutional Democrat or Kadet Party, hoped that work within this unrepresentative and rigged assembly could persuade the Tsar to make further constitutional concessions. The majority of labour movement politicians, however, rejected such a reformist strategy and supported the view of the Bolshevik faction of the Russian Social Democrats that the only way forward in Russia was for there to be a second revolution. For all Russian revolutionaries, the 1905 Revolution was merely a 'dress rehearsal' for the real event. What did that dress rehearsal show Russian workers? It showed that the opposition to the Tsarist autocracy could only remain united for a limited period; it showed that while initially united and nationwide, the fissures between the liberal and socialist opponents of the Tsar quickly became acute; and it showed that the 'muscle' of the revolutionary struggle, which the organised working class provided, felt let down by the actions of the liberal elite in October 1905. As the political outlook of organised labour stabilised during the course of 1905, so most workers favoured advancing their own socialist programme rather than joint action in coalition with the liberals. This evolution was clearly seen in the events of 1905 itself, but was as clear in the events which followed, in particular the short-lived 'parliamentary' months of spring 1907; the revived labour unrest of 1912–14 after the Lena Gold Fields massacre; and the election of a workers' group to the War Industries' Committee in 1915. On all four occasions, when faced with a choice between reform and revolution, Russian workers opted for revolution.

THE ST PETERSBURG SOVIET IN 1905

The 1905 Revolution is best remembered for Bloody Sunday, 9 January 1905, the day a demonstration of unarmed workers tried to present the Tsar with a petition calling for political reform, but were met instead by a hail of bullets; 96 demonstrators died instantly and a further 34 later succumbed to their wounds, while 333 were injured. That petition was a strange document, a confusing combination of reformist and revolutionary demands, beginning with a plea to seek 'justice and protection' for 'our wives, children and helpless old parents' but also listing a series of revolutionary demands – for freedom of speech, for a free press, for freedom of religion and for freedom of association – and linking those demands to the need for an accountable government formed through a Constituent Assembly elected on universal, secret and equal suffrage; such an assembly would then legislate for free universal education, the eight-hour day and a social insurance system administered by elected worker representatives, these being the measures felt to be most essential in improving the workers' lot.[1]

The origins of that petition went back to the last months of 1904, when liberal-led opposition to the Tsar was beginning to mobilise. In January 1904, Imperial Russia had gone to war with Imperial Japan over rival claims for influence in Manchuria and Korea. The war did not go well for the Tsar, with the sinking of the Pacific fleet and the eventual fall of the besieged naval base at Port Arthur. Soon, opposition began to mobilise around liberal members of Russia's local government councils. Ever since these elected local councils – called *dumas* in the towns and *zemstvos* in the countryside – had first been established in the 1860s, liberal politicians had argued that it was anomalous that the Tsar allowed elected councils, albeit on a very restricted franchise, to operate at local government level, while insisting that at national level no representative assembly was possible. Ever since 1879, when for reasons of international diplomacy the Tsar encouraged the formation of the new Bulgarian state as a constitutional monarchy but still insisted that Russia should have no constitution itself, there had been demands from liberal politicians that the Tsar call a national *Zemstvo* Congress. By autumn 1904, unrest provoked by the war with Japan was such that, from 6 to 8 November 1904, a *Zemstvo* Congress was finally held. It reached two broad conclusions: first, that pressure needed to be put on the Tsar to agree to the formation of a legislative assembly, putting on one side for the moment the question of how representative that assembly should be; and second, that all public bodies should send petitions to the Tsar, urging him to make these changes.

The more radical among the liberals decided to broaden this petition campaign and imitate the actions of the French liberals before the 1848 Revolution and organise a Banquet Campaign: since public assemblies were unlawful, notionally 'private' banquets should be held with doctors, lawyers and other professionals and these banquets should then draw up further petitions to be sent to the Tsar. Could the industrial working class be included in this petition campaign? Back in February 1904, the St Petersburg authorities had allowed the Russian Orthodox priest Father Gapon to establish an Assembly of St Petersburg Factory Workers. His vision was that a Christian trade union movement might evolve in Russia on the basis of this initiative, loyal to traditional social values but prepared to confront exploitative employers. At first the Assembly grew slowly, with only three branches being formed between February and September, but then it grew exponentially: eight more branches had opened by December with a total membership of 10,000. Liberal activists, concerned to involve the labour movement in their struggle, saw the potential offered by Gapon's Assembly and encouraged him to become involved in the petition campaign, providing some working-class muscle for the broad 'all-class' opposition movement against the Tsarist autocracy. Gapon hesitated at first, but was persuaded.

Father Gapon was not alone in trying to organise the working class. By the start of the twentieth century, underground socialist parties were emerging, most notably the Socialist Revolutionary Party (SR), which identified the peasantry as the revolutionary class and sought to strengthen links with it, and the Social Democratic Party, which followed Karl Marx in identifying the urban working class as the vanguard for revolutionary change. Many Social Democrats and SRs also joined the Gapon Assembly, hoping gradually to take control of the organisation and push it away from what they saw as Gapon's Christian reformism. It was Social Democrat activists in the Assembly who persuaded the hesitant Gapon to join the petition campaign. Their task was made easier by the actions of the St Petersburg industrialists. They had become increasingly wary of the Gapon Assembly, which appeared determined to lay the groundwork for a trade union movement in Russia, and on 27 December the administration of the massive Putilov Works, one of the biggest employers in the capital, decided to sack four members of the Gapon Assembly as 'trouble-makers' in a move designed to break its influence. Within days, 25,000 workers had downed tools in protest and by the end of the first week in January 1905 over 400,000 workers were on strike. Gapon held talks with the Putilov director on 5 January, but when these failed, the Assembly committed itself to marching with a petition to the Winter Palace. Gapon ran the final text of the petition past his political advisors before the march began.[2]

After Bloody Sunday, revolutionary events in St Petersburg went in two, parallel directions: first, the Social Democrats and SRs captured control of the labour movement; and second, the various liberal groups opposing the Tsar showed themselves ready to do a deal with the Tsar before the concerns of the workers had been addressed. To calm the strike wave unleashed by Bloody Sunday, the Tsar agreed to reduce the length of the working day in the capital and to establish a commission of enquiry. However, he was also determined that the work of the commission of enquiry should not be politicised and so, before it met, he closed down all 11 branches of the Gapon Assembly. When moves to establish the commission of enquiry began, it was announced that workers would be invited to elect their own delegates to it, and workers used these elections of 13 February at first to demand that the ban on the Gapon Assembly be lifted, and when this did not happen, and in part because this did not happen, the workers turned instead to the Social Democrats and SRs. To quote the historian Gerald Surh, 'St Petersburg workers were not only organizing but reaching toward new organizational forms, of which the Soviet of Workers' Deputies would later prove to be the most developed and popular embodiment.' For the first time, Russia's illegal revolutionary parties were able to emerge from underground and agitate among the masses: when the 417 elected worker representatives assembled for a series of pre-meetings on 16–17 February, the assembly was chaired by a radical lawyer, G. S. Nosar, who assumed the identity of one of the worker electors, P. A. Khrustalev. At this meeting it was agreed to demand the reopening of the closed Gapon Assembly branches; immunity from prosecution for all members of the commission of enquiry; and the release of all those arrested since 1 January 1905.[3]

The second demand of the workers' representatives on the commission of enquiry proved to be one the Tsar simply could not meet. The workers insisted that their representatives should have immunity from prosecution because they intended to repeat the demand of the Gapon petition that a Constituent Assembly was the only way to bring harmony and prosperity to Russia; since this demand could be interpreted as anti-state propaganda, they did not want to be arrested for raising what they saw as an essential issues. The Tsar wanted his commission of enquiry to consider only the social causes of unrest and not to become a focus for political agitation, and so this second workers' demand was never agreed to and as a result the commission of enquiry was boycotted by its worker representatives. The 417 worker electors, on the other hand, did not return quietly to their factories: they continued to meet, if infrequently, and, particularly within the factories from which they had been elected, they began to form the nucleus of trade union representation. The Tsar's commission of enquiry fiasco opened the way for the start of a legal labour movement in Russia which radical socialists were increasingly able to dominate.[4]

These events within the factories of St Petersburg were not making the headlines in the first half of 1905. It was the various liberal opponents of the Tsar who were making the running. More *zemstvo* congresses were held and under this pressure the Tsar decided to make a concession: on 6 August he agreed that elections could be held to a nationwide assembly, to be called the State Duma; however, the powers of this assembly would be entirely consultative. The Tsar hoped that this would be enough to divide his liberal opponents. On 25 August the war with Japan was brought to an end and when the Fourth *Zemstvo* Congress met on 12–15 September, the liberals did indeed split into a more conservative wing, ready to accept the Tsar's offer of a consultative assembly, and those more radical liberals who wanted to continue the struggle for a legislative assembly.

The Tsar's strategy was blown off course by the re-emergence of labour unrest in the autumn. What began on 19 September as a localised printers' strike in Moscow, prompted by the employers' attempt to claw back some of the salary increase offered at the start of the year, quickly spread. Disentangling economic from political motivations for striking was impossible in autumn 1905. As part of the Tsar's response to Bloody Sunday, a review of strike legislation was underway and on 20 September the minister of justice made public a circular instructing its representatives to cease prosecuting strikers; then, early in October, the minister of the interior agreed to release the leaders of a strike at the Obukhov Works. In this climate, any strike had political connotations and the whole of Moscow was soon supporting the striking printers, and the printers in St Petersburg came out in sympathy with their Moscow comrades on 3 October. Then other workers joined in, including the railway workers who took up the printers' cause. By 9 October, railway workers in Moscow were on strike, joined three days later by St Petersburg railway workers. Russia's first ever nationwide general strike was underway.[5]

The ad hoc strike committee, established in the capital to co-ordinate activity and enforce discipline, decided to increase its authority by establishing an elected workers' council. This called for elections to be held on the same basis as those that had been held in February for the earlier commission of enquiry. In this way the St Petersburg Soviet was established, which at its height in November 1905 was composed of 562 delegates from 181 factories and 16 trade unions. Ura Shuster has suggested that many of the 'electors' of February became 'representatives' within their factories over the summer months and were then elected once again to the Soviet in the autumn.[6] Such continuity was reinforced by the decision of the St Petersburg Soviet to elect Khrustalev-Nosar as its chairman; his subsequent arrest led to the future Bolshevik leader Leon Trotsky taking his place. The Soviet's executive also included representatives from the illegal Social Democrat and SR parties.

By 17 October the strike in St Petersburg was so solid that the Tsar had to retreat further. His October Manifesto issued that day made clear that his planned State Duma would go ahead, but that now 'no law shall take effect without confirmation by the State Duma' and elected deputies would 'participate in the supervision of the legality' of the actions of his 'appointed officials'. The manifesto also referred to 'granting the population the essential foundations of civil freedom, based on the principles of genuine inviolability of the person, freedom of conscience, speech, assembly and association'. However, the manifesto did not specify how any of this was to be guaranteed.[7] As Trotsky famously declared on 18 October at a rally in the grounds of St Petersburg University, the Tsar's October Manifesto was nothing but 'a scrap of paper' offering no clarity on the precise powers of the proposed State Duma nor the franchise on which it was to be elected; it was a far cry from the demand in the Gapon petition which had clearly called for a Constituent Assembly.

For the majority of liberals, however, the Tsar had crossed the Rubicon; the State Duma would have legislative power and this was something with which they could work, so they proposed that the strike be called off. The St Petersburg Soviet, on the other hand, called for the strike to continue. Although Trotsky and the other leaders of the St Petersburg Soviet hoped in their heart of hearts that the Tsar might yet be forced to abdicate, they focused on a more immediate demand, that of an amnesty for all political prisoners. On 21 October, Trotsky and the St Petersburg Soviet leadership met the Tsar's newly appointed prime minister and pressed their case, and although there was no blanket amnesty, on 22 October the Tsar did issue a decree releasing from prison those, including Trotsky's wife, who had been arrested since the spring. There was another partial victory when at the end of October mutinies occurred at the Kronstadt naval base situated on an island just outside St Petersburg in the Gulf of Finland; sailors had wrongly assumed that the promised right to form associations might include them. Although the release of the arrested 'mutineers' was beyond the Soviet's power, the authorities were forced to reassure the Soviet on 5 November that none of those involved would be executed. Despite such successes, by early November it was clear that the workers' appetite for the general strike was running out of steam and so Trotsky decided that the time had come to organise a return to work. Threatened strike action called by the Soviet could force concessions from the authorities as late as 23 November, but gradually, things moved in the Tsar's favour.[8]

The end of the war with Japan meant that battle-hardened troops could be brought back from the Far East. On 3 December the leaders of the St Petersburg Soviet were arrested, and when, in protest, the Moscow Soviet took up arms on 7 December, the insurgents were shelled into submission. With the revolutionary movement cowed, the Tsar could fill in the blank spaces of his October Manifesto. On 20 February 1906 the details of the promised franchise for the State Duma were published, and it became clear that the proposed structure of electoral colleges would mean that the voting system would be quite unlike the 'equal suffrage' referred to Father Gapon's petition; the votes of the propertied classes would count for significantly more than the votes of workers or peasants. Then the 'Temporary Provisions' concerning freedom of association and the formation of trade unions were published on 4 March 1906; these made clear that trade unions could only act on a local basis, there were to be no national trade unions or federations of trade unions, and police officials were to oversee all meetings to prevent trade union discussions spilling over into politics.

THE 'PARLIAMENTARY' INTERLUDE

When the State Duma was summoned, the Tsar made clear that he would not let it be used to introduce radical reforms. The elections to the First State Duma in early spring 1906 were a rushed affair. The franchise became clear only after the electoral process had begun, and several of the revolutionary parties decided to organise a boycott in protest. As a result, it was the various liberal parties which dominated that assembly, which opened on 27 April. The Tsar dissolved the First State Duma on 9 July 1906 when it became clear that it intended to press ahead with a radical land reform. Over the summer of 1906, the Tsar used his emergency powers to introduce his own proposals for land reform, proposals drafted by his prime minister, Petr Stolypin. These proposals were then brought to the Second State Duma, which opened on 20 February 1907. The elections to the Second State Duma were not boycotted by any of the revolutionary parties, and saw the election of 55 Social Democrats, 37 SRs and 105 peasant 'Labourites' – the Labourites were reformist SRs. There were also 98 Kadets, the most radical of the liberal groups represented in the Duma. For the next few months, parliamentary politics came to Imperial Russia and, as this happened, divisions which had long existed within the Social Democrat Party became increasingly acute.

The Social Democrats had to decide whether it was better to form an alliance in the Second State Duma with the Kadets, or the SRs and Labourites. The more moderate reformist Social Democrats, belonging to the Menshevik faction, favoured siding with the Kadets and supporting their struggle to force further reforming concessions from the Tsar. The more radical Social Democrats, belonging to the Bolshevik faction, favoured an alliance with the SRs and Labourites, an alliance of working-class socialists and peasant socialists for revolutionary change. Of the 55 Social Democrat deputies, 36 supported the Mensheviks, 18 the Bolsheviks and 11 identified with neither faction. The Social Democrats, led by the Menshevik Irakli Tsereteli, took their new parliamentary work extremely seriously. They participated in four major subcommittees – the budget, local government, labour legislation and land reform – and dominated the work of the unemployment commission. The Social Democrats also put down 14 parliamentary questions in attempts to embarrass the Tsar and his approach to Duma politics. However, in carrying out this parliamentary activity the Social Democrats found themselves increasingly subject to criticism from the liberals, their supposed allies, who accused them of blocking orderly, legislative activity and interfering with the liberals' programme of reform.[9]

At the start of the Second Duma's work, the Social Democrat deputies joined the 'inter-faction information bureau' and in doing so had to decide which other Duma groups to inform about their plans. The Bolsheviks were clear that only the SRs and Labourites should be informed about Social Democrat initiatives, but the Mensheviks successfully argued that all Duma groups should be informed.[10] However, as Alfred Levin has clearly shown, although in principle the Mensheviks wanted to support the liberals, 'the entire Social Democrat group found itself aligned against the Kadets' in vote after vote.[11] Thus on 12 April 1907 the Social Democrats put a question to the government on why workers at a St Petersburg factory had been beaten up during a strike; the Kadets refused to recognise this question as 'urgent', but on this occasion the Social Democrats managed to win over sufficient support from other deputies to get the question accepted as urgent.[12] More frequently a lack of Kadet support frustrated the Social Democrat plans. On 24 May when the Social Democrats raised the idea of supporting the Labourite proposal for a bill freeing all political prisoners, the Kadets refused to support it; nor would they support the Social Democrat proposal for a vote of no confidence in the Tsar's governmental programme. When there was discussion of the Tsar's budget, relations with the Kadets broke down again. The Social Democrats were clear that they should be rejected as a point of principle; the Kadets insisted this was empty gesture politics. Agreement proved impossible. Some Mensheviks suggested a semi-compromise of voting in favour of the budget allocation for 'cultural needs' but nothing else; however, the majority of Social Democrats opposed this fudge and it did not happen.[13]

Disagreement followed on disagreement. The Kadets and Social Democrats could not come up with a joint response to the question of famine relief; in the end the Social Democrats worked with the Labourites on this, while the Kadets ended up voting together with the government. When another great social issue of the day, unemployment, came up for discussion, the Kadets insisted on raising what the Social Democrats saw as petty legislative points; the Kadets refused to support granting unemployment benefit to those who had been sacked as a result of their political agitation – although on this occasion the Kadet vote split and some Kadets did join with the Social Democrats, SRs and Labourites in supporting a proposal for unemployment benefit to go to all unemployed. It was the same with the most contentious issue debated in the Second Duma: land reform. Initially the Mensheviks were keen to work with the Kadets and prevented the Bolsheviks from supporting the law proposal put forward by the SRs and Labourites. However, when the debate began, the Kadets not only attacked the SR–Labourite proposal but came up with a proposal of their own which all Social Democrats felt was derived from the 1861 legislation to liberate the serfs and which would force peasants to buy any land they were allocated by the reform. When Tsereteli wound up the debate, he found himself attacking the Kadets, not supporting them.[14]

An issue that particularly infuriated the Social Democrats was the refusal of the Kadets to back them on what they saw as the persecution of workers. On 2 April the Social Democrats tried to raise a parliamentary question about a riot that had taken place in Riga prison after the alleged torturing of an arrested worker. Under Tsereteli's guidance, they agreed to a Kadet request that the question should be treated as non-urgent; then, when the question was debated a week later, the Social Democrats, SRs and Labourites drafted a common statement, which the Kadets refused to support, preferring to abstain. Later, when the Social Democrats tried to ask a parliamentary question about the use of gendarmes to discipline strikers, the Kadets would not support it since the use of gendarmes in industrial disputes was not prohibited by law.[15]

Once it had become clear that the Second State Duma would not pass the land reform proposed by Prime Minister Stolypin, the Tsar resolved that it too should be dissolved. An excuse had to be found, and the Social Democrats were the chosen target. They were accused of having undertaken agitation among soldiers in order to encourage mutiny; they had certainly used their position in the Duma to argue that in an autocratic state the army would always be used to oppress the people and that the only way to prevent this was to democratise the country. On 30 May 1907, Stolypin instructed the Duma that unless the 55 Social Democrat deputies were excluded from the Duma and handed over to the authorities by 2 June, the Duma would be dissolved; 15 of the deputies, headed by Tsereteli, were to be arrested as soon as their exclusion made this possible. When the Duma set up a committee to plan its response to this threat, the SRs and Labourites argued that the committee should stress the innocence of the Social Democrats; the Kadets insisted that the committee should investigate whether there was any basis to the government's charge. On the very last day the Duma met, 2 June, the Social Democrats, SRs and Labourites tried to change the order of the day's business so there would be a chance to reject the Tsar's budget before the Duma was dissolved; but the Kadets insisted that the published agenda could not be tampered with.[16] Although the Social Democrat deputies took no decision of principle to support the peasant deputies, the SRs and Labourites, this is what happened – in practice, they worked with the peasants' representatives and clashed with the liberals. The experience of the Second State Duma helps explain why, when the Social Democratic Party held its Fifth Congress in London in May 1907, the Bolsheviks had a clear, albeit slim, majority. Working with the Kadets had proved to be a dead end.

The Second State Duma was dissolved on 3 June. Using his emergency powers, the Tsar then changed the electoral franchise, reducing worker and peasant representation still further, even though the Tsar's own constitution made clear that the one thing he did not have the power to change through his use of emergency powers between Duma sessions was his own constitution. After this 'coup d'état of 3 June' a third State Duma was elected on 1 September and this much tamed assembly duly passed Stolypin's land reform. A crackdown on labour activism then followed. Already in September 1906, Trotsky and the leaders of the St Petersburg Soviet had been put on trial and sentenced to long terms of exile. An attack on trade union activity came next. Although negotiating the Temporary Provisions of 1906 was not easy, by May 1907 3.5 per cent of the labour force was enrolled in trade unions, nearer 10 per cent among skilled metal workers, and some 904 trade unions had been registered with the authorities. Between 1907 and 1910, 430 of these trade unions were closed down, and over the five-year period 1907–12 some 604 newly formed trade unions were refused legal registration, 206 union activists were imprisoned and 357 were given terms of administrative exile.[17]

THE LENA MASSACRE STRIKES, 1912–14

The lessons a majority of workers drew from the political upheavals of 1905–7 were that the liberals could not be trusted and that their best interests would be served by forming an alliance with the peasantry. This had been clear both during the revolutionary politics of 1905, when the liberals were so quick to leave the Soviet alone in the struggle for genuine democratic change, and in the parliamentary politics of the Second State Duma, when a majority of Social Democrat deputies preferred to back the peasant-based SRs and Labourites over the liberal politicians. When the labour movement began to recover towards the end of 1910, the issue of reform or revolution was once again before the Social Democrats. During the years 1908 to 1910, the period Soviet historians used to dub 'the years of reaction', labour militancy disappeared. During 1908–9 there were only 14 recorded strikes in metalworking factories, and in 1910 only two. It was developments in international politics that changed the situation. In 1908 the Austro-Hungarian Empire annexed the Slav-inhabited territory of Bosnia-Herzegovina, until then formally part of the Turkish Ottoman Empire. Unable to respond because of the state of the Russian army and navy in the aftermath of the defeat at the hands of the Japanese, the Tsar was resolved that he would never let the Balkan Slavs be treated in this way again, and a massive rearmament programme began producing an industrial boom in St Petersburg. In February 1911, workers at the Baltic Works took successful strike action to defend rates of overtime pay, the first successful strike in several years and the first sign of a new militant mood.[18]

Despite the best efforts of the authorities, some trade unions did survive the government onslaught of 1907. And, alongside the trade unions, the 1906 Temporary Provisions on freedom of association had made it legal to establish other labour organisations, such as workers' clubs and co-operative societies. Between 1908 and 1911 these legal workers' organisations – trade unions, clubs and co-operatives – sent delegations to a series of public congresses held to discuss the leading social issues of the day: the Congress of People's Universities (1908), the Congress of Co-operative Societies (1908), the Women's Congress (1908), the Congress of Factory Panel Doctors (1909), the Temperance Congress (1910) and the Congress of Handicraft Trades (1911). The workers' groups at these congresses used the opportunity to advance Social Democratic demands, in particular on the question of social insurance. Gapon's petition had raised the issue of social insurance, and a bill on the question was introduced into the Third State Duma. In March 1909 the Central

Bureau of St Petersburg Trade Unions, with the support of the Social Democratic Group in the Third Duma, published some 'Theses on Insurance', which would, it was hoped, inform the Duma's debates. Those 'Theses on Insurance' were presented to the Congress of Factory Panel Doctors in April 1909. Although this sort of activity was notionally legal, if the workers' groups at these congresses raised any issue that was considered 'political' by the authorities, they would be liable to arrest. The arrest of those taking part in the activities of workers' groups at legal congresses became entirely routine.[19]

Early in 1911 some Menshevik journalists proposed that, because it was five years since the Tsar had introduced his 'Temporary Provision' on freedom of association, the time had come for the Third State Duma to review these provisions and pass a bill on freedom of association. They suggested that trade unions, workers' clubs and co-operatives should send petitions to the president of the Third State Duma requesting such an initiative. The Social Democrat Group within the Third State Duma was not impressed: it called instead for workers' petitions to be sent to the Social Democrat Group, rather than the State Duma president; addressing petitions to the State Duma president suggested giving authority to a body that was illegitimate from a worker's perspective because of the unrepresentative electoral system on which it was based. Although the then leader of the Metal Workers' Union, Kuz'ma Gvozdev, supported the idea of petitioning the State Duma president, most underground Social Democrat groups did not; in the end only 1,295 signatures were on the petition sent to the State Duma president, while a few months later the Social Democratic Group collected 14,000 signatures for a petition demanding legalisation of the right to strike. This petition campaign raised once again the issue of how to bring about change in Tsarist Russia. If the way forward was through joint activity with liberals in the Third State Duma, then sending petitions to the State Duma president made sense. However, if the future could only be attained through revolutionary struggle, with the peasantry as an ally, then the petitions should go to the Social Democrat Group in the Third Duma, for the propaganda purpose of showing the powerlessness of the Duma and the need for a genuinely democratic assembly. After some hesitation, the majority of workers active in the legal labour movement sided with the revolutionary option.[20]

The importance of genuine freedom of association for workers was made abundantly clear in spring 1912 when the Lena Gold Fields massacre occurred. On 4 April 1912, over 200 striking miners working in the gold fields of the river Lena in Siberia were shot down in cold blood when they took part in a demonstration in support of their long-running pay dispute. A wave of sympathy protests followed and for the next two years St Petersburg experienced a recurrent strike wave, as anniversaries of Bloody Sunday and the Lena massacre mingled with more narrowly economic concerns. In St Petersburg in 1912 there were 743 strikes; in 1913, 1,073; and in the first half of 1914, 908. As World War I began, St Petersburg was experiencing a city-wide general strike.[21] This strike wave caused some concern to those Mensheviks working for a political understanding with the liberals. Both Bolsheviks and Mensheviks welcomed the initial strike wave since these strikes almost always included the demand for new legislation on freedom of assembly, a demand regularly repeated by the Social Democrat and Labourite deputies to the Fourth State Duma, which began its work on 15 November 1912.

However, even during summer 1912 the Menshevik press began to warn of the danger of alienating liberal support unless more discipline was shown on the question of strikes, and this issue became even more acute in spring 1913. At this time the St Petersburg Metal Workers' Union was re-established after one of its intermittent periods of closure at the hands of the government. As preparations began to elect a new leadership, the Bolshevik newspaper *Pravda* attacked the previous Menshevik leadership of the union, singling out Gvozdev and his stance during the petition campaign, and calling on workers to elect a new leadership. The triumph of the Bolsheviks in the Metal Workers' Union that April reopened the issue of strikes. The Bolsheviks were ready to call on union members to take a more disciplined attitude to strikes, insisting that the union would only support strike action cleared with it in advance, but they rejected the argument of Gvozdev's supporters that political strikes should be avoided. This issue came to a head when workers at the Aivaz Factory went on strike: this strike had not been cleared in advance with the union as it should have been, but it was a strike in defence of existing working conditions and thus legal under a clarification to the law on strikes issued in 1911. On these grounds, the Metal Workers' Union decided to support the strike. In response, Gvozdev's supporters claimed 'strikomania' had seized the new Bolshevik union leadership.[22]

When the Metal Workers' Union held a general meeting in August 1913, the issue of strikes dominated the agenda. According to Gvozdev, the new Bolshevik leadership had squandered money on supporting some 60,000 strikers and had spent nothing on raising the cultural and educational level of the membership; the Mensheviks believed that suitably educated workers would understand the cultural need for a political arrangement with the liberals. When other speakers, including one of the Social Democrats elected to the Fourth State Duma, suggested that economic and political issues needed to be kept separate where strikes were concerned, they were whistled at and shouted down. One of the first acts of the Social Democrat Group in the Fourth State Duma had been to introduce a parliamentary question about why the Metal Workers' Union had been closed down in summer 1912. This parliamentary question was co-ordinated with protest strikes, strikes which the 'culturally educated' like Gvozdev were quick to condemn as manifestations of 'anarcho-syndicalism'. By August 1913, workers did not want to be told not to strike and at the end of the general meeting, further elections were held and the Bolsheviks won an even clearer victory than in the April elections. Success in the Metal Workers' Union was quickly followed by success in the St Petersburg Printers' Union, and then the Bolshevik success in the trade unions spread to the textile workers. Indeed, in July 1914 the Bolsheviks informed the Socialist International that they controlled 14½ of the 18 trade unions operating in St Petersburg and 10 of the 13 in Moscow. Defeated Mensheviks conceded with concern that the Bolsheviks were 'close in spirit to the masses' and that they had found their support 'in the masses' state of mind'.[23]

One of the last acts of the Third State Duma, as it closed on 9 June 1912, had been to enact the proposed law on social insurance. That law retained just an echo of the Gapon petitioners' demand that workers should have elected representatives involved in the social insurance system. Workers' delegates were to be elected to sit on insurance boards, although those representatives would be outnumbered by employers' representatives and their powers would be severely limited. Nevertheless the law offered the first officially sanctioned factory based elections since the commission of enquiry into Bloody Sunday in February 1905. In the first stage of this process, the authorities simply selected some of the workers who had taken part in the election meetings for the Fourth State Duma, but in January 1913 the first elections were held in the eight factories chosen to run a pilot project and, following the 'Theses on Insurance' drafted in 1909, the worker delegates decided that their policy should be to merge the factory based insurance funds envisaged by the legislation into a broader territorially based general fund. However, the employers had no interest in establishing a general fund, so discussions got nowhere. When in autumn 1913 the insurance campaign was extended to all eligible metalworking plants and factory based elections took place throughout the city, the question of the general fund took on a political complexion.

The Metal Workers' Union had endorsed the idea of a territorially based general fund as recently as September 1911; such a fund had an obvious benefit for workers since it would allow the contributions of better paid workers to be pooled with those of the lower paid and therefore the overall level of benefits to be increased. In autumn 1913, however, some Mensheviks suggested that, since the authorities were clearly never going to agree to a territorially based general fund, it was time to campaign instead for a 'professional fund', a way of linking together factories in similar industries; they suggested that such a proposal just might be acceptable to the employers – the territorially based general fund would be relegated to a distant 'final goal'. To the uninitiated, the difference between a general territorial fund and a professional fund must have seemed marginal; however, the politics of these issues were clear to worker activists in St Petersburg at the time and, faced again with the choice between a reformist or a revolutionary action, they voted for the revolutionary option. Behind the 'professional fund' was the notion that real progress could be made by co-operating with liberal forces within the existing context of the State Duma; the 'territorial' fund recognised that this political regime had nothing to offer workers and only its radical transformation would achieve improvements to their living conditions. By the end of September 1913 the 12 largest metalworking plants in the capital had all voted for a city-wide fund, four of them overturning earlier decisions in favour of a professional fund.[24]

THE WORKERS' GROUP ON THE WAR INDUSTRIES COMMITTEE

Between 1912 and 1914, on the issues of petitions, of 'strikomania' and of the territorial insurance fund, workers had shown their preference for the revolutionary rather than the reformist option. That same revolutionary–reformist divide was evident during World War I and the workers made the same choice for revolution. As in all countries on both sides of World War I, the outbreak of fighting had been met with an outburst of patriotic enthusiasm. On top of that, the war started relatively well for the Tsar, with dramatic advances at the expense of Austria–Hungary on the territory of present day Poland. Then, in spring 1915, Russian forces began to retreat and by the autumn not only had all the territory which had been gained been lost, but the slow retreat had continued until the front stabilised not far short of Riga; as this disaster unfolded, a million Russian soldiers were killed and a further million taken prisoner. The reason for these military failures was not hard to fathom, at least for the popular press. There was a chronic shortage of shells: the military needed 3.5 million shells per month, and by summer 1915, despite apparently determined efforts on all sides, only 1 million shells per month were being supplied.

It was to address this crisis that the Tsar agreed to broaden the brief of the locally elected provincial and town councils, the *zemstvos* and town *dumas*. Initially they had been charged with caring for the sick and wounded, but in spring 1915 the Tsar agreed that these councils could establish a nationwide co-ordinating body – given the acronym *Zemgor* – which would support the war effort in every conceivable way. *Zemgor* soon grew into a massive organisation, eventually employing tens of thousands of personnel including lawyers, doctors, engineers and technicians. Spring 1915 also saw the emergence of a second 'voluntary organisation' alongside *Zemgor*. In May 1915 the Association of Trade and Industry decided to establish a hierarchy of War Industries' Committees, linked to local chambers of commerce. The main 'War Industries' Committee' sought to co-ordinate its activity with *Zemgor* and suggested mutual representation on their ruling councils; thus the *Zemgor* chairman, Prince G. E. Lvov, was also a member of the War Industries' Committee Central Council. The War Industries' Committee was a highly political organisation; its chairman was A.

I. Guchkov, a former member of the Third State Duma's Defence Committee which in 1909 had become involved in a long-running battle with the Tsar over the powers of the State Duma over defence allocations. For liberal politicians like Guchkov, building up *Zemgor* and the War Industries' Committee was not simply about winning the war but proving the incompetence of the Tsar's administration. Yet in summer 1915 the Tsar allowed Guchkov to go ahead with the idea of electing worker representatives to form a workers' group on the War Industries' Committee.

The climate in which these elections took place was inauspicious and helps explain why the result was yet another triumph of revolution over reform. On the evening of 30 August 1915 the police raided the workers' sickness insurance fund office at the Putilov Works. There they found representatives from the Nevskii Shipbuilding Works and several other metalworking plants discussing how best to co-ordinate their activity. Fearing that an attempt was being made to establish a new Soviet, the police arrested 23 labour militants. Those who avoided arrest alerted the informal sickness insurance fund network and the capital was hit by a wave of strikes which disrupted production for the first half of September. These strikes alarmed the reformist worker representatives in the Fourth State Duma. The Menshevik leader Nikolai Chkheidze toured the factories urging that the strikes be called off for the good of the war effort. He was accompanied by Alexander Kerensky, the leader of the Labourites in the Fourth State Duma, who had made his name taking up the cause of the Lena strikers. Local Bolshevik militants, on the other hand, called for the strikes to continue.[25]

Thus political tension among workers was already high when Guchkov decided to press ahead with his election, appropriating the system of election used in 1905 for the commission of enquiry and therefore the same system as had been used for the election of the St Petersburg Soviet; not surprisingly, there was more talk in labour circles at this time of reconstituting the Soviet.[26] Although some activists considered boycotting the whole process of electing workers' representatives to support the activities of the industrialists, the opportunity presented by factory based elections was too attractive an opportunity for most labour militants to pass up.[27] Never before in the history of the labour movement had Russian workers been presented with such a clear choice between collaborating with the liberal bourgeoisie for the good of the nation, or defending their class interests; for the Bolsheviks, the sole purpose of this electoral process was not to aid the country's defence, but to open the way to establishing a Petrograd Soviet as the first step towards revolution.[28]

The elections took place as planned and when the conference of electors opened on 27 September, it was Gvozdev who took the chair. However, as the electors assembled it soon became clear that the Bolsheviks had won in at least 16 of the major factories, including in the Putilov Works. Then, when the proposal to take part in the work of the War Industries' Committee was put to the vote, the electors defeated Gvozdev's proposal by 95 votes to 81. This, however, was not the end of the story. Before the conference began, the Bolsheviks had persuaded one of the Putilov workers chosen as an elector to transfer his mandate to S. Ya. Bagdatiev, a member of the St Petersburg Committee of the Bolshevik Party. Using the worker's name as a pseudonym, Bagdatiev was elected to the post of conference secretary and co-chair. Such a procedure was not unusual; indeed this was what Khrustalev-Nosar' had done at the time of the commission of enquiry into Bloody Sunday in February 1905. Nor was Badgatiev an unknown quantity: many of those at the conference knew precisely who he was since he had previously served on the St Petersburg Committee as a Bolshevik from 1907 to 1910 and had taken part in the workers' groups to the Women's Congress and the Temperance Congress. However, the Mensheviks decided to raise a complaint.[29]

Gvozdev wrote a letter about Bagdatiev's impersonation of an elector in the Menshevik press on 5 October; the police investigated, and the Putilov worker concerned, when interrogated, maintained that he objected to the use made of his mandate by Bagdatiev. In these circumstances, Guchkov decided that there were sufficient grounds to rerun the elections. When a second conference of electors was held on 29 November, only 153 of the original 218 electors attended, and more than half of them followed the revolutionaries in staging a walk-out in protest at Gvozdev's behaviour. The rump of the meeting then voted to send worker representatives onto the War Industries' Committee. Many of those who stayed and voted for participation, however, did so not because they favoured co-operation with the liberals in the war effort but in the belief that any form of workers' representation was better than none. Not surprisingly, the spokesman for the Workers' Group, the chairman of the ten worker representatives elected to the Central Committee of the War Industries' Committee, was Gvozdev.[30]

To the Bolsheviks, 'Mr Gvozdev and Co.' were renegades 'acting behind the backs of the working class' in order to 'lounge in the soft easy chairs' offered them by the War Industries' Committee; Gvozdev himself was threatened with being carted in a wheelbarrow from the Ericsson Telephone Factory where he worked unless he resigned, a threat from fellow workers that he chose to ignore. When the Workers' Group met the full central committee of the War Industries' Committee for the first time on 3 December 1915, they made clear that they saw their participation as provisional until it could be endorsed by a Soviet style workers' congress yet to be summoned.[31] That the November 1915 vote did not reflect true working-class feeling became clear a year later in October 1916 when the existing mandate of the social insurance councils ran out. Elections were held to choose worker representation on the Petrograd City Insurance Board and the Petrograd Provincial Insurance Board and on both occasions the majority of those elected were Bolsheviks.[32] And by autumn 1916, strike activity was again on the rise. During the war the level of labour unrest declined: just 55 strikes in St Petersburg during the second half of 1914 and 146 in 1915. However, during 1916, and markedly during the second half of the year, the rate of strikes rose again to 684.[33] By autumn 1916, the 'strikomania' that had so concerned reformists like Gvozdev was a problem once again.

On the eve of 1917, the Russian labour movement was as militant as it had been in 1905. Then the liberals had let the workers down by accepting the Tsar's October Manifesto before the powers of the State Duma had been determined. In 1907, during the short life of the Second State Duma, the attempts by the Mensheviks to work with the Kadets had ended in frustration. And so, in 1912–14, and again during World War I, whenever workers had been given the chance to vote, they had voted for revolution rather than reform. Given that tradition, it was unlikely that joint work between liberals and socialists would be easy once the Tsar was overthrown.

2

THE PROVISIONAL GOVERNMENT

REVOLUTION FROM ABOVE

The British ambassador noted early in 1917 that the only moot point about the forthcoming Russian Revolution was whether it would come 'from above or from below'.[1] Initially a revolution 'from above' seemed the more likely course as the voluntary organisations, *Zemgor* and the War Industries' Committee, challenged the Tsar's administration ever more forcefully and seemed in doing so to have the support of the growing liberal opposition in the Fourth State Duma. The liberal opposition had initially taken heart from the Tsar's decision in summer 1915 to allow the Duma to reconvene on 19 July. Ministerial changes encouraged such optimism: in August, General Aleksei Polivanov was made minister of war, someone the liberals felt they could work with, and other ministerial changes suggested a willingness on the Tsar's part to work with rather than against the Duma. At this stage, relations between the Duma and the voluntary organisations were also excellent: just before the session began, the Duma established a Special Commission on Defence on which both *Zemgor* and the War Industries' Committee were represented. This honeymoon did not last long. Duma politicians began to campaign for the government to be made responsible to the Duma, for the establishment of what they called 'a Government of Confidence'; they even circulated in the press the names of a possible new 'Defence Cabinet'. This was too much for the Tsar, who suspended the Duma on 30 August and promptly sacked all his moderate ministers.[2]

How best to respond to the Tsar's hardening attitude then resulted in divisions among his opponents. The suspension of the Duma provoked both strikes from the working class and resolutions of protest from the voluntary organisations, like those passed at the *Zemgor* congresses in September. The Duma politicians, however, responded with more caution, hoping that the Tsar might somehow be persuaded to resume his liberal stance, even though the omens for this were not good since a Duma session planned for November was abruptly cancelled. The Duma did, however, meet again in February 1916, and for a while it seemed that the Tsar was again ready to work with elected politicians, although the more radical liberals cautioned that this harmony had only been achieved by the Duma deciding to shelve discussion of all controversial issues; at this time, for example, liberals decided to drop the demand for 'the immediate removal of all religious and national restrictions' and to campaign instead for 'a gradual advance along the road to Jewish equality'.[3]

That there was no depth to the Tsar's reconciliation with the Duma became apparent in summer 1916. On 20 June the Duma was suspended again and ordered not to reassemble until November. Then, on 1 July, the Tsar appointed 'a dictator' to head a new more forceful administration committed to driving forward the war effort. By September, the beginning of a new stand-off was clear. An unofficial Duma session was held on 10–11 September at the instigation of the liberals, a session which demanded the urgent recall of the Duma and condemned the incompetence of the Ministry of Supply. Immediately after this, the Tsar appointed a new confrontational minister of the interior, Alexander Protopopov, one of whose first acts was to ban a congress of the War Industries' Committee; Guchkov took no notice and organised the congress anyway. Not surprisingly, the congress voted to struggle against the autocracy, and at the same time *Zemgor* called on the Duma to act and confront the Tsar. The response of the Tsar's dictator was to threaten to dissolve the Duma and send all the deputies of military age to the front.[4]

With liberal members of the Duma being bombarded with telegrams from town *dumas*, provincial *zemstvos* and voluntary

Fig. 1: Pavel Milyukov, leader of the Kadet liberals and foreign minister in the First Provisional Government

organisations calling for decisive action, the Kadet leader Pavel Milyukov felt something dramatic was needed when the Duma reconvened on 1 November. In a famous speech, which was widely circulated, he asked rhetorically whether it was 'stupidity or treason' which had led the Tsar to behave as he did. The Tsar's response was to suspend the Duma once again, and on 5 November the minister of the interior banned a planned conference of the voluntary organisations. Yet, the Tsar's new hard-line response seemed strangely hesitant. He sacked his 'dictator' on 8 November and established a new ministry which appeared to be more conciliatory; he even allowed the Duma to reconvene on 19 November. During the following month, hoping to build on the Tsar's apparent conciliatory mood, the Duma raised no controversial issues until it was suspended for the Christmas vacation on 16 December. Voluntary organisations were astonished and incensed at how the Duma politicians could so quickly back away from confrontation with the Tsar. The signs that he was ready to work with the Duma seemed ephemeral at best, and in the meantime the Ministry of the Interior was frustrating every initiative the voluntary organisations took.[5]

When World War I began, the rural peasant economy was relatively prosperous. The land reform introduced by Stolypin after his repeated clashes with the Second State Duma had done nothing to address the huge inequalities between noble and peasant landholding, but it had both relieved peasants of debt and enabled them to purchase additional land. By 1914, Russian peasants had never had it so good. Then, as the war developed the situation changed. Peasants formed the backbone of the ever-growing Russian Army, and the expansion of the war industries sucked more and more of those peasants who escaped conscription into the urban labour force. By 1916 some 70 per cent of those left working on the land were women, and because of the army's insatiable need for horses, these too were in short supply. On top of this, the reorientation of the economy towards war production meant that there was no chance that the shortage of manpower and horsepower could be met by increased mechanisation. The result was predictable. The area of land under cultivation declined in 1916 by 12 per cent and the 1916–17 harvest was 20 per cent down. The situation was made worse by the government's purchasing policy. It attempted to restrict inflation by taking monopoly powers in grain purchasing and paying peasants a low price for grain, but that price was soon so low that peasants refused to sell their grain, which in turn forced the government to start requisitioning. At the end of 1916, army rations had to be reduced, and in January 1917 Petrograd had been supplied with only half the number of grain wagons usually required to feed the city.

This situation of objective shortage was exacerbated by the intensifying clash between the Tsar and his opponents. Those surrounding the Tsar felt that liberal-dominated voluntary organisations were entering the war effort simply so that they could take credit for victory and force political concessions from the Tsar once peace was restored; the voluntary organisations argued that patriotism was their motive pure and simple. When first set up, *Zemgor* had no responsibility for food supplies, but by the end of 1916 this was its single most important concern. In summer 1915 the government had established a Special Council on Food Supply within the Ministry of Agriculture. Initially the Ministry encouraged *Zemgor* to help with the stockpiling of grain, but problems developed early in 1916 when *Zemgor* began to criticise the government's pricing policy which it felt was distorting the market and reducing the provision of grain. In March 1916, therefore, at its Moscow assembly, *Zemgor* established an Economic Department, to assess the grain available and deploy personnel, and a Supply Department to ship grain to the army. In doing so, *Zemgor* chose to bypass the Ministry of Agriculture and its Special Council on Food Supply, which, to the Tsar at least, suggested a political motive. Certainly, during spring 1916 *Zemgor* activists in the countryside chose not to implement the Ministry's instructions on compulsory purchase. In response, the government decided that the 'anti-government mood' in *Zemgor* meant that the Ministry of Internal Affairs and its new Special Committee to Fight Inflation should have a greater say in grain purchasing; by the end of October 1916 the Tsar wanted the Ministry of Internal Affairs to be fully responsible for food supply, but opted in the end to strengthen the powers of the Ministry of Agriculture.[6]

The day after the Duma was prorogued in the middle of December, Rasputin was murdered. For the elites of Imperial Russia the apparent powers of the 'mad monk' Rasputin seemed to explain why the Tsar could not see what the British ambassador could see only too clearly: that unless some sort of accommodation was reached between the throne and the War Industries' Committees and *Zemgor*, then revolution from below would follow. What blinded the Tsar had to be the malign influence of Rasputin who was able to comfort the heir to the Romanov throne when attacks of haemophilia overcame him, enabling him to become a close confidant of the Tsaritsa. Under his guidance, she had lobbied hard for the Tsar to take a firm stand against liberal critics and she had been instrumental in the appointment of Protopopov. Thus, for many of Russia's elites, the answer to Milyukov's question was not so much 'stupidity or treason' as 'stupidity and treason': the Tsar was foolish enough to fall under the influence of his wife who was not only German in origin but under the influence of Rasputin, who was addicted to Madeira which he sourced through secret channels from Germany.[7] For many among the Imperial Russian elites, Rasputin had to be killed and the Tsar forced to come to his senses; just before the murder of Rasputin, the Congress of Nobility had attacked the 'dark powers' which surrounded the throne.[8] The removal of Rasputin was not the only element of a palace coup at this time. There were also moves from within the army to make the Tsar see sense. Many generals recognised that it was only *Zemgor* and the War Industries' Committee that kept the army fighting efficiently. Guchkov established a relationship of sorts with General Mikhail Alekseev while he was army Chief of Staff; Guchkov may even have mentioned to him a plan he developed with young officers towards the end of 1916 to intercept the Tsar's train and force him to abdicate. This plot was an open secret, but none of those who learned of it felt it their duty to inform the authorities.[9]

Learning of Rasputin's death, the Tsar left the front, where he had been since the height of the munitions crisis, and returned to the capital where he stayed until 23 February 1917. On 27 December he changed his government once again, appointing new reactionary ministers; at one of its first meetings, on 3 January, the minister of the interior demanded that the Duma be closed. This extreme stance was not taken, but it was decided to delay the reconvening of the Duma until February. At the same time the Tsar gave his government the powers to get rid of the Duma whenever it thought fit: he signed papers enabling them to suspend the Duma indefinitely, suspend it until the end of the war, or to dissolve it completely, whichever of the three should prove necessary. The Tsar's hard-line stance did not weaken. On 26 January the minister of the interior arrested leading members of the Workers' Group. Yet the liberals were still confused about how best to respond. Guchkov and the voluntary organisations tried to organise a protest meeting, but Milyukov refused to address it. He also appealed for no demonstrations to take place when the Duma opened on 14 February lest this provoke the minister of the interior into dissolving the Duma. It was left to Kerensky to take the lead in defending the arrested workers, accusing Milyukov's liberals of being completely out of touch: 'your speeches on the necessity for calm at all costs are either the naïve sentiments of superficial thinkers or just an excuse to avoid the real fight, just a pretext to stay safely in your warm armchairs'. The Duma's only significant act at this time was to support the voluntary organisations by passing a bill that transferred responsibility for the food supply of the capital to *Zemgor* and the City Duma.[10]

The impact of that decision could be seen in the contradictory actions and pronouncements of the Commander of the Petrograd Military District, the Fourth State Duma and the Petrograd Duma as the February Revolution began. As one of the SR leaders Pitirim Sorokin recalled, the Russian Revolution was begun on 23 February 'by hungry women and children demanding bread and herring', yet on 24 February 1917 the Commander of the Petrograd Military District had notices posted on the streets stressing that there should be no shortage of bread since sufficient flour had been delivered to the bakeries; any shortages were due to people 'having laid in reserves' or hoarding. That same day, the president of the State Duma, joined by the prime minister, toured the city and decided it was necessary to convene an extraordinary conference to examine what were referred to as 'the food complications' in the capital. At the same time the Petrograd Duma had announced that it had decided to take into its own hands the question of food distribution and establish public committees for the regular distribution of food; it complained that although the law made clear that food supply was one of its legal responsibilities, other institutions were preventing it from carrying out this responsibility. There might be food, but its distribution had collapsed amongst political intrigue.[11]

REVOLUTION FROM BELOW

The hesitation of liberal politicians in forcing a showdown with the Tsar was not mirrored in the actions of workers. The Menshevik and Labourite Duma deputies had concluded in October 1916 that the 'on off' liberal policy of sometimes confronting the Tsar and then welcoming his every conciliatory gesture had left the popular masses hostile to the Duma. After nothing was done to build on Milyukov's 'stupidity or treason' speech of 1 November 1916, the Menshevik deputy Mikhail Skobelev accused the liberals of listening to the government not the people.[12] And it was in this context that on 22 February 1917 a delegation of workers from the Putilov Works sought to contact the two Duma deputies they felt would be most sympathetic to their cause, Kerensky and Chkheidze. An observer at the meeting with Kerensky recalled the workers' determined mood. They were insistent that the situation was serious and they therefore 'declined responsibility for the possible consequences'. They made it clear that the strike they were embarking on was not simply the result of economic grievances, nor even the desperate food supply situation; their strike had political motives, it was aimed at fundamental political change – and those deputies representing workers in the Duma needed to be aware of this. Calmly and firmly they explained that, while they were not entirely clear how things would end, something very serious was about to happen.[13]

Reasons for working-class unrest were not hard to find, for bread and herring were indeed in short supply. Between December 1916 and February 1917 the price of potatoes rose by 25 per cent, bread by 15 per cent, sausage by 50 per cent and milk by 40 per cent, prompting a rash of strikes. However, on 22 February the Putilov workers were clear that they had a political agenda and the fact that they felt the need to warn politicians like Kerensky and Chkheidze reflects the fact that they could not assume that their intentions would necessarily be supported. In September 1915 both Kerensky and Chkheidze had tried to discourage the strikes caused by the arrest of sickness fund activists. Gvozdev and others on the Workers' Group on the War Industries' Committee had called for an end to strikes for the duration of the war. That 'no strike' appeal had been criticised by the Menshevik deputies to the Duma, who by contrast had called on those members of the Workers' Group on the War Industries' Committee active at district level to form 'support groups' in the Petrograd factories and to organise strikes and protests to commemorate the twelfth anniversary of Bloody Sunday. Encouraged by the participation of some 132 enterprises in that event, the Menshevik deputies and the Workers' Group on the War Industries' Committee resolved to organise similar strikes and demonstrations when the State Duma reopened on 14 February. It was to prevent such an occurrence that the arrests of 26 January took place, when the authorities detained three members of the central leadership of the Workers' Group on the War Industries'

Committee and its representatives for Petrograd Province. Despite these arrests, when the State Duma reopened some 58 factories went on strike.[14] Were the Menshevik deputies still ready to back militant action? The Putilov workers visited Kerensky and Chkheidze in order to make clear that they should.

Amongst underground activists, it was assumed that the growing labour unrest would be linked in some way to activities in the State Duma. It was female textile workers who hijacked this agenda. Bolshevik women had to push hard to persuade a cautious underground leadership to make International Women's Day, 23 February (8 March according to the Western calendar), a day of street demonstrations about food shortages. On 23 February some 90,000 workers, both men and women, downed tools and staged a rally outside the Petrograd Duma, so recently made responsible for the city's food supply. These strikes and demonstrations continued on the 24th when almost half the city's workers were on strike. After factory meetings in the morning, workers again downed tools, toured neighbouring factories to rally support and then marched to the city centre and Nevskii Prospekt, the city's main street, where the hall of the Petrograd Duma building was situated. Although mounted Cossack troops were in attendance on the 24th, their swords were sheathed and the Military Commander of Petrograd, General S. S. Khabalov, did not call for any military action. Activists sensed this at once: what was distinctive about the events that day, one recalled, was not the scale of the demonstrations but 'the irresolution of the authorities who were obviously neglecting to deal with the movement'; indeed, there were the first signs of insubordination as 'the movement swept over Petrograd like a great flood'.[15] Another activist sensed this mood, recalling that on 24 February, while soldiers had clearly been ordered to control movement within the city and not let people through to certain strategic points, people kept getting through nonetheless by pleading with the soldiers who, when their officers were not watching, would quietly let them pass.[16] By the end of the 24th, one of the leaders of the unrest was already convinced that a revolution had begun.[17]

These demonstrations continued on 25 February, with factory production at a virtual standstill and meetings and rallies being held both in the city centre and local squares; Petrograd 'seethed' as activists recalled the events of autumn 1905. With rumours again circulating that the soldiers hesitated to back the police, the time had come for the Tsar to act. On the evening of the 25th, he instructed General Khabalov to respond at once and 'as from tomorrow' bring the disturbances in Petrograd to an end. General Khabalov did as he was told. He issued an order threatening that those who had not returned to work by 28 February would be drafted into the army, and promptly arrested 100 of the most prominent labour activists that could be found, including five members of the Bolshevik St Petersburg Committee and those members of the Workers' Group on the War Industries' Committee who were still at liberty. The city was informed that henceforth street demonstrations were banned and the authorities would open fire on those who broke this ban. To hamper the progress of any demonstrators, the bridges connecting working-class suburbs to the city centre were lifted.

On 26 February 'the whole city was full of troops', an observer confided to his diary, and there were no newspapers to be had. Nonetheless, demonstrators continued to demonstrate. Unable to reach the city centre across the bridges, they crossed the frozen River Neva on the ice, marched up to road blocks and were met with lethal fire. Some 40 demonstrators were killed in the first clash, and that morning there were three subsequent clashes, all resulting in heavy casualties: an activist recalled that just after midday there was intense rifle fire on Nevskii Prospekt, after which 'the corpses of innocent passers by' were removed. It looked as if the Tsar's forces were successfully regrouping, yet activists on the street were still convinced that the troops lacked determination. They were right. Not all the troops could bring themselves to fire on the unarmed demonstrators. On the evening of the 26th there was a mutiny in the Fourth Company of the Pavlovskii Regiment of the Imperial Guard. After units from this company had opened fire on demonstrators on Nevskii Prospekt, a workers' delegation went to their barracks to protest. The tactic worked: a junior officer agreed to return to Nevskii Prospekt and order his fellow soldiers to leave their posts and return to barracks. For a moment there was an exchange of fire between the mutineers and fellow regiment members still supporting the police.[18]

By the morning of the 27th the mutiny was beginning to spread. The Volhynian Regiment refused to provide any troops for the suppression of demonstrators and lynched the officer who had issued the order. The Volhynian Regiment then sent delegates to the Lithuanian and Preobrazhenskii Regiments, which joined the mutiny. 'The breakdown of discipline was reaching extreme limits,' an activist recalled, 'large numbers of soldiers had left their units and were strolling about singly and in pairs, with or without arms.' Nonetheless, other units were still obeying orders and plenty of demonstrators were still coming under fire. In response, demonstrators were no longer simply demonstrating but attacking police stations and setting fire to them. Spectacularly, demonstrators forced their way into the remand prison and freed all political prisoners. At one point the District Court was ablaze and arms were seized; soon 'arms were visible in great quantities in the hands of workers'.[19]

The Tsar's government had been uncertain how to respond to the crisis. On 25 February, the Council of Ministers had considered opening talks with the State Duma as a way of restoring its authority, but after the Tsar's decision to clamp down on the demonstrations it fell in with the new hard line and issued a decree on 26 February suspending the State Duma. Despite its suspension, however, the State Duma continued to meet on 27 February, although it was careful to explain that this was an unofficial session. After months of indecisiveness it was uncertain how to act. Should the revolution be supported? It was only when mutinous soldiers tried to force their way into the State Duma building, the Tauride Palace, that Kerensky persuaded his fellow deputies that it was indeed time to act. With little difficulty, Kerensky persuaded the soldiers that those who had mutinied needed the protection of the State Duma; with more difficulty he persuaded his fellow deputies that he should inform the mutineers that the State Duma was taking political responsibility for the situation. As a result, at 3.30 pm on the afternoon of the 27th the State Duma announced that it had established a Provisional Committee of the State Duma.

Typically, the first act of this liberal-dominated body was to give the Tsar one last chance: it sent him a telegram calling for the suspension of the State Duma to be lifted and requesting that he form a 'government of confidence' from State Duma politicians. Long before a reply was received, however, events had moved forward. Kerensky had agreed to the arrest of one of the Tsar's ministers who had been captured by some revolutionary students and brought to the State Duma. By 2 am on the morning of 28 February, when still no response had been received from the Tsar – and with ever more arrested members of the old regime turning up at the State Duma under the guard of soldiers, sailors or armed workers – the Provisional Committee announced that 'it has found itself compelled to take responsibility for restoring national and public order'. As dawn came on the 28th, the Provisional Committee sent commissioners to the various government ministries to take over their business. The Tsar's surviving ministers were barricaded into the Admiralty building, where a stand-off between troops loyal to the government and those loyal to the State Duma briefly occurred; then the loyal troops dispersed and the revolution had been accomplished.

The Tsar, however, still imagined he was in charge. On 27 February he sacked General Khabalov and appointed in his place General Nikolai Ivanov, who was instructed to move troops from the front line and march on Petrograd. This order, however, was countermanded by the Commander-in-Chief, General Alekseev, who had been assured by the Provisional Committee that order was gradually returning to the capital. After discussions with General Alekseev, the Tsar agreed on 1 March to sign a decree establishing a 'responsible ministry', finally meeting the Provisional Committee's request that he form a 'ministry of confidence'. The Provisional Committee then had to make clear to the Tsar that things had moved on dramatically since that request of 27 February; it resolved at a meeting held on the night of 1–2 March that the Tsar's abdication was now the only way forward. On 2 March the Tsar was informed that Alekseev and all front commanders agreed that his abdication was essential. The Tsar accepted this, and made clear that he would abdicate in favour of his son, who would be represented by the Tsar's brother Michael acting as regent until he came of age. However, when a representative of the Provisional Committee arrived and made clear that under the terms of the regency that they envisaged the Tsar would be separated from his son, the Tsar changed his mind and abdicated in favour of his brother Michael. On abdicating, the Tsar appointed Prince Lvov the new prime minister. When Michael met his government on 3 March, he also agreed to abdicate, his only act being to summon a Constituent Assembly.[20]

THE PETROGRAD SOVIET

What changed between the Provisional Committee calling for a 'government of confidence' on 27 February and the Tsar agreeing to a 'responsible ministry' on 1 March and then abdicating on the 2nd was the formation of the Petrograd Soviet, which gave political form to Russia's revolutionary minded workers. The origins of the Soviet can be traced back to 24 February, the second day of disturbances, when worker representatives on a number of social insurance funds in the capital came to the State Duma to get the assistance of Skobelev in forming some sort of working-class co-ordinating centre; in some parts of the capital the election of factory delegates took place that day. The idea was already in the air, of course: it had been raised in 1915 and in 1916 and some insurance fund delegates at the Putilov Works had again raised the issue of reviving the Soviet at a meeting held on 30 January 1917. By 25 February the Vyborg District Committee of the Bolshevik Party was encouraging the election of such delegates and the same day Chkheidze met a second delegation from the social insurance funds making similar proposals. Later on the 25th, it was agreed to use the social insurance funds as a base for electing delegates to a new Petrograd Soviet which would meet on the 26th.

However, as the members of the social insurance funds returned to their factories on the evening of 25 February, over half of them were arrested, victims of the Tsar's new hard line. Because of those arrests it was only on the afternoon of 27 February that the Mensheviks in the State Duma, and those associated with the Workers' Group on the War Industries' Committee who had not been arrested, declared themselves to be the Provisional Committee of the as yet unelected Petrograd Soviet. It called on all factories to elect delegates on the basis of representation used in the elections to the Workers' Group on the War Industries' Committee and that same evening, at 9 pm, some 40 or so delegates officially declared the formation of the Petrograd Soviet, with Chkheidze as president and Skobelev and Kerensky as vice presidents. They were joined by Gvozdev, who had been released from prison earlier in the day.[21]

Called in extreme haste, that first meeting of the Soviet chose as its provisional leaders the obvious public faces of the labour movement. However, these were politicians whose tradition of reformism did not fully reflect the views of many of the labour militants who were still on the barricades.[22] They were, in a way, accidental leaders; it was chance events that had brought them to the fore. When World War I began, the Bolshevik and Menshevik deputies to the Fourth State Duma had issued a joint statement condemning the war; the authorities, however, arrested only the Bolshevik deputies and exiled them to Siberia, so the Bolshevik deputies could play no role in the overthrow of the Tsar and the formation of the Soviet. The Bolsheviks had won the first elections to the Workers' Group on the War Industries' Committee, but Gvozdev's action had ensured it was only Mensheviks who took up their seats. By default, the public face of the labour movement in Petrograd in February 1917 was Menshevik and reformist, even though this was completely out of line with the tradition of labour militancy established since 1905.

What was the purpose of the Soviet? For its Menshevik and SR leadership it was about giving cohesion to the strike movement and co-ordinating street action with the high politics of whatever form post-Tsarist governance took. Far more radical ideas about the purpose of the Soviet were bubbling up from the labour activists on the street – the disconnect between the revolutionary instincts of labour activists and the caution of reformist leaders was also present as the

Fig. 2: State Duma deputy and Soviet leader Nikolai Chkheidze addressing soldiers

Soviet was founded. In the militant Vyborg Side industrial suburb, the leading Bolshevik underground activist Alexander Shlyapnikov had to restrain local militants who on 25 and 26 February called for developing the street action into an armed insurrection. The following day the only Social Democrat group that had managed to circulate leaflets on 23 and 24 February called for the establishment of a provisional revolutionary government. Some workers' meetings adopted resolutions calling for the establishment of a revolutionary Soviet government.[23] A general assembly of the Vyborg District Committee explicitly stated that soviets across Russia should be united into a Provisional Revolutionary Government which would hold power until the Constituent Assembly could meet.[24]

The precise relationship between the Provisional Committee of the State Duma and the Petrograd Soviet was unclear from the start. After the arrival of the soldiers' delegation at the Tauride Palace and Kerensky's talks with it, it was logical that Kerensky should take the initiative in forming a Military Commission. When the Soviet was established later on the 27th, it too sent representatives to this Military Commission. But, as the Provisional Committee of the Duma moved to take over the Tsar's ministries in the early hours of 28 February, it also took formal control of the Military Commission.[25] As this happened, the Military Commission began to call on soldiers to return to barracks and surrender their weapons to their officers. Fearing that those who had mutinied could be disciplined as soon as they had surrendered their weapons, soldiers began to protest. They mobbed a meeting of the Petrograd Soviet held at midday on 1 March. This meeting decided to formalise what was becoming a *de facto* reality: the extension of the Petrograd Soviet to include soldiers' deputies, renaming it the Petrograd Soviet of Workers' and Soldiers' Deputies. As this happened, the Petrograd Soviet drafted what became known as Order Number 1: this made clear that arms would not be handed over to officers and that 'the armed forces were subordinate to the Petrograd Soviet in all their political actions' and that 'the orders of the Military Commission of the Duma were to be carried out in so far as they did not conflict with the orders of the Petrograd Soviet'. Order Number 1 also called for the establishment of soldiers' and sailors' committees in the armed forces and for them to be represented in the Petrograd Soviet.

The issue of arms came up again in the early hours of 2 March when the Petrograd Soviet and the Provisional Committee of the State Duma met to discuss how a Provisional Government might be formed. The Petrograd Soviet took the initiative in these talks, believing that a new government administration was essential for the revolution to move forward, but it was also clear that none of its members should be included in the government, even though the Provisional Committee was keen to involve them. The Petrograd Soviet Executive voted 13–8 that no socialist should join the Provisional Government, although it also acquiesced to Kerensky's insistence that, as an individual rather than a Soviet representative, he could accept the post of minister of justice. The demands that the Petrograd Soviet put to the Provisional Committee of the State Duma during these talks on the formation of a government were mostly uncontentious: a political and religious amnesty, guarantees of basic freedoms, police reforms, democratic local government and plans for a Constituent Assembly. The controversial elements, which the Provisional Committee of the State Duma felt it had no choice but to accept, were full political and civil rights for soldiers and a guarantee that those army units that had taken part in the revolution would not be disarmed and would not be withdrawn from Petrograd.[26]

The Petrograd Soviet leaders were keen to keep their distance from the Provisional Government partly for ideological reasons: the reformist Mensheviks and even the SRs argued in quasi-Marxist terms that this was a 'bourgeois' revolution overturning a 'feudal' regime and therefore not the concern of the workers. However, at least until the abdication of the Tsar on 2 March, there was also a very practical reason for keeping clear of the government. There was always the danger of a military counter-revolution. Even once it was clear that General Ivanov's march on Petrograd had been called off, there were persistent rumours of counter-revolutionary military action. It was widely accepted at this time, in the words of Tsuyoshi Hasegawa, that 'the Petrograd Soviet could not have established a revolutionary government without inviting a counter-revolution'.[27] Petrograd Soviet activists were convinced that if the revolution showed any sign of turning into a socialist seizure of power, the entire middle class would turn against the revolution and look to action from the Tsar.[28]

Not all were agreed, however. From the factories radical voices could still be heard. Even as the Provisional Government was formed, on 2 March, radical Social Democrats issued a pamphlet calling for no co-operation with the Provisional Government and for the Petrograd Soviet to establish its own Provisional Revolutionary Government.[29] Thus although the Petrograd Soviet immediately recognised the Provisional Government and called on workers to support it, they did not give it carte blanche. On 3 March the Petrograd Soviet Executive declared that the Provisional Government had made a good start by introducing an amnesty and promising to call a Constituent Assembly, and 'in so far as the emergent government acts to further these obligations' it should be supported.[30] This conditional, 'in so far as' support reflected the fact that there was a gulf in perception between the reformist leadership of the Petrograd Soviet, and the more radical rank and file. As Hasegawa noted, 'the discrepancy between the Executive Committee's wish and the irresistible pressure from the insurgent masses created an ambiguous, inconsistent position – this was the direct cause of the birth of dual power'.[31] Dual Power was evident from the very start of the new government. As the Soviet activist and radical journalist Nikolai Sukhanov noted, during the course of 48 hours, from 28 February to 1 March, the Provisional Committee of the State Duma 'found the time to publish a whole pile of decrees, appointments, orders and proclamations [...] but in those crucial hours of convulsion it was absolutely unable to govern'. That was because 'it was clear to everyone that all effective workers' organisations were at the disposal of the soviets, and that it was for it to set in motion the immobilised tramways, factories, newspapers and even to restore order and safeguard the inhabitants from violence'.[32]

DUAL POWER

The membership of the Provisional Government, agreed on 2 March, was made public on 3 March. Kerensky had his place as minister of justice, while the remaining nine ministers were mostly liberals of various shades with two, including the prime minister Lvov, claiming no party affiliation. Lvov had been a Kadet deputy in the First State Duma and as chairman of the *Zemstvo* Union, a member of the *Zemgor* Board and the leadership of the War Industries' Committee he was perhaps the most prominent member of the liberal opposition that had grown up towards the Tsar in the two and a half years of war. The initial acts of the Provisional Government were to enact and extend the list of liberal freedoms granted under the earlier agreement reached with the Soviet. Sometimes this was done in acts of public theatre, as when on 3 March the Imperial coats of arms were taken down on Nevskii Prospekt and burnt, or when the text of the abdication was read out loud in every school in the country.[33]

Step by step the old order was dismantled and new freedoms introduced. On 4 March the system of provincial governors was abolished and their powers transferred, temporarily, to the provincial *zemstvo* chairman. On 6 March an amnesty was granted to all those accused of political crimes. On 8 March the Tsar was put under house arrest. On 10 March the old Police Department was abolished. On 12 March the death penalty was abolished. On 13 March the powers of courts martial were restricted to the front line. On 17 March flogging in prison was abolished. On 19 March the old gendarmerie was abolished. On 20 March all the former restrictions on religion were lifted. Alongside this string of civil rights reforms, measures were taken to end the wealth of the former Tsar. In a series of moves announced on 12, 16 and 27 March, all crown land was taken over by the state. In other moves to dismantle the structure of the old regime, the autonomy of Finland was restored and Russian Poland was declared to be independent.[34] However it took three weeks of active campaigning by women before it was confirmed that women could vote for the planned Constituent Assembly.

The watchword of this liberal Provisional Government was 'freedom' and, as minister of justice, Kerensky was responsible for implementing many of these changes. In an important early speech he commented:

> The first act of the new government is an immediate amnesty. Our comrade deputies of the Second and Fourth Dumas who were illegally exiled to the Siberian tundra will be liberated and returned to the capital with honour.
>
> Comrades, I have under my control all of the former ministers and

Fig. 3: A women's rally. The banner reads: 'electoral rights for women'

representatives of the Council of Ministers. They will answer, comrades, for all crimes before the people, but in accordance with the law.

Comrades, free Russia will not resort to the shameful means of struggle typical of the old order.[35]

In some ways the minister of trade and industry expressed the liberals' optimism most clearly:

Confidence and harmony in the relations of the citizens among themselves and towards the Provisional Government, is the basis upon which the new structure of free Russia will be erected. But the old order had left us a heritage of discord [...] There is only one way to overcome this [...] namely for the representatives of various groups and classes to approach one another without distrust, to openly and frankly set forth their views, and after getting mutually acquainted, combine their efforts to the common cause of all Russia.[36]

The dominant liberal group within the Provisional Government was still the Kadet Party, and its programme sought compromise and balance. Peasants should receive land, but only if landowners were adequately compensated. Workers should benefit from shorter working days and improved conditions, but the profitability and stability of the industrial order should not be upset. Ethnic and national groups should be respected and free from oppression, but without undermining the integrity of the Russian Empire.[37] When the Kadet liberals held a party congress on 25 March, they were adamant that their party stood above class. Although some on the left of the party felt it was better to seek 'friends on the left', a clear majority felt it essential to reassert the view that they put what they saw as the interests of the newly free nation above the narrow concerns of class, even though, as William Rosenberg has pointed out, 'whether the Kadets admitted it or not, by now advancing "above class" in defence of "stable" social and political relations, they were attempting to hold back revolutionary energies'. Appeals for reason, patience and overcoming distrust, at one level unexceptional policies, became in the context of 1917 an appeal that the revolutionary process should be slowed and even halted.[38] That, at least, is how things seemed to many members of the Petrograd Soviet, especially as it quickly acquired an authority which rivalled that of the Provisional Government.

When, on 3 March, the Petrograd Soviet began to function on a regular basis, establishing commissions on most aspects of administration, the divisions between the reformist leadership and more radical rank and file, visible in its origins, came to the fore once more. The Commission on the Resumption of Work was headed by the Bolsheviks' old bugbear Gvozdev, yet in the first weeks after the February Revolution the majority on the Petrograd Soviet Executive was comprised of radicals including several Bolsheviks; as Sukhanov recognised, the Bolshevik leader Shlyapnikov, a member of the Soviet's Propaganda Commission, headed 'the most influential workers' organisation' in Petrograd. On 4 March the Petrograd Soviet Executive considered the question of power and heard the Bolsheviks suggest that political power ought to pass 'into the hands of democracy', in other words to the Petrograd Soviet and other yet-to-be-formed bodies representing the peasantry and other mass social groups. The majority would not go that far, but felt there should be some degree of representation for the Petrograd Soviet in the ministries. To this end an agreement was reached to establish a Liaison Commission, linking the Provisional Government and the Petrograd Soviet; it started to operate on 7 March.[39]

Bringing life back to normal was largely the work of Gvozdev and the Petrograd Soviet rather than the Provisional Government. The trams resumed on 7 March, but it was only on the night of 10–11 March that the Petrograd Soviet and the Petrograd employers finalised the understanding on which the majority of workers would return to work. This recognised the eight-hour day for workers in Petrograd, but equally accepted that in wartime conditions longer shifts would continue but henceforth with proper overtime arrangements in place. The employers also agreed to recognise elected factory committees with which they would negotiate through conciliation boards made up of equal numbers of workers' representatives and employer delegates.[40] The Petrograd Soviet continued to play a crucial role in other ways. Because of the existence of the Liaison Committee with the Provisional Government, the Petrograd Soviet very quickly found itself carrying out quasi-governmental functions. Many routine aspects of daily life only functioned with the sanction of the Soviet: trains, for example, only travelled with the agreement of the Soviet; telegrams could only be sent with the endorsement of the Soviet; and nothing could be printed without the Soviet's say so. The Soviet became the place to which the population surged with greetings, proposals and complaints. Despite being an unofficial body, the Soviet sent a revolutionary guard to the State Bank, the State Treasury and the State Mint in order to monitor activity: if the Soviet's brief was to support the Provisional Government 'as long as' it implemented a democratic programme, the Soviet felt it was quite legitimate to monitor that performance.

This became a particular issue on matters concerning the army. Guchkov, the minister of defence, established a commission headed by Polivanov, the former minister of defence dismissed by the Tsar in 1915, which was to consider how best the army might operate in a democratic state. The Polivanov Commission was due to receive submissions from all interested parties, and well into April it was still considering various proposals and working on a draft government statement. However, on 10 March the Petrograd Soviet adopted a Declaration on the Rights of Soldiers. This was, at least in theory, a contribution to the work of the Polivanov Commission, but as soon as the Soviet had adopted it, it became the norm for the behaviour of soldiers. The Declaration of the Rights of Soldiers took away from officers the right to have orderlies, gave soldiers and officers the right to wear civilian clothes when off duty, deprived officers of the right to impose disciplinary punishments, abolished compulsory saluting, ended political censorship and confirmed the right of soldiers to set up committees. Although Guchkov still hoped that the Provisional Government might issue its own Declaration of the Rights of Soldiers, the Soviet decision of 10 March had usurped this power.[41]

Although the power of the Petrograd Soviet was substantial, it was no longer as wary of liberal politicians as it had been during the transfer of power. Within it the influence of reformist elements began to grow as the immediate revolutionary crisis passed and it began to operate on a more orderly basis. The reformist Menshevik leadership had long had a troubled relationship with radical labour militants, but with the formation of a Soldiers' Section in the Petrograd Soviet, more and more soldiers became involved in its activities and they reinforced the position of the reformists. That process was strengthened still further on 14 March when the Mandate Commission of the Petrograd Soviet decided to establish regular representational norms for factories and weed out those elected with no clear mandate during the chaos of the revolution. On top of this, as more and more exiled revolutionaries returned from Siberia, they were co-opted to the Executive of the Petrograd Soviet, and many of the more prominent Siberian exiles were reformists. Sukhanov commented that 'During the first weeks it was painful to watch the proletariat in the soviet, at the core of the revolution, being more and more submerged among the impenetrable little peasants in their grey great coats.' These peasants in uniform, he suggested, were wooed by Kerensky and the reformist leaders of the Petrograd Soviet to moderate the more militant instincts of the working class.[42]

For all Sukhanov's concerns, it was important for the fate of the revolution that the soldiers were wooed by the Petrograd Soviet rather than military figures opposed to it. On 2 March, General Lavr Kornilov was plucked from the obscurity of the 48th Artillery Division in Galicia and, on the orders of the Duma president, made Commander of the Petrograd Military District. On 10 March he addressed the Executive of the Petrograd Soviet, warned of the danger of an imminent German offensive and called for 'discipline and solidarity'. Sukhanov was sceptical about the reality of such an offensive, but the speech had its impact. From 12 March, regiments began to lobby the Petrograd Soviet on a daily basis with their patriotic slogans. As Sukhanov and the left in the Petrograd Soviet saw things, what was developing was 'a struggle for the army between the Soviet and the propertied classes'. Soldiers were subjected to propaganda about the 'idle' workers who demanded the eight-hour day and thus did not do their bit for the war effort. Groups of armed soldiers began to visit factories and insist on inspecting production to check that everything needed for the front was in hand. Workers responded by explaining that the eight-hour day was purely notional since overtime was still worked on a regular basis, and that workers had voluntarily agreed to shorten the Easter holiday; there were, of course, production delays, but these were the result of breakdowns in the supply chain and had nothing to do with the attitude of workers.[43] As Sukhanov later recalled:

> Doggedly, step by step, the Petrograd workers explained the real state of affairs to the soldiers – in private conversation, in mass meetings, in the Soviet, in the barracks and in the factories themselves. In every factory special meetings were devoted to 'the soldiers' and the bourgeois-baiting campaign, and resolutions were passed making a special appeal to the soldiers' intelligence and sense of justice.[44]

Although during the second half of March the situation was critical, the danger of the soldiers turning against the workers gradually passed; after soldier delegations had actually met the workers and held talks with them, their mood usually changed. By the start of April, Sukhanov believed 'the primitive instincts had been neutralised which would have swept away' the revolution: 'within the first days of April it began to be clear that democracy, even if it had not yet won, was undoubtedly going to win in the struggle for the army [...] At the factories, instead of brawls, there was triumphant fraternisation between soldiers and workers.' The 'patriotic bourgeoisie had played on the foreign peril' in an attempt to weaken the Petrograd Soviet and had failed.[45]

THE APRIL CRISIS

It was in this atmosphere of potential tension between workers and soldiers that the issue of peace came to the fore. On 14 March the Petrograd Soviet had issued a manifesto to the peoples of the world urging them to take part in a common struggle to re-establish peace. This would not be a unilateral peace – there was no suggestion that revolutionary Russia would simply pull out of the war – but Russia's war aims needed to be reconsidered for the new democratic order. Russia was now a democratic state fighting two archaic semi-feudal empires to establish a democratic world order. At the very least, revolutionary Russia should announce that it was fighting for a democratic peace and call a conference of its allies to clarify its war aims; it was possible such a conference would seek a negotiated end to the fighting. Through its appeal, the Petrograd Soviet hoped workers in Britain and France might pressurise their governments to adopt a similar stance. The SR leader Victor Chernov commented at about this time somewhat rashly that 'we need to combine the Russian Revolution with an Anglo-French one'.[46]

On 21 March, radicals within the Executive of the Petrograd Soviet decided to push the issue of peace one stage further. They introduced a motion calling for the Petrograd Soviet to initiate a nationwide campaign for peace: the Tsar's programme of alliances should be rejected and a joint call issued by the allied powers for a peace 'without annexations or indemnities'. The leadership of the Petrograd Soviet, which had recently been reinforced by the return from exile of Tsereteli, the leader of the Social Democratic Group in the Second State Duma, opposed this motion. After much debate, the Petrograd Soviet agreed a compromise: there would be no special initiative on peace by the Petrograd Soviet, but it would ask the Provisional Government 'to repudiate all aggressive treaties'. The necessity of this became clear when, on 24 March, the foreign minister and Kadet Party leader Milyukov gave a press interview to mark the occasion of the United States entering the war. Although he referred to the need for 'peace without annexations', he also listed three territories that the free Russian state needed to acquire: those parts of Austria–Hungary inhabited by Ukrainians; Armenian-speaking parts of Turkey; and control of the Bosphorus, the straits linking the Black Sea and the Mediterranean. The next day, Kerensky and a majority of government ministers persuaded Milyukov to clarify that this was his personal view and not that of the government, but the damage was done.[47]

On the evening of 24 March, the Liaison Commission between the Petrograd Soviet and the Provisional Government met, now reinforced by the presence of Tsereteli. Although Milyukov was adamant that there was no need for a government document outlining revised war aims and that there was no way he would sign such a document, Tsereteli demanded a new and clear statement of war aims, arguing that Soviet support for such a statement would help inspire the army. Milyukov's fellow ministers were persuaded and declined to back Milyukov: a statement was duly drafted on 26 March, which came close to the views of the Soviet, but contained no clause specifically rejecting the acquisition of territory. Debated by the Executive of the Petrograd Soviet on 27 March, the statement was first rejected, then, after a telephone call from Lvov and certain minor amendments had been made, the Petrograd Soviet changed its mind and agreed to endorse the Government Declaration on War Aims, issued later on the 27th.[48] The statement read: 'the objective of the free Russian state is not the subjugation of other nations, it is not the expropriation of their national possessions, nor is it the conquest by force of arms of foreign territories: it is the establishment of a lasting peace based on the rights of nations to self-determination'.[49] Was this clear enough? The Executive of the Petrograd Soviet was bitterly divided on the issue.

Tsereteli suggested that he had forced a major concession from the Provisional Government and that this form of words was in line with Soviet policy. Those to his left saw only minor, even trivial amendments to the Provisional Government's earlier statement. In retrospect, the left's anger was largely prompted by the change in the balance of forces within the Soviet. It saw this as the moment when reformists won firm control of the Executive of the Petrograd Soviet. This victory was reinforced by the First All-Russian Conference of Soviets, which took place in Petrograd from 29 March to 2 April. The 479 delegates represented 138 local soviets, 7 armies, 13 rear units and 26 front units. The conference endorsed the earlier decision of the Petrograd Soviet that the Provisional Government would be supported 'in so far' as it implemented 'the programme of revolutionary democracy', and at its close on 3 April adopted a programme calling for 'peace, land and bread'. However, the new Soviet Executive, when elected, cemented the domination of the reformists.[50]

Issues of war and peace were highlighted early in April when the Bolshevik leader Vladimir Lenin and other Russian revolutionaries trapped in Switzerland by the war and unable to return to Russia were allowed to cross Germany in a sealed train carriage and thus make their way to Sweden, Finland and Russia. The patriotic press whipped up a campaign against the Soviet left. Baltic sailors, who had at first welcomed Lenin's return, were persuaded in the middle of April to pass a resolution expressing shock at his apparent connivance in his travel arrangements with the enemy power; hostile demonstrations were organised at Bolshevik headquarters, with crowds calling for Lenin's arrest. On 17 April a demonstration of the war-wounded lobbied the Petrograd Soviet and also demanded Lenin's arrest. In this climate an apparently trivial issue took on major importance. The Provisional Government decided to refuse to allow into Russia a Swiss socialist who had travelled with Lenin across Germany but had stayed behind in Stockholm for a few days. This decision was raised in the Liaison Committee on 10 April by Victor Chernov, the SR leader, just a couple of days after he too had returned from exile. Chernov had arrived in Russia in a militant mood. As soon as he could, he published an article in the SR press making clear that 'we support the Provisional Government, but not Milyukov'. On 11 April he got the Soviet Executive to raise in the Liaison Committee the idea of circulating the Declaration of War Aims of 27 March to the Allies in the form of a diplomatic note. In an extended personal clash with Milyukov, Chernov argued that since the government declaration had been addressed to the Russian people, the Allies would have had

Fig. 4: A meeting of the Soldiers' Soviet in the chamber of the State Duma

no reason to consider it. With some reluctance, Milyukov agreed to send a diplomatic note to the Allies drawing to their attention the declaration of 27 March. When the text of the note was made public on 19 April, for the left at least, 'it annulled everything the revolution had accomplished on behalf of peace up until then', for Milyukov had included with the note a covering letter.[51]

This letter made it clear that free Russia was a reliable ally, that any talk of a separate peace was 'absurd' and 'that the Provisional Government, while defending our country's rights, will fully observe the obligations undertaken toward her allies'. The war would end, it was hoped, in a 'durable peace' underpinned by 'guarantees and sanctions which are essential to the prevention of new blood-spilling conflicts'.[52] This reference to peace underpinned by 'guarantees and sanctions' was a far cry from 'peace based on the right of nations to self-determination'. Similarly, comment on observing 'obligations to the allies' seemed to refer to the secret treaties signed by the Tsar which allocated to Russia territory that was currently part of the Austro-Hungarian Empire and Turkey, the very territory referred to by Milyukov in his interview of 23 March. There was some justification in terms of self-determination for the notion of areas of Austria–Hungary inhabited by Ukrainians joining the Russian Empire or even for Turkish Armenians joining together with Russian Armenians, but Russia acquiring the Bosphorus and naval access to the Mediterranean was naked imperialism.

Protests at the implication of Milyukov's note began at once. On 20 April between 25,000 and 30,000 soldiers, all in uniform and some of them armed, demonstrated outside the building of the Provisional Government, the Mariinskii Palace. They demanded Milyukov's resignation, but the demonstrators were not particularly threatening since several military bands also attended. When the Provisional Government met to consider its next step, it heard General Kornilov request permission to disperse the demonstrators by force. Lvov and Kerensky dismissed such a proposal out of hand and insisted on a negotiated settlement. Thus Petrograd Soviet vice chairman Skobelev took to a podium at the Mariinskii Palace and explained that negotiations to clarify the situation were already underway. He was followed by General Kornilov who called on the soldiers to return to their barracks at once and leave the resolution of the crisis to their elected representatives in the Petrograd Soviet: 'It is your legitimate right to voice your needs peacefully and in order, but that does not mean coming forward with weapons in your hand. You must wait in your barracks for the legitimate resolutions made by your legitimate representatives.'[53]

Most soldiers obeyed these instructions, but the following day, 21 April, workers rather than soldiers organised a demonstration that planned to march both to the Mariinskii Palace and then on to the Tauride Palace, where the Petrograd Soviet was based. They too called for the resignation of Milyukov, but unlike the unarmed demonstrators of the previous day, they were accompanied by armed Red Guards. And, unlike on the 20th, these demonstrators faced a counter-demonstration organised by Milyukov's Kadet Party. Most of the Kadet demonstrators were well behaved and well dressed and listened politely to speeches from Milyukov himself and Minister of War Guchkov.[54] Others, however, were interested in direct action. Three separate groups of demonstrators were involved. Those from the Vyborg Side crossed the river Neva at about 3 pm and marched along Sadovaya Street towards Nevskii Prospekt. When they reached Nevskii, a group of army officers and Kadet demonstrators tried to bar their way. A scuffle broke out. The Kadets tried to seize a banner reading 'Down with the Provisional Government!', and as they did so some officers drew their sabres, others pulled pistols from their holsters and a shot rang out from a building on Sadovaya Street. Despite this, the demonstrators forced their way onto Nevskii Prospekt and marched down towards the Admiralty Building and the Mariinskii Palace.

Frustrated at their failure to stop the demonstrators from reaching Nevskii Prospekt, the Kadets and their officer supporters held a rally outside 'The Passage', Nevskii Prospekt's premier shopping arcade. Learning that a second group of demonstrators was about to enter Nevskii Prospekt from Sadovaya Street, they rushed to meet them. The two groups clashed outside the Kazan Cathedral. Banners were seized, and this time the workers began to retreat. As they retreated, some of the Red Guards dropped to the ground and opened fire. Officers rushed to seize their weapons, and shots were exchanged, before the shaken workers were allowed to pass. In buoyant mood after what seemed to them to have been a successful clash with the workers, the Kadets and officers marched first to the Mariinskii Palace to show their support for the Provisional Government, and then to the home of Defence Minister Guchkov nearby on the Moika

River Embankment. From there they held a rally outside the Kazan Cathedral.

Early in the evening, just as the Kadets and officers were about to disperse, a third workers' demonstration arrived. This came from Vasilevskii Island and therefore entered Nevskii Prospekt from the Admiralty end, not Sadovaya Street. As the demonstrators approached the Kazan Cathedral there was another armed clash, before they were allowed to advance towards Sadovaya Street. Here they were stopped by more Kadets and officers. After negotiations, the demonstrators made clear that they were heading home and were allowed past. However, the tail end of the demonstrators got separated from their Red Guard escort and some Kadets and officers grabbed their banner and headed back to Nevskii Prospekt. In pursuit of the banner, Red Guards drew their weapons and soon there was a gun battle, with the Kadets and officers taking shelter in the Gostiinii Dvor shopping gallery and the demonstrators taking shelter by the public library. After an exchange of fire lasting some five minutes, the Red Guards retreated.[55]

Moves to bring the crisis to an end had been underway since the night of 20 April when the Provisional Government and Petrograd Soviet representatives had drafted a 'supplementary note' that would be sent to the Allied governments. This text was endorsed by the Executive of the Petrograd Soviet on the afternoon of the 21st, after hearing a report from Tsereteli. On the 22nd it called on the soldiers to remain in their barracks unless given written instructions calling on them to demonstrate: 'only the Executive Committee has the right to give you orders', the appeal stated, 'your guns are for the protection of the revolution – you do not need them for demonstrations or meetings'. However, although the issue of the 'Note of 18 April' was now closed by the Executive of the Petrograd Soviet, it was also decided on 21 April that as a matter of principle 'it is necessary to adopt resolute measures at once for increasing control over the activities of the Provisional Government' and that 'no major political act must be published without first notifying the Soviet Executive'. The logic of this decision was that the Petrograd Soviet should now join the government, but such a move was still hotly debated by liberal and Soviet politicians alike.[56]

After the April Crisis was over, the Provisional Government drafted a declaration which was issued on 26 April. This asserted that the Provisional Government had assumed power with 'the unanimous support of the people' and that it had a clear programme: summoning the Constituent Assembly; introducing civil liberties; establishing democratic local government; introducing civil rights to the army while retaining discipline; and fighting the war to a victorious conclusion. The declaration suggested that much had already been achieved, but expressed 'anxieties' about certain issues: 'The power of the state should be based not on coercion, but on the consent of free citizens to submit to the power they themselves created', and yet 'less conscious and less organised strata of the population threatened to destroy the country's internal civil cohesion and discipline'. To prevent anarchy at home and defeat abroad, order was needed, but for that order to be achieved the Provisional Government felt the need to expand its membership. This declaration was tantamount to an appeal for the formation of a Coalition Government with the moderate socialists of the Soviet. Liberals like Lvov were happy with the declaration and its stress on the support of the masses, but this was not a view shared by liberals closer to Milyukov, who saw the legitimacy of the state resting on the constitutional transfer of power from the Tsar to the Duma politicians rather than deriving from the sovereignty of the popular masses.[57]

On the night of 28–9 April the Executive of the Petrograd Soviet voted 23–22 not to join the government; on the night of 1–2 May it reversed that decision. This change of heart was largely due to the work of Tsereteli, who had learned that Milyukov and his supporters were developing a plan for the liberal ministers to stage a mass resignation from the Provisional Government aimed at forcing the Soviet to assume power.[58] When on 2 May Lvov tried to carry out a government reshuffle and move Milyukov to head the Ministry of Education rather than the Ministry of Foreign Affairs, divisions among the liberals became acute. The Kadet Central Committee tried to persuade Milyukov to accept this demotion, but he would not and resigned in protest. However, the Kadet Central Committee did not endorse his resignation and prevented it leading to the sort of mass resignation Milyukov wanted by making clear that it had no intention of calling on other ministers to resign. Milyukov's departure in fact opened the way for the formation of a Coalition Government on 5 May.

3

THE SUCCESS OF COALITION

COALITION POLITICS

The decision of the Soviet Executive to take part in a Coalition Government marked an important milestone: reformism had firmly triumphed within the Soviet leadership. The driving force of the February Revolution had not been the hesitant moves of the liberal politicians in the Duma, but the determined action of the working-class rank and file. Yet as February turned to March, that determination was filtered through a hybrid Petrograd Soviet, whose 'accidental' leaders hardly reflected the militant mood on the streets. The formation of the Soldiers' Section of the Soviet, and the prominence given to returning reformist exiles, changed the make-up of the Soviet still further and paved the way for reformist socialists joining the government. In government, history repeated itself. During 1907, Tsereteli found it intensely frustrating working with the Kadets in the Second State Duma. Now, working with the Kadets in government proved no easier. In 1907, the failure of Tsereteli's travails enabled the Bolsheviks to prosper and win control of the Social Democratic Party. Would history repeat itself in this way too? Lenin was certainly determined that it should.

As the Coalition Government set about its work, the Mensheviks and SRs found the pedantic legalism of the Kadets infuriating, as Tsereteli must have suspected they would. The Kadets insisted that there could be no enactment of social reform until the Constituent Assembly had met. The two socialist parties argued, on the other hand, that some social reforms were so urgent that they needed to be implemented at once, if only in a provisional manner; the Constituent Assembly, which was bound to be far more radical than any of the four State Dumas since all adults would have an equal vote, could endorse such urgent reforms retrospectively. What made Tsereteli and the other supporters of the Coalition persevere with the difficult work of coalition politics was their shared commitment to victory in World War I. The war was the cement that held the coalition together, and it was opposition to the war which enabled the Bolshevik opponents of the coalition to make their mark. With Lenin in Switzerland and the Bolshevik Duma deputies exiled to Siberia, the Bolshevik response to the February Revolution had been radical but ill-disciplined and confused. However, the return of Lenin, followed a month later by the formation of the Coalition Government, helped bring clarity to their stance. In line with the revolutionary tradition established in 1905, the Bolsheviks opposed co-operation with the liberals and therefore wanted to bring down the coalition government. By the end of June they were well on the way to achieving this and ending the Coalition Government between socialists and liberals, that embodiment of reformist politics.

Tsereteli played a key role in forming the Coalition Government. It was he who insisted that the Soviet parties should not demand a majority in the government. The Soviet had joined the government not because it wanted to exercise power, but because its leaders were afraid that mass resignation on the part of the liberal ministers might create a power vacuum in which they were to assume power. Tsereteli saw himself as responding to the Government Declaration of 26 April on the need to broaden the government. He was broadening the government by making Soviet support more tangible than working through the Liaison Committee, but this was support rather than responsibility. Tsereteli also insisted that in supporting the government, the socialist ministers were still accountable to the Petrograd Soviet. This was because the Petrograd Soviet had laid down some conditions before it agreed to send Menshevik and SR ministers into a coalition with 'the bourgeoisie'. There was agreement on the need to introduce at once a new democratic structure for local government and to press ahead with work on summoning a Constituent Assembly. A minimal social programme was also agreed: the government would in future 'oversee' the workings of commerce and industry in order 'to protect' labour, while also preparing for the transfer of land to the peasantry in a way that would ensure the greatest possible production of grain for the war effort. The problem with this social programme was that the socialist ministers were in a minority. Of the 15 ministers, there were only two Mensheviks, three SRs and one Popular Socialist – the Popular Socialists had inherited the reformist SR tradition of the Labourites in the State Dumas. While the liberal-dominated Coalition had no qualms about democratising local government as the first stage in summoning the Constituent Assembly, it had little interest in addressing the social concerns which the Mensheviks and SRs put forward. Skobelev, the Menshevik minister of labour, could raise workers' concerns; Chernov, the SR minister of agriculture, could stress the need to address the question of land; but the liberals could always trump their socialist colleagues by insisting that such major transformations of the country had to await the Constituent Assembly.[1]

The liberal policy of stabilisation rather than reform pushed the party towards a position where it seemed to be defending privilege. When the Kadets met in congress on 8 May, the majority favoured support for Milyukov's rather sour verdict on recent events: 'what reason is there for continuing the revolution'? Industry became an immediate battleground. For liberals, too much interference in industry risked disrupting markets and profit, so there seemed no alternative to continuing the Tsar's system of economic regulation. The minister of trade and industry, a leading member of the War Industries' Committee, dismantled only those Tsarist institutions which had frustrated the work of the War Industries' Committee, leaving the others in place. In early May, liberals began to campaign for workers' 'interference' in production to be curbed and for the rights of 'spontaneously formed' organisations, factory councils, to be limited. The minister of trade and industry was clear that employers would rather close their enterprises than accept more regulation. Yet on 16 May the Soviet demanded 'the immediate, total and systematic' extension of state supervision over the economy. Two days later, the minister resigned in protest and the liberal press attacked both the Soviet and the Coalition Government for not being 'impartial' in their approach to economic policy. The new minister of trade and industry was no softer on the Soviet, drafting by early June 'measures to end worker radicalism and reverse the disruption of industry'; he also hoped to persuade the Coalition Government of the need to make a public statement opposing 'socialism', a policy in line with the contemporaneous First All Russian Congress of Trade and Industry which had urged the Coalition Government to recognise that 'no economic organisation other than capitalism is possible in Russia'. Liberal talk of standing 'above class' was slipping further towards acting as a bulwark against change.[2]

The Coalition Government did not issue a statement condemning 'socialism', and it survived the liberal–socialist tensions largely because of the commitment of two key Soviet politicians who were determined to make the Coalition work: Tsereteli and Kerensky. Even before the April Crisis, Tsereteli had taken measures to make the Soviet more effective. Nominally the ruling body of the Soviet was its Executive Committee which met about three times a week. From 14 April onwards, however, Tsereteli established an informal inner bureau, soon branded the 'Star Chamber', which met daily at the house he shared with Skobelev and 'prepared business' for Soviet Executive meetings. One of its first moves was to bring the Soviet newspaper *Izvestiya* firmly under its control.[3] Tsereteli's formal position was minister of post and telegraph, but he left the running of the ministry to his deputies and devoted his time instead to the Soviet and its work in supporting the principle of coalition. He dominated the events of May and June: Chernov called him the 'minister of general affairs'; for Sukhanov he was 'commissar of the government within the Soviet'. Unlike the liberals, who argued that 'spontaneous bodies' like the soviets weakened the authority of the state, Tsereteli wanted to create a strong government that would be based on those new bodies thrown up by the revolution. And this is precisely what happened. After the First Congress of Soviets, which opened on 3 June, had established a new Central Executive Committee, this body was quickly expanded into a massive administrative organisation: it soon consisted of 18 departments employing several hundred personnel; with an Agrarian Department, a Transport Department and an Economic Planning Department it was, as Tsereteli intended it to be, a shadow government.[4]

Tsereteli argued that 'either revolutionary democracy gets the anarchistic elements under its control, or it will fall together with them'.[5] Therefore it was essential to build up the authority of the Soviet. This was first put to the test when on 16 May the local soviet in the naval base at Kronstadt announced that it no longer recognised the authority of the government. On 22 May, Tsereteli went to Kronstadt and addressed the sailors assembled on Anchor Square, threatening to declare the area 'an insurgent province' unless the Kronstadters backed down. He risked unpopularity again when at the First Congress of Soviets he told delegates that in the present circumstances 'responsible workers' could not press for the eight-hour day, something that went down no better than when Gvozdev had condemned 'strikomania' on the eve of World War I.[6] As his biographer W. H. Roobol noted, Tsereteli 'was not sufficiently attuned to the sentiments that lived among the masses'. Nevertheless despite everything, Tsereteli achieved some famous victories. Behind the scenes, when Prime Minister Lvov began to have doubts about his minister of agriculture, Chernov, Tsereteli made clear that all the Soviet ministers would resign if Chernov were to be dismissed, and he was equally forceful on the question of the timing of the Constituent Assembly. On 4 June the First Congress of Soviets set the date for the Constituent Assembly as 17 September, but earlier a Kadet congress had voted to delay the Constituent Assembly until after the war had been won; on 14 June, Tsereteli and the socialist ministers raised the timing of the Constituent Assembly in cabinet, and the government agreed to set the date of 17 September.[7]

Tsereteli was totally committed to the war and the idea that the Coalition Government should launch an offensive. Once *Izvestiya* was firmly in his hands, it supported the offensive campaign initially pencilled in for mid-June. From the very moment the new Coalition cabinet was formed, 'Take the Offensive' became the order of the day. As Sukhanov commented, 'the Coalition had grouped itself around the offensive'.[8] Even as the Coalition was being formed, Tsereteli attended a joint meeting with military commanders at which he insisted that a democratised army was still an army that was capable of fighting. He was confident that 'an offensive strengthens the revolution'.[9] The offensive, however, was the primary concern of the second pillar of the coalition: Kerensky became minister of war in the Coalition Government. He was, with Tsereteli, the driving force behind those successes which the Coalition had.

Kerensky's predecessor, Guchkov, had only very reluctantly agreed on 16 April, some ten days before his resignation, that 'while preserving the fundamental principle of combat' that 'the unquestioning execution of orders' was essential and that the spontaneously formed 'system of elective military organisations' would be standardised and systematised so that soldiers could 'exercise their civil and political rights'. This order of 16 April

Fig. 5: Iraklii Tsereteli, leader of the Social Democrats in the Second State Duma and effective Soviet leader during the First Coalition Government

made clear that general meetings of soldiers 'should not interfere with combat work'.[10] Kerensky, by contrast, embraced the soldiers' committees and was determined to show that this new democratic army could fight, and fight effectively. One of Kerensky's first moves as minister of war was to sign the Declaration of the Rights of Soldiers, something which Guchkov had steadfastly refused to do. However, he only signed the declaration after adding two new clauses which made clear that no one other than commanders had the right to nominate officers, and that officers had the right to use force if they faced disobedience during combat; this final clause, known as 'paragraph 14', was much criticised by the Bolsheviks. On 7 May, almost as soon as he had been appointed, Kerensky visited the Petrograd regiments and then set off on a whistle-stop tour of the front, taking with him a group of pro-war socialists which included Grigorii Aleksinskii, once Tsereteli's protagonist as the Bolshevik leader in the Second State Duma. It was on 12 May that Kerensky signed the document committing the Russian Army to an offensive, and later the same day he addressed troops on the South West Front, before moving on to Odessa, Sevastopol and Kiev. By 20 May he was at General Staff Headquarters in Mogilev and, on 23–5 May, he visited the Northern Front, before returning once more to Mogilev.[11]

During this tour Kerensky was at times so close to the front that his life was in danger, but the purpose of these visits was to meet front-line soldiers. He met elected soldier delegates and he met with entire regiments. These meetings were not simply aimed at boosting moral, but at persuading the soldiers to agree on the need for an offensive. After hearing Kerensky speak, meetings of regimental committees or mass general meetings of soldiers would discuss the offensive and debate whether or not they were willing to take part. Indeed, the start of the offensive was delayed more than once so that Kerensky could address what were felt to be key groups of soldiers. Although Kerensky later recalled that during the offensive 'whole divisions would rebel and were only formally subservient', the impression not only of the contemporary press, which was biased in favour of the offensive, but of contemporary letters and diaries, confirms how effective his speeches were, even if the upbeat mood did not always survive long after a meeting was over.[12]

The meetings could be extraordinarily successful. One English commentator noted, 'When he left, they carried him on their shoulders to his car. They kissed him, his uniform, his car, the ground on which he walked.'[13] When the offensive began, even units that were felt to be at risk in fact fought well. As even the Bolsheviks conceded, Kerensky's May visits had succeeded since 'soldiers believe the Minister of War and go where he orders'. And the tenor of Kerensky's campaign was clear: 'Let all the peoples know that we are not talking about peace from weakness. They should know that freedom has increased our strength.' The offensive would show Russia's strength to the Allies and put her in a position where she could force war aims to be clarified. The democratic powers of Europe and America were standing up to the archaic empires of Germany and Austria–Hungary. And the soldiers would repeat his slogans: 'Peace to the whole world! Peace without annexations and reparations! Freedom for all people.' As the SR minister of the navy declared, 'With the Red Flag of Freedom, the Russian Army is Bringing Peace to the World.' For Kerensky the offensive meant that peace could come with victory in two to three months' time. Some of those around Kerensky even hoped that the offensive would force a German revolution, presenting Kerensky as the leader of a world revolution.[14]

Albert Thomas, the French socialist, accompanied Kerensky on one of these trips to the front and noted, 'Has he any aspirations to dictatorship? I do not think so, but he savours and maintains his popularity.' Certainly he used his position as minister of war to reinforce his position in the government; between trips to the front he formed an inner cabinet with Tsereteli to deal with the war and foreign affairs. During his first days in office he also brought together the staff who would remain with him until October. The SR Party had always supported the use of terror as a political weapon, and using the former terror section of the SR Party as a basis, Kerensky established a new Political Department within the War Ministry to act as commissars and mediate between officers and men. Such commissars would be the key to persuading a democratic army to fight, since through their actions soldiers would become aware of what they were fighting for and why discipline was essential. One of these commissars was Boris Savinkov, who in July 1904 had assassinated the then minister of the interior, Vyacheslav von Plehve; Savinkov served as commissar of the Seventh Army.[15]

Although Kerensky had served as a Labourite deputy to the Fourth State Duma, he was a long-term member of the SR Party,

Fig. 6: Kerensky during a tour of the front

serving on its Central Committee. The enthusiasm with which he took to the role of minister of war seemed to some party members like incipient Bonapartism, and this did not help his standing in the SR Party. At the end of May he was in Moscow for the party's Third Congress, and when elections were held to the Central Committee on 1 June, he failed to get elected by just two votes. Kerensky had looked certain to be elected until those on the left of the party suggested he was not fit for election because of the penalties which that very day had been introduced for those soldiers accused of desertion. The actual penalties were pretty uncontroversial: the deserter would be deprived of the right to vote, and his family would be deprived of the soldier's benefit, which was often desperately needed to feed his children. However, because of what Kerensky felt was inept chairing of the congress session on the part of Chernov, the impression was given that Kerensky was threatening to restore the death penalty in order to combat desertion. Personal relations between Kerensky and Chernov were never restored and Kerensky felt he had been stabbed in the back, comforted only by the decision of one of his closest colleagues to resign from the Central Committee as an act of solidarity.[16]

Preceded by a spectacular two-day-long artillery bombardment, the offensive began on 18 June. The Russian Army had never been better supplied with shells and guns, but it was a bloody affair because the Germans were well aware of what was planned and had moved troops from France to meet the challenge; with Kerensky visiting the front so often and so many meetings taking place, it was hard to retain any element of surprise. Where the fighting was most intense, on the South West Front, 12,000 Russians died and 90,000 were wounded; on the opposing side 16,000 died and 77,000 were injured. Although up to the very last minute Kerensky was not sure that his soldiers would go into battle, they did and with unexpected élan.[17] Kerensky was briefly the hero of the hour. When he met General Kornilov, now commanding the Eighth Army, red flags were flying and Kornilov himself shouted, 'Long live the people's leader Kerensky!' Although on 24 June Kerensky could report that 'the operation which has started is developing significantly less successfully than one might have hoped', on the 25th Kornilov's troops staged a dramatic advance, taking some 20 miles of territory.[18]

Then the offensive began to unravel. Although the 150th Infantry Regiment could resolve on 29 June that it would 'unequivocally fulfil the orders of People's Minister Kerensky' and go wherever they were ordered, by 3 July the collapse of the offensive was clear to all.[19] Kerensky was then with General Kornilov on the South West Front, but he returned to General Staff Headquarters on the 4th to analyse the situation. The offensive had been what kept this first Coalition Government together: it was the number one priority of the Coalition, the glue that held the disparate elements of the government together. If that coalition had held, if the Bolsheviks had remained as they were at the start of May, a small but determined opposition, the outcome of 1917 might have been very different. However, the Coalition could not withstand the collapse of the offensive.

LENIN AND A SOVIET GOVERNMENT

The formation of the Coalition Government on 5 May helped Lenin impose his analysis of events on the Bolshevik Party. By the

Soviet Executive joining the government it seemed symbolically to be distancing itself from the workers and allying itself with the bourgeoisie. For Bolsheviks, as Sukhanov put it, the formation of the Coalition Government ushered in 'the triumph of reaction'. The Bolshevik Party's strategy in the immediate weeks after the Tsar's overthrow had been confused and inconsistent. According to the hierarchical principle on which the party operated, in Petrograd there existed both a Russian Bureau of the Central Committee and a St Petersburg Committee; below that there was also a series of district committees. The Tsar's clampdown on the night of 26 February resulted in the arrest of the entire membership of the St Petersburg Committee, which had already been weakened by earlier arrests. So it fell to the Vyborg District Committee, the strongest in the capital, to give what cohesion the Bolsheviks could to the revolutionary movement as the Petrograd Soviet was formed. During 27 February the Vyborg District Committee issued leaflets calling for the formation of soviets in the factories and for Petrograd as a whole, and at a meeting on 1 March it made clear that the party wanted these soviets to come together and form a Provisional Revolutionary Government that would administer the country until a Constituent Assembly could be held.[20]

Unlike the Petrograd Committee, the members of the Russian Bureau of the Central Committee, which included Shlyapnikov, had escaped arrest on the 26th and it was able to give some guidance during the February Revolution, issuing a manifesto which appeared in the first issue of the Petrograd Soviet paper *Izvestiya* on 28 February. This also called for the formation of a Provisional Revolutionary Government, rather than the Provisional Government then in the process of formation; this Provisional Revolutionary Government would be composed of members of the Petrograd Soviet and would introduce the immediate demands of the Bolshevik programme. The wording of this manifesto was confirmed by the Russian Bureau at its meeting on 1 March. Thus both the Vyborg District Committee and the Russian Bureau were agreed that the Petrograd Soviet should be transformed into a revolutionary government.

The St Petersburg Committee, on the other hand, when it was reconstituted, was made up of people who had been arrested on or before 26 February and who therefore had little experience of the mood on the streets during the Tsar's overthrow. Perhaps for that reason they were much more cautious about proposing that the Petrograd Soviet form a revolutionary government. On 3 March the St Petersburg Committee voted completely differently to the Russian Bureau and the Vyborg District. There was no mention of the Petrograd Soviet forming a Provisional Revolutionary Government; on the contrary, the St Petersburg Committee proposed supporting the Provisional Government 'in so far as' its activities corresponded with the wishes of the masses. Two days later the Russian Bureau tried to persuade the St Petersburg Committee to fall into line, but it refused. Thus the Bolshevik Party was very obviously divided on the most fundamental issue of the day. Things did not improve when, on 12 March, Stalin and other exiled members of the Central Committee like Lev Kamenev returned from Siberia to swell the ranks of the Russian Bureau; enlarged from three members to fifteen, seven members remained opposed to the Provisional Government, two supported it and the others had no clear stance. With the Russian Bureau still hostile to the Provisional Government, the St Petersburg Committee also stood its ground and on 18 March it voted to offer 'conditional support' to the Provisional Government.[21]

Bolshevik policy turned back to its more radical stance on 22 March when the Russian Bureau adopted a resolution on the Provisional Government which it planned to present to a Conference of Bolshevik Party Workers on 29 March. The resolution made clear that the Provisional Government could not solve the tasks of the revolution; that the soviets were, in embryo, a new source of power; that in the meantime the Petrograd Soviet should hold the Provisional Government to account; and that for this to happen, the power of the soviets needed to be consolidated and a workers' Red Guard formed. However, under the surface disagreements continued. When Stalin presented the resolution to the conference on the 29th, he made clear that he actually preferred a different form of words that was less antagonistic to the Provisional Government and repeated the earlier formula of the St Petersburg Committee: that is, support for the Provisional Government 'in so far as' it supported the revolution. In the run up to the conference of 29 March, Stalin had been working closely with what became known as the *Pravda* group within the Bolshevik leadership. Led by Kamenev, who had taken over control of the Bolshevik newspaper *Pravda*, this group was even more supportive of the Provisional Government than the St Petersburg Committee. From 14 March onwards, *Pravda* editorials used the phrase 'conditional support' when referring to the Provisional Government. When Lenin sent *Pravda* a series of articles known as 'Letters from Afar', which repeated the earlier calls of the Russian Bureau and the Vyborg District for the soviets to become a Provisional Revolutionary Government, the *Pravda* editorial board decided his views should not be published in full.

As soon as Lenin was back in Russia, on the evening of 3 April, he brought this debate within the Bolshevik Party to an end by throwing his weight decisively behind the call for the Soviet to become a Provisional Revolutionary Government; henceforth the slogan 'a Soviet Government!' was primarily associated with the Bolsheviks. Lenin's arrival in Petrograd was suitably dramatic. Under Shlyapnikov's leadership the Bolsheviks had mobilised vast crowds in front of the Finland Station to welcome him, filling the entire square. There and then Lenin called for the soviets to be transformed into organs of state power, and he outlined these ideas in full the next day in a text which became known as the April Theses. It was clear to Lenin that it was not the Provisional Committee of the State

Fig. 7: Lenin addressing a crowd.

Duma that had taken power during the February Revolution but the Petrograd Soviet, and that the Petrograd Soviet had then handed that power back to the Provisional Committee of the State Duma. Real power lay with the armed soldiers, and the Provisional Government, formed as the result of negotiations between the Petrograd Soviet and the Provisional Committee of the State Duma, ruled only because the soldiers supported it. Thus what Lenin now advocated was 'systematic and patient work': strengthening the soviets and building workers' militias; establishing peasant soviets; winning over soldiers; exposing the reactionary nature of the Provisional Government.[22]

Although such an open call for the overthrow of the Provisional Government shocked many contemporaries, it did not mark a radical evolution in Bolshevik thought. During the 1905 Revolution, Lenin, like all Bolsheviks, had argued that the natural ally of the working class was the peasantry, not the liberal bourgeoisie. For that reason they did not see the St Petersburg Soviet as some sort of trade union institution but as a 'provisional revolutionary government in embryo'. In the years between 1905 and 1917, Lenin continued to insist that the soviets were a concrete manifestation of the worker–peasant alliance in action and that a countrywide union of soviets would, as the revolution progressed, constitute 'a democratic dictatorship of the proletariat and the peasantry'; a government formed in this way, he insisted in a 1909 article, would inevitably be led by the proletariat. His views were essentially the same when he wrote in 1915 that 'the social content of the approaching revolution in Russia can only be the revolutionary-democratic dictatorship of the proletariat and the peasantry'. By the second year of World War I, Lenin had linked a revolution in Russia to a prospective European revolution: a revolutionary-democratic dictatorship of the proletariat and peasantry was necessary in Russia 'in order to kindle the socialist revolution in Europe'. By 1917 he was suggesting that these revolutions would be roughly contemporaneous: in the case of the first revolution the ally of the Russian workers would be the Russian peasants, whereas in the case of the second it would be the workers of Europe.[23]

In those 'Letters from Afar' of mid-March 1917 which *Pravda* had been so unwilling to publish in full, Lenin first raised the point he would make on 4 April, a point which really was new

– Russia was about to experience a socialist revolution. The slogan 'a revolutionary dictatorship of the proletariat and the peasantry' needed to be updated. Lenin argued that, in reality, although for now just in a passive form, the dictatorship of the proletariat and peasantry had already been established in Russia through the nationwide network of soviets that were already in place and already had an effective veto on the power of the Provisional Government. This meant, therefore, that 'the bourgeois democratic revolution in Russia was already completed' and it was necessary to think of what should happen next. And in his view what came next was not 'a democratic dictatorship of the proletariat and peasantry' but a socialist revolution. The key to the success of a socialist revolution, he stressed, was to ensure that, as the socialist revolution progressed, it was the workers who led the peasants rather than the peasants who 'swamped' the workers with 'petty bourgeois' concerns about owning land. Already in March 1917 from Switzerland, Lenin had instructed that the new Bolshevik formula should be 'the revolutionary dictatorship of the proletariat and the *poorest* peasantry', not the peasantry as a whole.

In his speech on 4 April, Lenin explained why this was so important: when it came to land reform and the division of the nobles' estates, an alliance with the peasantry as a whole would result in land being divided equally among all the peasants, whereas an alliance with the poor peasants and village labourers was more likely to result in the formation of large model farms administered by soviets of farm labourers. In his view, 'worker-peasants are bound to be against the war, peasant proprietors for the war'; this was the essence of the future class conflict within the Russian Revolution, he argued, and to bring together the proletariat and the whole peasantry under some all-encompassing description like 'Democracy' was to deny class conflict. Bolsheviks needed to be clear – the future Soviet Government would be made up of just two groups, the working class and the poorer peasants.[24]

The April Theses, which Lenin propounded the day after his return to Russia, were summed up thus: 'The specific feature of the present situation in Russia is that the country is passing from the first stage of the revolution – which, owing to the insufficient class-consciousness and organisation of the proletariat, placed power in the hands of the bourgeoisie – to its second stage, which must place power in the hands of the proletariat and the poorest sections of the peasantry.' Two basic demands therefore followed: 'no support for the Provisional Government' and 'patient, systematic and persistent explanation' to the masses that the soviet was the 'only possible form of revolutionary government', exposing the errors of previous tactics and preaching 'the necessity of transferring the entire state power to the Soviets'.[25] The aim was to work towards establishing a state like the Paris Commune, which 'provides us with an example of a state like the Soviet of Workers' Deputies – the direct power of the organised and armed workers, the dictatorship of the workers and peasants'.[26]

Lenin's theses were not universally welcomed by his party comrades. On the right of the party, for example, the St Petersburg Committee rejected Lenin's April Theses on 8 April by 13 votes to 2.[27] However, when the Seventh Bolshevik Party Conference was held on 27 April–5 May, the April Theses were formally adopted as policy.[28] In the intervening weeks, Lenin had made clear that 'systematic and patient explanation' would take some time, and that the socialist revolution was still some way off. It was, he suggested, only Blanquists who stood for an attempt to seize power while the Bolsheviks remained in a minority in the soviets: 'we are still in a minority, we recognise the necessity to win a majority'. Lenin's appeal for time and preparation was reinforced by incidents during the April Crisis. Many of the Bolsheviks who took to the streets during the events of 20–21 April encouraged the use of slogans like 'arrest the Provisional Government' and seemed ready to establish a revolutionary administration at once. When Lenin wrote in *Pravda* on 23 April about 'The Lessons of the Crisis', he stressed that it was necessary to oppose both those in the party who had a 'policy of support' for the Provisional Government, and those who raised the demand 'Down with the Provisional Government' before the majority of the people were firmly united behind it; there was a danger of Blanquism in talk of 'seizing power' or 'arresting the Provisional Government'. Such 'Blanquists' did exist: they were grouped around the then secretary of the Central Committee, Bagdatiev, whose behaviour during the elections to the War Industries' Committee in 1915 had been so controversial. To the views of Bagdatiev, Lenin countered that 'in Russia the state of freedom today is such that the will of the majority can be ascertained by the composition of the soviets, that is to say that the Party, if it wishes seriously, not by Blanquism, to obtain power, must fight for influence within the soviets'.[29] The logic was clear: once the Bolsheviks had a majority in the soviets, the campaign for a Soviet Government would begin.

THE COALITION CHALLENGED

What Lenin called patient work in the soviets began in early May. From then on some partial re-election of Soviet deputies began to take place in the factories of the capital, and these gave greater weight to the Bolsheviks, who, as Sukhanov noted, 'had begun realising their programme of conquering the soviet'.[30] Patient work in the Soviet was already reaping rewards. Thus in the Pipe Factory a re-election took place on 17 May which became particularly heated. When a Soviet representative tried to persuade some of the workers to delay the re-election by a day, he was bundled into a wheelbarrow and pushed towards the River Neva; prompt intervention by more moderate voices, and a brief fist fight, prevented the Soviet representative being soaked or possibly drowned.[31] This incident was exceptional; most of this patient explanatory work was carried out at factory committee level and this work in the factories began to have an impact on the Workers' Section of the Petrograd Soviet: 'day by day it was irresistibly filling up with Bolsheviks', Sukhanov recalled. It was the Bolsheviks who took the initiative in organising the First Conference of Factory Committees, on 30 May, where nearly three-quarters of the delegates supported the Bolsheviks. In Sukhanov's words, that assembly 'reflected with precision the real physiognomy of the Petrograd proletariat'.[32] For Sukhanov, as for the Bolsheviks, by early summer the working class was moving away from its brief willingness to accept joint work with the liberals and back to its traditional stance of hostility to the liberals. Tsereteli really was 'not sufficiently attuned to the sentiments that lived among the masses'.

At the same time there were also the first signs that some soldiers, especially garrison soldiers, were moving over to the Bolsheviks and away from their almost instinctive support for the Soviet leadership. As soon as Lenin got back to Russia, the importance of the soldiers became obvious to him. He grasped at once that soldiers had to be incorporated into the revolutionary equation.[33] The Bolshevik Military Organisation was established on 31 March and from mid-April onwards its newspaper *Soldatskaya Pravda* began to appear; between April and June, 2,000 garrison soldiers were persuaded to join it.[34] In a few places whole military units backed the Bolsheviks: in Petrograd the First Machine Gun Regiment moved to support them in May,[35] as did the Latvian Riflemen regiments.[36] Bolshevik support among the sailors at the Kronstadt naval base was also soon very clear.[37] From the middle of May onwards, the Bolshevik Military Organisation took the lead in organising those soldiers opposed to Kerensky's attempts to restore aspects of pre-revolutionary discipline, and to prevent any move to send Petrograd garrison troops to the front in readiness for the offensive; as early as 23 May the Bolshevik Military Organisation had agreed to organise an armed street demonstration if there was an attempt to mobilise garrison soldiers. By 1 June the Bolshevik Military Organisation had held talks with representatives from the Kronstadt naval base and could inform the Bolshevik Central Committee that over 60,000 troops could be called onto the streets in the event of a clash with the government.[38]

When the First All-Russian Congress of Soviets took place from 3 to 24 June, its composition reflected none of the recent increased support for the Bolsheviks among workers and soldiers; of just over 1,000 delegates, only 105 were Bolsheviks. When it came to the vote on support for the Coalition Government, only 19 per cent of delegates voted against, although delegates did remind the socialist ministers that they had clear responsibilities to the popular masses and should see any decisions passed by the Soviet Congress as mandatory on them to implement. The moderate socialists, the Mensheviks and SRs, had total control over the Soviet apparatus, which meant that the newly formed Central Soviet Executive became a body quite unlike the revolutionary organ established at the end of February. More than ever before, decisions were taken through Tsereteli's 'Star Chamber', which critics argued served as 'the formal crystallisation of the dictatorship of a narrow little circle of opportunists'. Sukhanov suggested that 'the Praetorian Guard' of the Coalition Government was the Soldiers' Section of the Soviet. This could almost always be relied on to support the government, apart from odd incidents like the one when the Soviet Presidium tried to prevent Lenin concluding a speech to the Soldiers' Section in late May because he had run out of time, and the Soldiers' Section members voted to allow him to finish his speech.[39]

While the First Congress of Soviets was underway, to embarrass and challenge the Star Chamber 'opportunists', the Bolshevik Military Organisation decided on 4 June to stage a demonstration to honour the fallen heroes of the February Revolution. Several hundred Bolshevik-led Kronstadt sailors, joined by hundreds of garrison troops, marched to the Field of Mars in central Petrograd. There, those who addressed the crowd referred to the Bolshevik Military Organisation as 'the bulwark of the revolution'. This demonstration proved such a success that on 6 June the Bolshevik Military Organisation raised with the Bolshevik Central Committee the idea of holding a further demonstration with a clearly anti-government message, opposing the Coalition Government and demanding the formation of 'a Soviet Government' in its place. Although right-wing Bolsheviks like Kamenev opposed the idea of such a demonstration, Lenin favoured it and on 8 June a meeting of the Central Committee, the St Petersburg Committee and the Military Organisation agreed to press ahead and started to plan the details. With working-class areas like the Vyborg District clearly in support, on 9 June the Bolshevik press gave details of what was to happen and when: demonstrators would assemble at 2pm on Saturday, 10 June. In readiness, the Bolshevik Military Organisation prepared its forces for a possible armed clash, while the powerful Vyborg District Bolshevik Committee distributed arms and laid plans to seize control of vital public services.[40]

These activities were halted at the eleventh hour by the Central Committee and the party's delegation to the First Congress of Soviets, without the St Petersburg Committee and the Military Organisation being consulted. This radical about-turn took place because, on 8 June, the First Congress of Soviets, after its overwhelming vote in favour of support for the Coalition Government, had at the same time voted to ban any armed demonstration not specifically authorised by the Petrograd Soviet. In line with this, on the afternoon of 9 June the Soviet resolved to take measures to resist the planned Bolshevik demonstration. Those Bolsheviks opposed to the demonstration, including Kamenev, succeeded in convening an emergency joint meeting of the Central Committee and the Military

Organisation, but their proposal to cancel the demonstration was resisted. Then, just after midnight on 9–10 June, a full meeting of the First Congress of Soviets, rather than the Soviet Executive, appealed to the Bolsheviks to call off the planned demonstration. In the face of this public appeal the Central Committee met again in the early hours of the 10th and this time cancelled the demonstration. That decision would not have been taken without Lenin's intervention. He made clear that not enough patient and persistent work had been done and there was a danger of walking into a trap. The Soviet leadership was involved in a campaign against the Bolsheviks, and 'the proletariat must reply by showing the maximum calmness, caution, restraint and organisation' – they should give 'no pretext for attack'.[41]

How should the Soviet leadership respond to this Bolshevik retreat? The challenge had been met, but should the Bolshevik concession be met with magnanimity and reconciliation, or should the Soviet press home its advantage? At the opening of the First Congress of Soviets, when Tsereteli had suggested that there was no political party in the Soviet ready to take on the responsibility of political power, Lenin had intervened to say that the Bolsheviks were ready to take power at any moment. This was a case of rhetorical overstatement, rather than a direct threat, but the planned demonstration of 10 June and the military style preparations for it meant that Tsereteli was not so sure.[42] Both Tsereteli and Kerensky favoured taking a hard line with the Bolsheviks. For Tsereteli it was clear: 'this has been a conspiracy, nothing else, a Bolshevik conspiracy to overthrow the government and seize power'; 'the counter-revolution can appear in our midst via one door only, via the Bolsheviks', he suggested. The Bolsheviks now represented the anarchy against which he had repeatedly warned, and which he felt would provoke some sort of counter-revolutionary action from the right. If the Bolsheviks had moved from ideological propaganda to what he called 'conspiracy', then they should be disarmed, for 'revolutionaries who are not worthy of the arms they bear must have them confiscated'.[43]

The First Congress of Soviets would not agree to the radical action which Tsereteli and Kerensky proposed. Instead it voted on 12 June, by a large majority, to respond in a very different way. The Soviet would organise its own march, on 18 June, as a symbol of unity and reconciliation. Tsereteli opposed this weak

Fig. 8: The demonstration of 18 June, called by the Soviet Executive to support
the First Coalition Government but subverted by the Bolsheviks. The banner
reads: 'Down with the ten capitalist ministers, all power to the soviets of workers',
soldiers' and peasant deputies'

response vehemently. It seemed to him a preposterous idea that the
planned demonstration on 18 June would 'take the wind out of the
Bolsheviks' sails'. The Bolsheviks, naturally enough, agreed to take
part in the 18 June demonstration, but they did so on their own
terms. They resolved to carry banners emblazoned with the slogan
'All Power to the Soviets'. The Bolsheviks' success in subverting the
18 June demonstration was recognised by all. Sukhanov, like other
contemporary commentators, saw what contemporary photographs
confirm: the predominance on the 18th of banners demanding 'All
Power to the Soviets'.[44]

COMBATING THE OFFENSIVE

The decision of the Soviet Executive on 12 June not to confront
the Bolsheviks over the issue of their planned demonstration but to
join with them instead in organising a shared demonstration on 18

June was linked to Kerensky's success that same day in persuading the First Congress of Soviets to support the long planned military offensive; unity rather than disunity seemed more important with the offensive about to begin. A week later, the news of the offensive was made public in Petrograd and, with the exception of the Bolshevik press, the announcement was greeted with patriotic fervour. This fervour was not matched during the debates of the First All-Russian Conference of the Bolshevik Military Organisation, held from 16 to 23 June. Delegates to this conference were in militant mood and were determined to resist the offensive and remove those politicians who had called for it. In particular, they would resist any attempt to transfer garrison troops to the front.

Just after the offensive was announced, Lenin had to use his address to the Conference of the Bolshevik Military Organisation on 20 June to persuade delegates that an immediate armed uprising was not the correct response to the current crisis. It was still his view that insufficient patient preparatory work had been done. However, some sort of response was needed, since, also on 20 June, the Coalition Government had presented the Bolshevik-dominated First Machine Gun Regiment with a plan for its 'reorganisation': despite the understanding reached at the beginning of March that no troops would be moved from Petrograd without the agreement of the Soviet, this 'reorganisation' suggested that two-thirds of its personnel should prepare to be moved to the front to help with the offensive; they were also called on to send over 500 machine guns to the front immediately. The First Machine Gun Regiment responded by sending delegates to other Petrograd regiments proposing a joint protest demonstration, and it was with some difficulty that, on 21 June, emissaries from the Bolshevik Military Organisation and the Bolshevik St Petersburg Committee persuaded the machine gunners not to undertake 'isolated actions' against the government. Divisions within the Bolsheviks were becoming visible. As *Soldatskaya Pravda* campaigned angrily against the offensive, *Pravda* warned against the impulsive actions of soldiers new to the party who wanted 'the immediate realisation of slogans, whose complexities they did not understand'.[45]

Crisis point was reached when, on 30 June, the Soviet sent representatives to the First Machine Gun Regiment to try and persuade them to respond to the needs of the offensive and accept 're-organisation'. Amid rumours that the whole regiment would soon be transferred to the front, preparations for a protest demonstration resumed on 1 July. On 2 July, the Bolshevik Military Organisation asked the Central Committee for guidance, since it saw no way of preventing the First Machine Gun Regiment from taking to the streets. Unhelpfully the Central Committee suggested that the Military Organisation should try and distance itself from the plans of the First Machine Gun Regiment, advice it chose to ignore, since to do so would have meant losing all credibility with the machine-gunner rank and file. A 'wildly anti-government' rally was staged on the 2nd, and the First Machine Gun Regiment made clear that it would begin an operation on 3 July to overthrow the Coalition Government, and in this, by default, they had the support of the Bolshevik Military Organisation.[46]

The Coalition Government was in no position to respond to this emerging threat to its authority. Since the end of March, nationalist groups in Ukraine had been involved in establishing a provisional council or 'Rada' to articulate their demand for some sort of autonomy for Ukraine within the new revolutionary Russia. On 10 June the Rada had adopted what was designated the First Universal; this asserted Ukraine's right to autonomy, an assertion partly prompted because, for fear of disrupting the offensive, Kerensky had banned a congress of Ukrainian military units. The Rada was hoping to bring military units operating in Ukraine under its authority.[47] On 26 June the Coalition Government agreed to send a delegation, which included Tsereteli and Kerensky, to Kiev for talks. The talks opened on 28 June and three days later a compromise had been reached which ceded Ukraine limited autonomy, but resisted the Ukrainianisation of the army and shelved any further discussion until after the Constituent Assembly had met. When this compromise was discussed by the Coalition Government on 2 July, the liberal ministers were furious and resigned en masse. For moderate socialists there was no problem about granting autonomy to Ukraine; for both SRs and Mensheviks it was obvious that revolutionary Russia would transform the old Russian Empire into some form of federal state. For the liberals, however, it was a point of absolute principle that the new Russia had to be 'one and indivisible'; no concessions on this were possible, at least until the Constituent Assembly had spoken.

On the morning of 3 July, abandoned by the liberals, the Soviet ministers met for a 'Star Chamber' session. Tsereteli proposed that a full plenary session of the Soviet be called for mid-July, but that in the interim the existing ministers should form a caretaker administration which would draft what he called a radical democratic programme as the basis for forming a second Coalition Government. The 'Star Chamber' agreed to this way forward, but before any progress could be made, the Soviet ministers were forced to confront the revolutionary demonstrations prompted by the actions of the First Machine Gun Regiment.

4

THE FAILURE OF COALITION

THE JULY DAYS

The First Machine Gun Regiment began its demonstration on 3 July
as planned and sent delegates looking for support to the Kronstadt
naval base, as well as to the working class districts of the city. As
trucks carrying the machine gunners arrived in Vyborg District,
workers rallied to their support, joined soon afterwards, on the other
side of the city, by workers from the Putilov Works. The avowed
'Blanquist' Bagdatiev, now secretary of the Putilov factory committee,
was one of those calling for immediate action to overthrow the
Provisional Government, just as he had been in April.[1] Soon the First
Machine Gun Regiment had occupied the Finland Station and taken
control of the city's bridges. Columns of armed soldiers and workers
were marching towards Bolshevik headquarters in the Petrograd Side
district of the capital on the northern bank of the River Neva. How
would the Bolshevik leadership respond? Their focus on 3 July was
initially the Workers' Section of the Soviet, not the demonstration
by the machine gunners. The weeks of patient explanation which
Lenin had called for in April were about to bear fruit, for a session
of the Workers' Section of the Soviet was planned for the evening
of the 3rd, and the Bolsheviks were quietly confident that they had
done enough groundwork to get a resolution passed at that session
calling for a Soviet Government. When the Workers' Section meeting

began that evening, the call for a Soviet Government was indeed passed, but no Bolshevik leader was present to witness the Petrograd workers reassert their long-held hostility to collaboration with the liberals, for the demonstration by the machine gunners seemed to be spiralling out of control and the entire Bolshevik leadership had left the Soviet building and returned to the party headquarters to see what could be done.[2]

During the afternoon of 3 July a delegation from one of the demonstrating regiments burst into Bolshevik Party headquarters and announced they were 'coming out'. Disconcerted Bolsheviks responded at first by telling them not to do so but to observe the Soviet ban on demonstrations.[3] The Central Committee, St Petersburg Committee and Military Organisation then all met in crisis session and confirmed the ban, sending out delegates to the regiments to reinforce the message. But the demonstrators were not listening. Armed soldiers and workers rallied in their thousands outside party headquarters and, despite at first being urged to disperse, insisted that they should march to the Tauride Palace and call on the Soviet to take power. Realising that this action could not be stopped, the party decided it had no choice but to try to lead and control it, so the Military Organisation was instructed to head the movement. This impromptu decision was retrospectively endorsed by the Bolshevik Central Committee in the early hours of 4 July; the *Pravda* editorial appealing for calm was hastily rewritten. Understandably in these circumstances Lenin was called back to the capital from his walking holiday in Finland.

On 4 July the Bolshevik Central Committee, St Petersburg Committee, Military Organisation and the Board of the Workers' Section of the Soviet all called for 'a peaceful and organised demonstration' which would call on the Soviet 'to take power into its own hands'. Thus 'the movement which has sprung into being in the regiments and factories is to turn into a peaceful and organised expression of the will of all the workers, soldiers and peasants of Petrograd'. Precisely what this meant was unclear. Armed clashes had begun as early as 11 pm on the 3rd when demonstrating soldiers on Nevskii Prospekt, spooked by an apparent bomb explosion, had opened fire at random. By 2 am on the morning of the 4th, some 30,000 Putilov workers were on the streets and soon the number was 70,000 – this was high summer, the period of Petrograd's 'white nights' when the skies that far north hardly darken. As the throng approached the Tauride Palace, the Putilov workers vowed not to leave its precincts until a Soviet Government had been formed. The Soviet Executive, on the other hand, resolved at 5 am to reject this 'attempt to influence its will by force'.[4]

During the morning of 4 July, more and more reinforcements arrived to support the demonstrators. A steady stream of trucks fanned out across the city as new regiments backed the protests. Then 10,000 Kronstadt sailors disembarked, bringing with them 60,000 rounds of rifle ammunition, 500 revolver shells, a medical team with stretchers and a marching band. The Kronstadters went straight to Bolshevik headquarters to be addressed by several Bolshevik leaders, including Lenin, although he had to be persuaded to go onto the balcony. When he did so, he was greeted with a thunderous ovation, but his message was not well received. He stressed that the slogan 'All power to the soviets' would triumph in the end, but restraint, determination and vigilance were still the order of the day. It was left to others to issue some rather unclear practical instructions: 'demand that the capitalist ministers be thrown out of the government', the demonstrators were told, but if the Soviet ministers refuse to then form a government without the liberals, they should 'await for further instructions'. The demonstrators then marched on to join the crowds already gathered outside the Soviet building. They chose a circuitous route so as to take in the heart of the city, south across the River Neva, along Nevskii Prospekt and then past the Field of Mars to the Tauride Palace. This march was not without incident. Bagdatiev later told an Investigation Commission, established to ascertain Bolshevik aims during the July Days, that his men had made short work of a group of snipers who opened fire on the demonstrators; in this clash, 5 demonstrators were killed and 27 wounded. Later in the day, other demonstrators came under fire on Nevskii Prospekt: they responded at first with wild and random shots, but then an armoured car appeared and the building where the firing had started was sprayed with machine-gun fire; sailors then entered the building and lynched those believed to be responsible. In all there were some 400 people killed and wounded during the July Days.[5]

With the arrival of the Kronstadters at the Tauride Palace, Chernov, perceived by his fellow ministers as the most radical among them, came out to appeal for calm. In a short speech he blamed the current political crisis on the resignation of the liberal ministers. A voice from the crowd then demanded why, as minister of agriculture, he had not yet nationalised the land; this provoked the crowd to surge forward and grab Chernov, bundling him into a car and declaring he was under arrest. As this happened, some demonstrating workers got into the Soviet building and informed a meeting of the Soviet Executive about Chernov's fate. Trotsky, despite his commitment to the call for a Soviet Government, rushed to Chernov's rescue, climbing onto the bonnet of the open car and appealing to the sailors to release their captive. At first the sailors refused to shake Trotsky's hand and would not agree to his request; then, rather unwillingly, they did so and Trotsky was allowed to lead Chernov to safety back in the Tauride Palace. As tempers calmed a little, a delegation of demonstrators was received by the socialist ministers, but they refused point blank to agree to the demonstrators' demands that a Soviet Government be established at once.[6]

Around midnight the Soviet leaders received word that loyal army units were approaching Petrograd. Two hours later, the Bolshevik Central Committee met. At this meeting Lenin intervened decisively. He asked the leader of the Bolshevik Military Organisation to give him a precise and detailed picture of Bolshevik strength in the army: which troops could be relied on and which could waver, and, he demanded to know, what arms and other necessary supplies were currently available for a Bolshevik action. When the Military Organisation's leader could only reply in generalities, Lenin was clear that retreat was the only option. The Central Committee called on the soldiers to return to their barracks and end the demonstration. Before Lenin had gone onto the balcony to address the Kronstadters earlier in the day, he had been asked by a comrade whether the moment to seize power had come. He had responded equivocally: 'we shall see, right now it is impossible to say'. By the early hours of 5 July it was only too clear that the moment had not yet come.[7]

KERENSKY'S COALITION

Kerensky was with General Kornilov at the South West Front when news of the July demonstrations reached him. He issued a telegram on 3 July demanding 'the prevention of treasonable demonstrations, the disarming of mutinous detachments and the handing over to the courts of all instigators and mutineers'. He also called for 'the publication of the evidence in the hands of the Ministry of Foreign Affairs'.[8] This referred to the alleged 'proof' that Lenin was a German agent, and during the afternoon of 4 July the minister of justice duly issued a press release declaring that Lenin was a paid German agent and that the demonstrations then underway were part of a German plot. The impact was immediate. On the night of 4–5 July the *Pravda* offices were seized on the orders of the minister of justice, and then wrecked by an unruly mob. Later the Bolshevik headquarters, abandoned by the Bolsheviks, was taken over by government forces. Those Kronstadters who had not retreated to their island naval base, but instead had seized control of the Peter Paul fortress, were quickly persuaded to surrender their arms.[9] When the Soviet ministers assembled once again for a 'Star Chamber' meeting on 6 July, there was agreement on the need for a second Coalition Government. However, the demands of the Mensheviks and SRs sketched out on this occasion were hardly likely to impress their putative liberal coalition partners. They wanted an interim solution to the question of land reform, and raised the possibility of declaring the formation of a democratic republic.[10] By that evening, Kerensky had returned from the front and he introduced a renewed sense of urgency: an order was immediately issued for Lenin's arrest and the following day Lvov was persuaded to resign as prime minister.

There was a widespread perception that Lvov was simply not forceful enough to get to grips with the problems now besetting the revolution. He was, for many, a muddle headed idealist. He had told a meeting of deputies to all four State Dumas on 27 April that 'it is our lot to live under the influence of great ideas, to participate in the creative labour of popular forces and to cherish and guard the great spiritual blessings attained to that labour', adding the perhaps naïve hope that 'every day that passes renews the belief in the inexhaustible creative power of the Russian people'.[11] Kerensky felt he had tried the creative power of the Russian people when visiting the front in May and June and now it was time for some no-nonsense politics. He took on himself the task of organising a new interim administration until the next coalition government could be formed, a coalition which Tsereteli explained to the Soviet Executive would be comprised of ten members: five socialists and five liberals. In the interim administration, Tsereteli took the post of minister of interior and started to implement the determined action against the Bolsheviks which he had been calling for for some weeks. All demonstrations would be banned until further notice and all those involved in the July Days demonstrations would be punished.

Forming a second Coalition Government did not prove easy and it was not until 24 July, three weeks after the July Days crisis, that the new Coalition was finally agreed. The process began on 8 July when Kerensky issued a Declaration of Principles of the Provisional Government, on the basis of which he hoped the new Coalition might be formed. This built on the ideas advanced by Tsereteli on 6 July. It made clear that the new government would liquidate some of those archaic features of Tsardom that were still in existence – the division of society into social ranks, for example – and would push ahead with preparations for the Constituent Assembly. On the question of the war, the government now made an explicit appeal to the Allies to call a conference to discuss shared war aims. On social policy, the declaration made clear that the new government should introduce measures to regulate economic life and oversee industry: 'as a matter of urgency' it would introduce laws on the trade unions, on social insurance and on labour arbitration, as well as 'ending the old agrarian policy'.

Although the Declaration of Principles was acceptable to liberal politicians when it referred to the Constituent Assembly, just as when the First Coalition Government was formed, the liberals had qualms about the references to social policy: they still argued that all such issues should be postponed until the Constituent Assembly had met. However, given the increasingly radical mood of workers and soldiers, forming a Coalition Government without a social policy seemed out of the question. The official response of the Kadet Party was to take no part in Kerensky's proposed administration, even when on 12 July he showed his new firmness by agreeing to restore the death penalty at the front. On 13 July Kerensky's interim administration resigned and called on Kerensky to use his personal powers of persuasion, rather than inter-party negotiations, to establish a new coalition. As a result, a group of more radical Kadets did agree to talks with Kerensky in Moscow on 14–15 July. Their demands were wide-ranging: Chernov, the radical minister of agriculture, should be sacked; the Declaration of Principles should be withdrawn; and 'pluralism in the administration' should be brought to an end – this meant that Tsereteli's principle of the socialist ministers being responsible to the Soviet should no longer apply, even though the First Congress of Soviets had insisted on it. The liberals also demanded that there should be complete solidarity with the Allies and an end to soldiers' committees interfering in military tactics and strategy.[12]

Kerensky brought these demands to the Soviet Executive on 18–19 July, and during the subsequent discussion Chernov agreed that his position in the government was not sacrosanct and he would stand down as minister of agriculture; however, the Soviet Executive was clear that there could be no concessions on the Declaration of Principles. When the Kadets made clear that the Declaration remained unacceptable, an impasse had been reached and Kerensky resigned on 21 July. Kerensky's former deputy then summoned a joint emergency meeting of ministers, the Soviet Executive and the Provisional Committee of the State Duma in the Winter Palace. Recognising that it was impossible 'to imagine how a new government could be formed unless Kerensky withdrew his resignation', the meeting gave Kerensky full powers to form a government as he pleased. Kerensky then formed 'a government of individuals': the socialist ministers would not be representatives of the Soviet or responsible to it in any way, except that, as individuals, they could inform their colleagues in the Soviet of their actions; in a similar way, the government as a whole would not support the Declaration of Principles, but individual ministers could express their support for it.[13]

Kerensky's fudge enabled the Second Coalition Government to start its work on 24 July, but the government met without Tsereteli. It was for him a point of principle that the socialist ministers had to be responsible to the Soviet. He was convinced that, without the duty of regularly reporting to the Soviet Executive, the socialist ministers would end up being completely cut off from their constituency; time would show that he was right.[14] Of the 15 ministers, there were now eight socialists including Chernov. Yet the policies of this Second Coalition Government scarcely reflected its socialist majority. The government declared itself 'national and non-partisan', and in policy terms it was to the right of the First Coalition Government. One reason why, in the end and in opposition to the leadership of the party, a significant number of Kadets decided to acquiesce to the formation of the Second Coalition Government despite being outnumbered by moderate socialists was the result of local elections to town *dumas* and district *zemstvos*, which had been taking place at the end of June and early in July. These consistently showed the liberals winning only 16 per cent of the vote. At the Kadet regional party conference on 14–15 July, which considered the impact of these election results on party policy, it was suggested that the party's influence on the development of the revolution was falling away.[15]

THE KORNILOV AFFAIR

At the height of the crisis over the formation of a second Coalition Government, on 18 July, Kerensky decided to appoint General Kornilov as Commander-in-Chief of the army. Appointing as the country's new military chief the man who during the April Crisis had called for force to be used against the Petrograd Soviet was clearly a gamble, especially since when Kornilov resigned as Military Commander of Petrograd in protest shortly afterwards, he had told the then minister of defence Guchkov that 'he considered it impossible to be a witness and a contributor to the disruption of the army by the Soviet'. Early in May, Kornilov moved to the post of Commander of the Eighth Army on the South West Front. During the preparations for and implementation of the offensive, he had had several meetings with Kerensky, and after the July Days he was promoted to commander of the South West Front on 8 July. Kornilov's very first move as Commander-in-Chief suggested that the working relationship between him and Kerensky was not going to be an easy one. Kerensky wanted to appoint, as Kornilov's replacement to the post of commander of the South West Front, General A. V. Cheremisov, one of the few generals able and willing to work with soldiers' committees; Kornilov promptly vetoed Cheremisov's appointment. However, Kerensky needed above all else to win over the liberals to his Second Coalition Government, and the appointment of Kornilov would certainly appeal to them, even if it were to cause problems later.

Kornilov had been a consistent advocate of the reinstatement of the death penalty in order to re-establish discipline. He had made this demand in public before Kerensky's decision on 12 July to restore the death penalty at the front, and immediately after his appointment, on 19 July, he demanded the restoration of the death penalty in the rear, adding at the same time the demand that there should no longer be any government 'interference' in operational plans. On 3 August, Kornilov presented the Second Coalition Government with a memorandum on how to restore the fighting capacity of the army. This called for the death penalty in the rear as well as the front, and for the power of officers to be restored and the powers of government commissars to be reduced; soldiers' assemblies at the front would also be banned, and only certain newspapers permitted to circulate in the army. Kerensky did not dismiss this memorandum out of hand, but felt it needed to be 'toned down'. However, nothing was toned down; in fact Kornilov added to it, calling for the militarisation of the railway network as an essential element of his programme for military recovery, as well as powers to restore order in areas where peasant land seizures were disrupting essential food production.[16]

These, however, were Kornilov's public demands. From the moment of his appointment those closest to him were involved in plotting to end the power of the Soviet and establish an authoritarian government. Kornilov's orderly and close advisor was V. S. Zavoiko, a member of the Society for the Economic Rehabilitation of Russia, a group of industrialists and bankers established in April 1917 who were persuaded by Kornilov's behaviour during the April Crisis that he was the best candidate for the much needed post of dictator of Russia. Back in May, an Officers' Union had been established at General Staff Headquarters and its leader, a former Kadet deputy in the Fourth State Duma, was soon also involved in plotting. He committed the union to a secret programme of military dictatorship and brought his organisation into the work of another counter-revolutionary group, the Republican Centre, funded by the Siberian Bank. The Society for the Economic Rehabilitation of Russia and the Republican Centre acted quite separately until the middle of July when they made contact with each other and the Republican Centre effectively became a client of the wealthier Society for the Economic Rehabilitation of Russia. On Kornilov's appointment, the Union of Officers sent a telegram to all ministers, signed by its leader, calling for Kornilov's programme to be implemented or the ministers

Fig. 9: General Lavr Kornilov in dress uniform

'would answer with their heads'.[17] Serious plotting began at the start of August. As an initial preparatory move, on 6 August, Kornilov deployed the Third Cavalry Corps to Velikie Luki, a strategic location at a railway junction in easy striking distance of Petrograd, while the Union of Officers sent some of its members 'on leave' to Petrograd to await instructions.[18] The plotters then assembled in Moscow. Formally they were attending the Conference of Public Figures, which took place from 8 to 10 August and brought together the pre-revolutionary elites, members of the State Duma, landowners, industrialists and generals all keen for a government that would 'cut itself free from all traces of dependence on committees, soviets and the like'; the conference sent a telegram to Kornilov expressing the 'hope and faith' they entrusted to him. Behind the public sessions of the conference, in secret meetings, preparations for a military coup were discussed. However, these revealed both a poor level of preparation and doubts about the success of the venture; Milyukov for one commented that the plotters would probably lose their nerve at the last minute and run for cover.[19]

When Kornilov finally met with Kerensky on 10 August to discuss his proposed programme, a lot of work had been done on it by the new acting minister of war, Boris Savinkov. He had done much to make the programme more politically acceptable, but it still called for martial law to be declared on the railways and in those industries working on defence contracts, combined with a general ban on all factory meetings and an end to strikes until the war was over. Kerensky had warned Savinkov on 8 August that he could not sign such a document, and again refused to do so when he met Kornilov in person two days later.[20] Indeed, at this meeting Kerensky was forthright in his views: Kornilov should not be seduced by those in the Union of Officers who suggested staging a coup; if such an attempt were made, the railway network would cease to operate, as would the telegraph system, and the plotters would be left high and dry. Yet, Kerensky also offered an olive branch. He was still considering Kornilov's programme, he said, and he was not opposed in principle to taking it forward; the restoration of the death penalty and the militarisation of the railways could be part of his agenda.[21]

Kerensky's comments on 10 August did not impress Kornilov. The next day he informed his Chief of Staff that Kerensky was simply playing for time by asking Savinkov to carry out further work on the programme; he, Kornilov, was being 'led by the nose'. So he now confided to his Chief of Staff that the Third Cavalry Corps had been moved to Velikie Luki so that it was at hand to deal with the Bolshevik demonstration which all military and government figures assumed would be organised at the end of August to mark six months since the overthrow of the Tsar. It was, Kornilov said, 'time to hang the German agents and spies, with Lenin at their head, and to dispel the Soviet'. The Third Cavalry Corps, he added, would 'not hesitate to hand over all the members of the Soviet'. However, in spite of his comment about being 'led by the nose', Kornilov made clear to his Chief of Staff that his preferred option in confronting the Soviet was not to carry out a coup but to come to an understanding with Kerensky and Savinkov; if that failed, however, 'I may have to deal the blow to the Bolsheviks without their consent'.[22]

In line with this preference for acting with rather than against Kerensky, Kornilov was caution itself when he addressed the Moscow State Conference. Held from 12 to 15 August, the Moscow State Conference was Kerensky's way of rallying popular support behind his new Second Coalition Government, an idea he had first mooted as early as 12 July. The proposal brought him into open conflict with his former Coalition ally Tsereteli, who from early August had begun to see danger to the revolution coming not only from the Bolshevik left but also from the counter-revolutionary right. When Tsereteli had returned from exile he had explained to those who welcomed him that 'a bourgeois revolution is taking place [which] represents a stage of the social revolution [in which] you must strengthen your position in order to accelerate the progress of all Russia, the progress of all mankind toward the bright ideals of socialism'. Therefore 'as long as this government, under the impact of revolutionary events, is following the revolutionary path, as long as the interests of the bourgeoisie are embodied in acts which coincide with the common national interest' then the Provisional Government would be supported. However, 'should the moment arrive when this government renounces the revolutionary path [...] then we will march dauntlessly against this government'. That moment seemed to be approaching. On 2 August, *Izvestiya* urged the propertied classes to have the 'moral fibre' to 'come to the aid of the country', and two days later the Soviet passed a resolution warning of the danger of counter-revolution. Such warnings seemed to gain credence when on 9 August the Second Coalition Government postponed the Constituent Assembly elections from mid-September to mid-November. As preparations for the Moscow State Conference gathered pace, the Soviet Executive warned against those preparing for the betrayal of the revolution.[23]

Boycotted by the Bolsheviks because only 10 per cent of the seats had been allocated to the soviets, the Moscow State Conference was not a forum for all social groups, from land owners to peasants, and from industrialists to workers, to gather together in a quest for unity in the common national cause, as Kerensky had suggested when summoning it; it was in fact a mouthpiece for Russia's corporatist interest groups. Bankers and industrialists had more seats than the soviets, and a fifth of the seats went to deputies from the four State Dumas, all of which had given preference, if to different degrees, to the propertied classes. Against the background of a protest strike in Moscow organised by the Bolsheviks, Tsereteli used his speech to remind those present that the soviets were the popularly elected keystones of the revolution and it would be 'criminal' to try to undermine them. He singled out General Kornilov as one of those trying to blame the soviets for the present state of the army, and declared that order could not be restored at the cost of democratic values. Kerensky's tone was the very opposite. There was no homage to the revolutionary spontaneity of the masses; he preferred to echo Bismarck. In one of his most dramatic speeches ever, Kerensky stressed the 'hour of deadly danger' which the country faced; he spoke of the need for 'blood and iron' if victory were to be achieved; and he announced that, since 'we will pluck out our heart, yet save the state', the death penalty would be reintroduced in order to restore the army. If Tsereteli's heart was still with the revolution, Kerensky seemed to be flirting with counter-revolution.[24]

Sensing this, Kornilov continued his line of working with Kerensky. He arrived at the Moscow State Conference to the most enthusiastic welcome, but his speech, delivered on 14 August, was very bland: he stuck to the promise he had made to Kerensky and did not stray from military affairs, referring mostly to the problems in the rear and the shortage of ammunitions. While his public profile seemed in line with the policy of working with Kerensky, behind the scenes plotters continued to be active. There were more discussions of a possible military coup and even whether former State Duma deputies might give such a coup their blessing; once again Milyukov urged caution – the time for a military coup was not right, he said, the time for a public break with Kerensky had not yet arrived. When, at the end of the Moscow State Conference, Kornilov met the leaders of the Society for the Economic Rehabilitation of Russia, he assured them that things were falling into place. Troops were already stationed to deal with a Bolshevik demonstration anticipated at the end of August to mark six months since the overthrow of the Tsar; just in case the Bolsheviks did not stage a demonstration, officers had been dispatched in secret to Petrograd to organise one. These claims suggested Kornilov's determination to act, but did not clarify whether he would act with Kerensky or against Kerensky.[25]

Perhaps because of the caution of politicians like Milyukov about the advisability of a military coup, Kornilov returned from the Moscow State Conference apparently once more in favour of working with Kerensky. The issue was debated at a meeting held at military headquarters on 17 August. One of his advisors, I. A. Dobrynskii, suggested working with Kerensky in suppressing the anticipated Bolshevik demonstration, while Zavoiko was still wedded to the idea of a coup. Far from working with Kerensky, Zavoiko made clear that the safety of the socialist ministers could not be guaranteed once the proposed action began, so the liberal ministers should be warned in advance to resign and assemble at General Staff Headquarters for their own protection. Which plan to follow? Accommodation with Kerensky seemed the better option, for that same day news came that Kerensky was indeed ready to implement much of Kornilov's programme. Savinkov was to work as an intermediary once again and he was briefed that Kerensky would reintroduce the death penalty throughout the army and would also be prepared to put the Petrograd Military District, other than the very city centre, under Kornilov's control.

Savinkov left for General Staff Headquarters at once and agreed with Kornilov on 23 August that troops should be deployed to disperse any Bolshevik action. When that Bolshevik action began, steps would be taken to form a new government, with Kerensky possibly taking on more of a figurehead role as president of a new republic. When Savinkov set off back to Petrograd on 24 August, Kornilov must have felt that by working with Kerensky everything was falling into place. He told his Chief of Staff that Savinkov had met all his requests, with only the 'reduced' powers of the army commissars needing further clarification. Both sides realised that even before the six months' commemoration of the February Revolution the Bolsheviks might organise protests when it was announced that Kerensky had adopted Kornilov's programme, but Savinkov insisted that Kerensky was ready for this and would take determined measures so long as Kornilov had reliable forces in place; if the Soviet supported the Bolshevik protests, it too would be dispersed. These best laid plans were already falling apart, however. On 21 August, Kornilov's advisor Dobrynskii mentioned to V. N. Lvov, a former minister in the Provisional Government but no relation of former prime minister G. E. Lvov, that Kornilov's other advisor Zavoiko had spoken about not being able to guarantee the safety of the socialist ministers when the action began. Lvov decided to warn Kerensky of the possible danger he faced. At a meeting with Kerensky on 22 August, Lvov explained his fears and asked for permission to go to General Staff Headquarters to clarify the situation; Kerensky agreed he should go, and he met Kornilov on both 24 and 25 August.

On the 24th, Kornilov told Lvov, 'I know Kerensky and I know that one can reach an understanding with him', which put Lvov's mind at rest. The next day, however, Kornilov's tone was very different. Unlike the previous day, Zavoiko was present on the 25th and that appeared to have helped harden Kornilov's attitude to Kerensky. Kornilov now increased his list of demands: no regimental committees should have the right to interfere in military matters; Petrograd in its entirety should be included in the frontal zone and subject to martial law; and all regiments, both front and rear, had to be subordinated to the Commander-in-Chief. Kornilov was proposing a military coup, even if he did sugar the pill by suggesting that Kerensky could stay on as deputy prime minister and Savinkov as minister of war. From this encounter Lvov understood that Kornilov, under pressure from Zavoiko, had once again changed tack and veered away from working with Kerensky and back to the idea of a military coup followed by a dictatorship. Such a future became even more alarming for Lvov when Zavoiko confided in him as he prepared to return to Petrograd that he doubted if Kerensky's life could be saved once action began: 'Kornilov wants to save him, but he won't be able to', he said; his death was 'a necessary outlet for the pent up feelings of the officers'.[26]

On 26 August, Lvov returned to warn Kerensky that a coup was imminent and his life was in danger. Kerensky at once decided to contact Kornilov and confront him. He used what contemporaries called the Hughes apparatus, a sort of long-distance typewriter and printer. Kerensky typed a message into the Hughes apparatus in his office and it was printed out on another Hughes apparatus in Kornilov's office. However, when opening up the Hughes apparatus 'conversation', Kerensky identified himself as Lvov, not Kerensky. He then asked Kornilov to confirm what had been discussed between them the previous day, and Kornilov was happy to do so. Kerensky, now convinced that Kornilov was after all plotting a coup against him and had no intention of working with him to confront the Bolsheviks, used the Hughes apparatus to reveal his true identity and dismiss Kornilov as Commander-in-Chief on the spot.[27] Kornilov, realising that there was no time to lose, ordered the coup to begin at once, with the Third Cavalry Corps leading the way. However, just as Kerensky had predicted would happen when he met Kornilov on 10 August, there was no popular support for Kornilov; the railways and the telegraph were indeed paralysed by workers loyal to the Soviet. As the Third Cavalry Corps marched towards Petrograd it found the railway tracks torn up and a mass of agitators explaining to rank-and-file Cossacks that, in truth, there were no Bolshevik German agents in Petrograd organising illegal demonstrations as they had been told.[28] As to the officers sent in advance into Petrograd by the Union of Officers, evidence suggests they did little other than sing patriotic songs in restaurants; the Third Cavalry Corps had halted its advance on Petrograd by the time they set about staging a supposed 'Bolshevik uprising'. Kornilov's coup ended in a complete shambles.[29] As to the Bolshevik demonstration to mark six months since the February Revolution, the Soviet newspaper *Izvestiya* made clear on 26 August that, despite rumours to the contrary, and provocative acts by soldiers lobbying various factories, there never had been any plans to organise a demonstration on 27 August and there would be no such demonstration.[30]

At 4 am on the morning of 27 August, Kerensky summoned a cabinet meeting and was granted emergency powers to cope with the crisis. He appointed Savinkov Governor General of Petrograd, with all troops in the area supposedly subject to him; he also placed himself at the head of a quickly formed Directory, on which Savinkov also sat.[31] However, Kerensky's Directory was not the body which defeated Kornilov. Later on the 27th, Kerensky appealed to the Soviet Executive for support and the Soviet established a Committee for the People's Struggle against the Counter-Revolution and it was this committee that actually led the struggle against Kornilov. One of the committee's first moves was to revive the Red Guard as a workers' militia. This was deeply ironic, since, in the aftermath of the July Days, one of the Soviet's main concerns had been to disarm the Red Guards.

ARMING THE WORKERS

Kornilov's attempted coup was frustrated by the grass-roots mobilisation of workers and garrison soldiers, the same people who had carried through the February Revolution and who now refused to accept the replacement of an archaic Tsarist autocracy with a modern military dictatorship. Key to that mobilisation was the activity of workers' militias, many of which had originally been established in February, but which in the interim had faced a variety of moves to restrict their activities. The most dramatic of these came after the July Days, when searches, arrests and disarmings were the order of the day. It was not only the mutinous regiments and battalions that were disarmed in July; almost more attention was devoted to the working-class districts, where the workers' Red Guard were forced to hand over their weapons.[32]

During the height of the February Revolution, on the 26th and 27th, there had been discussion in Bolshevik circles about whether it was possible or indeed advisable to establish detachments of armed workers to help in the revolutionary struggle. Senior figures like Shlyapnikov counselled against this, advising that it was more important to persuade soldiers to change sides than to arm the workers as such. It was only as the soldiers did start to change sides in large numbers on the 27th that workers came into possession of significant quantities of arms, and by the 28th voluntary armed workers' militias were a common sight outside every factory. This was largely the work of the Soviet Executive, which on the evening of the 27th had designated arsenals throughout the city where arms could be issued and instructions received; Shlyapnikov, despite his earlier reservations about arming the workers, was one of those entrusted with this work. Soon these workers' militias were working in parallel with local militias established by the Petrograd City Duma, which from 28 February had been calling on citizens to form revolutionary militias for the preservation of order.[33]

A *modus vivendi* gradually evolved between the two militias, the workers' militias and the civic militia formed by the City Duma. Working-class districts were patrolled by Red Guards, middle-class districts by the civic militia, and there was a tacit agreement about what to do about overlap: on Vyborg Side, the workers' militia predominated; on Petrograd Side the civic militia predominated;

while on Vasilievskii Island there was a mixture of the two. One thing was very clear, however, as Shlyapnikov found when he helped to organise a conference of militias on 5 March: the workers' militias were determined to resist any proposal that they disarm and stand down in favour of the civic militia. The Soviet Executive supported the workers' militias in this stance and helped persuade the conference that the way forward was for the organisation of the militias to be as decentralised as possible. The Soviet plan was that, at local level, the militia would elect a council and those councillors would then elect a supervisory council for the whole city. Although this plan envisaged a common armband for militias throughout the city, in workers' districts a red armband would be worn as well.[34]

Pravda referred to the workers' militias as a 'Red Guard' for the first time in an article of 18 March, and the name stuck. The Bolsheviks called for the Red Guards to be offered basic military training by sympathetic revolutionary soldiers; that same proposal was endorsed by the Bolshevik Central Committee on 22 March. However, little was done in practice and the All-Russian Conference of Bolshevik Party Workers of 29 March took no clear decisions on the Red Guards, despite referring to their activities repeatedly. Indeed, when a city-wide conference of Red Guards was held on 17 April, it was an initiative of the Mensheviks, not the Bolsheviks, and the conference elected a commission made up of three Mensheviks and only two Bolsheviks. Since only 22 factories were represented, the conference decided it was not representative enough to make any policy decisions and issued a rather bland call for all factories to establish Red Guards and for a more representative conference to assemble on 23 April. By then, of course, the April Crisis had taken place, in which the Red Guards played a crucial role, and in these circumstances it was just the commission which met on the 23rd, with the conference being postponed until 28 April. On this occasion the commission passed a resolution which asserted that 'the Red Guard exists for the protection of the achievements of the Revolution and for struggle against counter-revolutionary attempts'.

The Bolsheviks won control of the Red Guard movement in the aftermath of the April Crisis. This was clear as early as the 23rd, when the Mensheviks had wanted to make the Red Guards a 'department' of the Soviet, but the Bolsheviks persuaded the commission that the Red Guards should operate 'in close unity' with the Soviet but retain a degree of independence. The influence of the Bolsheviks was even clearer on 28 April when the more representative General Conference of Red Guards was held. In the spirit of the moves being made at this time to establish a coalition government, and Tsereteli's attempts through the 'Star Chamber' to keep the left under control, the Soviet newspaper *Izvestiya* had published an editorial on 28 April which questioned the need for Red Guards: they were 'unnecessary and harmful' since they could damage the unity between workers and soldiers, and 'enemies of the revolution would say the workers were being armed against the soldiers'. This editorial embarrassed the Menshevik activists at the General Conference of Red Guards, who saw no reason why a specifically workers' militia should not continue to operate.

Arguing that *Izvestiya*'s policy was not necessarily that of the Soviet, the General Conference of Red Guards continued its work and pointed out that soldiers actually supported the formation of the Red Guards, an argument that was challenged by the Soviet representative in attendance. After acrimonious debate, the conference resolved to send a delegation to talk to the Soviet Executive and urge it to change its policy. When the Red Guard delegation met the Soviet Executive it was told by a former reformist trade union activist, who in 1911 had supported Gvozdev in sending petitions to the Duma president, that the Red Guard was 'a Bolshevik movement' and should not be supported for that reason; in vain the Menshevik Red Guardists argued that the Red Guards were a proletarian movement which the Mensheviks had once controlled and could control again. The Soviet Executive would not be moved. On 30 April, *Izvestiya* published an editorial calling on workers to take part in the establishment of the civic militia, on the model of the middle-class districts of the city. As Rex Wade has noted, 'the Soviet Executive's position on the Red Guards was an early example of a broader attitude of distrust about where spontaneous activity by the masses might lead and of an insensitivity to workers' concerns and fears'.[35]

In the era of the First Coalition Government, the Soviet leadership thought the best way forward was to go along with the plans of their liberal partners and encourage the formation of a professionally-based civic militia. That stance meant that the class-based Red Guard movement of February was now classified as something 'Bolshevik' which had to be stopped. The Soviet's hostile stance towards the Red Guards was successful to the extent that it slowed the momentum of the movement set in train by the two conferences in April, yet it did not stop the process completely, even among loyal Mensheviks and SRs. On 29 April the Vyborg District Soviet established a 'Workers' Guard', a name chosen with care. As *Pravda* noted on 5 May, this was an initiative taken by Vyborg District workers which had the support of local Mensheviks and SRs, not just the Bolsheviks, and they called it a 'Workers' Guard' rather than a 'Red Guard' as a transparent device for appearing not to go against the advice of the Soviet Executive. This sense of worker intransigence became even stronger when the City Duma announced on 1 May how new regulations to cover the operation of a professional civic militia would operate from 1 June. No longer a voluntary body composed of some 20,000 part-time staff, the militia would become a paid force of just 6,000, roughly the size of the old Petrograd police force. The salary, paid out of city funds, would be well below that of a skilled worker, and factory owners made clear that once the new militia was operational they were no longer prepared to cover the pay of those workers who volunteered for militia work. On 19 May a meeting of representatives of militia men and workers' organisations in 18 districts of Petrograd resolved to oppose the new law, while the commander of the civic militia confirmed to employers on the 23rd that, after 1 June, there would be no obligation to pay worker militia men.

The new law separated the Red Guards completely from the civic militia, but did not end their activities. The Bolshevik Military Organisation and Petrograd's short-lived anarchist movement stepped in to offer the Red Guards support, helping to organise two protest meetings, on 19 May and again on 25 May. When, in the area around the Putilov Works, an independent 'People's Militia' was established, with the support of the Bolshevik Military Organisation, the civic militia ordered on 23 May that anyone wearing an armband emblazoned with the words 'People's Militia' rather than the official 'Civic Militia' would be disarmed. Nonetheless, on 27 May a Conference of Petrograd People's Militias was held at the Durnovo Villa, the headquarters of the anarchist movement in Petrograd and a complex of buildings dedicated to the mission of developing popular rather than state initiatives of all kinds. The conference decided that the new plans for a civic militia were 'an attempt by the ruling classes to foist a form of militia organisation favourable to them on the Petrograd population'. It proposed that the reduction in the size of the militia should be negotiated through the district soviets and that employers should meet the cost; by 10 June, moves to establish a People's Militia were gaining pace and the rules that were adopted made clear that the People's Militia was to remain class-based: all those volunteering for it had to have the recommendation of either a socialist political party or a trade union or factory committee.[36]

On 3 June the First Conference of Petrograd Factory Committees backed the demand for a workers' militia, and that same day a second Conference of People's Militias was held at the Durnovo Villa at which a Council of Petrograd People's Militias was established; of its eleven members, five were Bolsheviks and the other six either anarchists or SRs. This council established offices in the Durnovo Villa and sent delegations for talks with both the Soviet and the Civic Militia headquarters.[37] However, the growth of this People's Militia movement was then cut short by completely extraneous developments. On 5 June a group of anarchists had tried, and failed, to seize control of the Russian Freedom printing works. In response, the minister of justice decided on 7 June that the anarchists should be taught a lesson: they should be evicted from the Durnovo Villa on the grounds that they had never had any legal entitlement to expropriate the building in the first place. Vyborg Side workers went on strike in protest, the anarchists threatened to resist by force of arms and a temporary stalemate was reached. Then, at the time of the Soviet's demonstration of 18 June, the anarchists refused to inform the Soviet in advance whether their black-flag-carrying comrades would be bearing arms or not, and during the demonstration itself an armed group of anarchists forced its way into the Kresty prison on the Vyborg Side and obtained the release of the editor of the Bolshevik Military Organisation newspaper distributed among front-line troops. The minister of justice ordered the immediate recapture of the liberated Bolshevik and at 3 am on the morning of 19 June soldiers surrounded the Durnovo Villa. After a short exchange of fire, some 60 anarchists were arrested and their headquarters closed down; the liberated Bolshevik was not recaptured.[38]

If the closing of the Durnovo Villa brought the People's Militia movement to an abrupt end, a fortnight later the July Days showed just how crucial the Red Guards were in their stated aims of defending the revolution and resisting counter-revolution, for they had been at the forefront of the action on 3–4 July. In the aftermath of the July Days, the Second Coalition Government was determined to disarm the Red Guards, but the Red Guards were in origin the creation of district soviets, not the Petrograd Soviet, and their disarming by representatives of the Petrograd Soviet in the aftermath of the July Days sparked hostility between these two levels of soviet organisation. Five of the seven district soviets for which records have survived agreed to partial disarming: they would hand over rifles and machine guns, accepting the Soviet's argument that these weapons were needed at the front; however they refused to hand over revolvers and other light weapons which they insisted were needed 'for self-defence'. The Vyborg District Soviet refused to make a policy decision on disarming and instructed individual factories to resolve the matter themselves, while a seventh district refused point blank to hand over any weapons. The issue of disarmament became a major cause of the loss of faith in the Soviet leadership on the part of the working-class rank and file, a mood from which the Bolsheviks could only profit.[39]

Although after the July Days leading Bolsheviks were quickly arrested and Lenin went into hiding, 'second rank' Bolsheviks remained at liberty. Indeed, although the Bolshevik Party was notionally banned by the simple expedient of changing its name to the Social Democrat Internationalists and renaming *Pravda* as *Rabochii put'* it continued to operate, even holding its Sixth Congress from 26 July to 3 August.[40] Nor had the Bolsheviks lost control of the Workers' Section of the Soviet, which they had won as the July demonstrations began. In the Workers' Section they established a separate executive with its own ruling presidium, and built on Lenin's 'patient explanatory work' within the soviets.[41] If in May and June there had already been a drift leftwards in elections to district soviets enabling the Bolsheviks to capture the Workers' Section, that trend accelerated in July and August. The Bolsheviks, often working closely with other radical activists, steadily increased their influence. From July onwards the district soviets issued repeated calls for the re-election and reorganisation of the central Petrograd Soviet on the grounds that it had lost contact with the masses and no longer represented the interests of 'revolutionary democracy'. This work within the district soviets was largely possible because the Bolsheviks won control of the so-called Inter-district Conference of Soviets.[42]

Back in April 1917, the Petrograd Soviet had established an Inter-district Conference of Soviets to help co-ordinate policy within the districts. Such co-ordination was no longer thought to be necessary after the First Congress of Soviets in June, and the conference ceased to exist. After the July Days, however, it was decided to revive the conference to help organise the collection of arms from the Red Guards; this move backfired spectacularly. When the reconvened Inter-district Conference of Soviets met on 17 July it had shifted to the left. Although it was not yet under Bolshevik control, it immediately challenged the authority of the Soviet and refused to go along with the instruction to collect arms from the Red Guards, asserting that the July Days and their consequences had shown 'a serious loss of contact between the Soviet and both the proletariat and the soldiers of the capital'; to put this right, it wanted representatives of the district soviets to be brought into the Soviet Executive. By early August, the Inter-district Conference of Soviets had chosen a new pro-Bolshevik leadership which elected a ruling presidium that was given the specific task of working out how to improve representation from the districts on the Soviet Executive. As August went on, the Inter-district Soviet Presidium became even more assertive, claiming the right both to co-ordinate the meetings of district soviets and even attend meetings of the Workers' and Soldiers' Sections of the Soviet. In other words it was, unilaterally, seeking to reorganise the Soviet leadership.[43] There were other clear signs of growing support for the Bolsheviks among the capital's working class at this time. When the Second Conference of Factory Committees was held on 7 August, it was entirely Bolshevik in composition.[44] Then, in the elections to the Petrograd City Duma on 20 August, the Bolsheviks won 33 per cent of the vote, nearly on a par with the SRs who secured 37 per cent.[45]

Given their key role in fighting to preserve the Red Guards, it was no surprise that during the Kornilov Affair the Bolsheviks dominated the Committee for the Struggle against the Counter-revolution; according to Sukhanov it was the Bolsheviks who defined its activities and character. In organising the defence of the capital, the committee 'had to set in motion the masses of workers and soldiers, and these masses, in so far as they were organised, were organised by the Bolsheviks and followed them'. Thus although the Bolsheviks were in a minority within the leadership of the Committee for the Struggle against the Counter-revolution, in practice they dominated it. 'Without them the committee was impotent; without them it could only have passed the time with make-shift proclamations and flabby speeches by orators who had long since lost all authority,' Sukhanov commented. It was the Bolsheviks who insisted that the workers had to be armed, and made it a pre-condition of their joining the committee. Since the Soviet leaders accepted that Kornilov had to be stopped, the SR chair of the committee had no choice but to agree to this Bolshevik demand. It was the Bolsheviks who controlled the Red Guards – by 29 August the Inter-district Conference of Soviets had re-established a Red Guard in every district of Petrograd. The Bolsheviks also had their Military Organisation, which during the night of 27–28 August was active in every barracks, organising mass meetings, urging the soldiers to take up arms to resist Kornilov and save the revolution. By the time on the evening of the 28th when some of the Third Cavalry Corps were approaching Petrograd, the suburbs of the capital were an enormous military camp with Red Guards and garrison soldiers preparing for action, while in nearby towns like Gatchina, Pavlovsk and Tsarskoe Selo the garrisons had come out in support of the Committee for the Struggle against the Counter-revolution. By the morning of the 29th, Kornilov had been arrested.[46]

The collapse of Kornilov's conspiracy brought the Bolsheviks back to the forefront of the Russian Revolution. Imagining that his newly formed Directory might still be able to make use of the current crisis to limit the sudden Bolshevik resurgence, Kerensky tried on 31 August to close the Bolshevik daily as well as the independent left socialist newspaper *Novaya zhizn'*. The decision was simply not implemented. On 2 September, and again on the 5th, Kerensky called for the Red Guards to be dissolved on the grounds that the crisis was over, but the Inter-district Conference of Soviets refused point blank to do so; a few days later the Bolsheviks' control of the Petrograd Soviet would be confirmed and an official Red Guard Department would soon be established. Armed workers had survived the attempts to disband them and would remain a permanent feature of the revolution for the next few months, an essential force for resisting a repeat of Kornilov's adventure. Sukhanov summed this up clearly:

The news of the bourgeois coup profoundly stirred the surface and the depths of Russia. The entire organised democracy rose to its feet. Hundreds of thousands and millions of workers, soldiers and peasants rose up in arms, for defence and from attack, against the class enemy. Their desire for a decisive battle grew irresistibly, hour by hour. Here there was a class instinct, a small portion of class consciousness, and the influence of the ideas and organisation of the gigantically growing Bolsheviks [...] After the Kornilov revolt Bolshevism began blossoming luxuriantly and put forth deep roots throughout the country.[47]

Kornilov was prevented from staging a counter-revolution by the mass action of those loyal to the revolutionary tradition of Russian labour.

5

SIX MONTHS OF SOCIAL REVOLUTION

The return to the revolutionary traditions of 1905, what Sukhanov called the blossoming of Bolshevism after Kornilov's failed military coup, was made possible because of the deep frustration the Russian masses felt at the slow pace of change under the First Coalition Government, and a sense that the government was beginning to chip away at the achievements of the revolution when Kerensky established his Second Coalition administration. The liberals, referred to in working-class circles as 'the bourgeois', still wanted to delay all serious discussion of social reform until the Constituent Assembly had met, and were even ready to flirt with counter-revolution to ensure this happened. The reality was, however, that, six months after the overthrow of the Tsar, the pressure for social change was becoming unstoppable. Workers, peasants and soldiers all faced issues which they increasingly felt brooked no further delay. The social impact of six months of revolution on the social classes which went to make up revolutionary Russia was to radicalise them to the point where a second revolution seemed the only way to defend the achievements of the first.

FACTORY COMMITTEES AND THEIR POWERS

Under the impact of the war, industrial output in Petrograd doubled and the workforce increased from 242,600 in 1914 to 392,800 in 1917, nearer 417,000 if the surrounding industrial suburbs are included. Expansion was greatest in those industries linked to the war effort: in metallurgy the workforce grew by 135 per cent; in chemicals by 99 per cent; but in the clothing industry the increase was only 44 per cent, and other consumer industries were static in output or even saw output decline. When the war broke out, 17 per cent of the capital's labour force were conscripted into the army, and replacing those workers resulted in significant social changes in the composition of the workforce. While 40 per cent of workers were core workers or 'cadre' workers, whose families were by 1914 in the second generation of urban life, the remaining 60 per cent were newly recruited. The bulk of these were unskilled labourers from Petrograd's rural hinterland, but there were also 'Chinese' workers, usually Koreans, brought from Russia's far eastern provinces. The number of women workers also rose significantly, from 25 per cent to 33 per cent of the workforce. As in all combatant countries, World War I saw rapid inflation. Goods costing 100 roubles in 1913 cost 221 roubles by the end of 1916 and 512 roubles by the end of 1917. Until spring 1916, cadre workers, essential for the war effort, were able to ensure that their wages matched inflation; thereafter, inflation steadily ate away at their real earnings until the February Revolution brought a temporary respite.[1]

Workers responded to the overthrow of the Tsar and the collapse of the old regime with euphoria. The moment had come to end the autocratic order in the factory and establish a 'constitutional' factory. Rule books concerning fines and other punishments were torn up, blacklists were published and denounced, and those who had imposed the old order in the factories – tyrannical overseers, bribe-takers, informers – were often physically expelled from the factories, roughed up and sometimes even killed. At the Putilov Works, the director and his aide were killed by workers and their bodies thrown into the nearby Obvodnyi Canal; some 40 other members of management were driven from the Putilov Works during the first three days after the abdication. Ultra-loyal workers could suffer a similar fate. Between 1905 and 1917 the Tsar had fostered an ultra-patriotic, anti-Semitic organisation known as the Black Hundred movement, which was always ready to help break a strike. In the Putilov Works' engine assembly plant, the man who had led the local branch of the Black Hundred was 'tossed into a wheelbarrow, red lead was poured over his head, and he was ignominiously carted out of the factory and dumped in the street'. In the Putilov Works' brick yard, the foreman was deposed because of his rude treatment of workers and his insistence on forced overtime. At the Baltic Shipyard at least 60 members of the administration were demoted, transferred or carted out of the factory in wheelbarrows. At the Cartridge Works up to 80 per cent of the technical staff were removed. At the Admiralty, New Admiralty and Galernyi Island Shipyards, 49 technical employees were sacked after mass meetings of workers, while at the Pipe Factory the director and 14 senior managers were temporarily removed from their duties.[2]

It was at radical, even riotous mass meetings such as these that the first factory committees were elected. Having removed whole sections of the old management structures, it was almost inevitable that some of the factory committees, from early on, began to take on quasi-management tasks. This was particularly true of the state-run arms manufacturers. In these plants the administration was seen by the workers as an extension of the state which they had just overthrown, and so much of the old administrative apparatus was removed that some factory committees were establishing 'executive committees' to keep production going. Thus at the Cartridge Works, the workers elected an 'executive committee' which appointed a new temporary director and set up two commissions, one of technical staff to ensure continuing production and the other of workers, to plan a new administrative structure for the plant. There were similar moves at the Sestoretsk Arms Works, the Pipe Factory and the Okhta Explosives Works. Although this situation would not last for long, for a few weeks in March 1917 factory committees found themselves virtually in charge of some of the big state enterprises and, as Steve Smith has suggested, 'that experience was crucial in giving birth to the idea of workers' control of production'.[3]

The reformist Soviet leadership did not encourage developments such as these. The decisions of the Provisional Government on labour matters were all about moderating the radicalism which had emerged during the overthrow of the Tsar. On 10 March, as part of the deal for an orderly return to work, the Petrograd Soviet and the Petrograd Society of Manufacturers and Factory Owners had jointly agreed to establish an eight-hour day in the capital.[4] Indeed, in practice, the eight-hour day was in operation throughout the country by the end of April.[5] However, rather than guarantee that provision in legislation, the Provisional Government preferred to establish a Commission of Enquiry to consider the many and varied consequences of such a dramatic change; under the old order the norm was eleven or twelve hours. There was no mention of the eight-hour day when on 29 March the minister of trade and industry published a programme promising to guarantee the rights of trade unions, factory committees and other mechanisms for the peaceful resolution of industrial disputes; the programme referred only to 'a shorter working week' and extending the existing provisions on social insurance established by the Tsar in 1912.[6]

On 15 April a meeting held by managers of factories working for the Navy Ministry and the Artillery Administration discussed the future role of factory committees and rejected any notion of 'self-management' or workers having responsibility for production; the meeting insisted that factory committees should limit themselves to overseeing the internal order of the factory and defined this as the regulation of wages, hours, hiring and firing and, more intangibly, 'informational supervision' of the factory administration. When on 23 April the Provisional Government enacted a law on factory committees, their activities were even more circumscribed and confined to traditional trade union matters: bringing complaints to managers, negotiating in demarcation disputes and educating their members. This was problematic because in the private sector, unlike the state sector, factory committees had not become involved in management issues, but they had asserted the right that no worker could be hired or fired without the agreement of the factory committee; several campaigns had been fought to reinstate 'trouble-makers' dismissed before the Tsar's overthrow.

On 28 April, as the moves towards the establishment of the First Coalition Government were underway, a meeting was held of the factory committees in the enterprises working for the Ministry of the Navy. The meeting was addressed by a Menshevik who since 1915 had been a leading member of the Workers' Group on the War Industries' Committee, and he criticised any move by factory committees to run the affairs of their factories themselves; factory committees should oversee, should supervise, should inspect, but not manage. He held up as a model the workers at the Obukhov Factory where the factory committee had left management structures intact but had asserted the right to ask questions and request access to financial information. He was therefore critical of the situation in the Baltic Shipyards where the factory committee insisted on taking part in all aspects of management, including the drafting of financial statements.[7]

Once the First Coalition Government was in place, it established for the first time a Ministry of Labour, headed by Skobelev and assisted by Gvozdev. Although there was talk of intervening in the economy and confiscating excessive war profits, in practice little of that rhetoric came into being. The First Congress of Soviets accepted that 'in the present circumstances' it was not the task of 'responsible workers' to press for the eight-hour day. This sort of attitude, reminiscent of criticisms of 'strikomania' in 1913 or opposing strikes for the duration of the war, meant that the Ministry of Labour achieved very little. By the time the First Coalition Government collapsed, only small amendments to existing Tsarist legislation had been made; thus on 11 July labour inspectors were established as a first step towards revamping the system of factory inspection established back in the 1880s.[8]

The 'present circumstances' were, of course, difficult for business. Employers struggled to adjust to the new situation. In February, workers had gained an average wage increase of 50 per cent although some individual enterprises had been forced to grant increases of 200–300 per cent. Wages were not the only cost to rise: between February and June 1917 the cost of fuel from traditional suppliers in the Donbas rose by 100 per cent. There were also financial issues. The wartime expansion of industry had largely been funded by the banks, with 75 per cent of their funds invested in war-related industries. By June 1917 the political instability in the country was such that the banks started to reduce credit, just as fuel and other fixed costs began to soar. On top of this the constant disruption to production meant that productivity was down 35–50 per cent. Many war-related enterprises had made substantial profits in 1916, but the 'present circumstances' meant that these profits were rapidly disappearing. Yet, when factory committees demanded 'to see the books', the profits made in 1916 convinced them that the employers were crying wolf when they said they were on the edge of bankruptcy.[9] During the lengthy talks resulting in the formation of the Second Coalition Government, there had been much discussion of Kerensky's 8 July Declaration which referred to the urgent need for social legislation. That Declaration, of course, had never been accepted by the liberals and they were determined to resist its provisions when the government was finally in place. Thus, in practice, all the new government did was, once again, amend existing Tsarist labour legislation: on 25 July the existing Law on Social Insurance was extended to all workers, not just those working in private industry who had been covered by the 1912 act. Later, on 8 August, night work was banned for women and minors, except in enterprises linked to the war effort. Such modest changes were hardly going to impress a workforce that was increasingly voting for Bolshevik resolutions.[10]

In the dying days of the First Coalition Government, on 28 June, Skobelev warned workers against 'arbitrary' actions which 'disorganised industry' and 'exhausted the exchequer'. Such 'spontaneous actions often take the upper hand over organised action; they are taken without consideration for the conditions of the enterprise involved [...] and bring damage to the class movement of the proletariat', he added. This marked turn to the right was even more apparent after the July Days, when the attitude of the Second Coalition Government towards labour issues hardened still further. In its circular of 23 August, the Ministry of Labour made clear that the Law of 23 April had established that factory owners had an absolute right to hire and fire all employees other than members of factory committees, unless by mutual consent some alternative arrangement had been reached. The factory committees, the Ministry of Labour asserted, had 'usurped' the right to be involved in matters of hiring and firing, which was a clear management prerogative. The circular ended with this threat: 'coercive measures on the part of workers for purposes of dismissal or employment of certain persons are regarded as actions to be criminally punished'.[11]

A further Ministry of Labour circular, issued on 28 August at the height of the Kornilov crisis, reminded workers that under the 23 April Law meetings of factory committees should only take place after work and should not disrupt the working day: 'it is the duty of every worker to devote his energies to intensive labour and not to lose one minute of working time'. These clarifications of the 23 April Law led to protests at the Langenzipen Factory, which called on the Soviet to revoke the circular and condemned it as counter-revolutionary; it was, the workers suggested, a malicious slander that the work of factory committees lowered productivity, and the Ministry of Labour had clearly been converted into the Ministry for the Protection of Capitalist Interests.[12] There were similar protests at the Putilov Works, the Admiralty Works, the Cable Works, the Nobel Works and the Lebedev Works. The Third Conference of Petrograd Factory Committees was called to condemn Skobelev's circulars, in the aftermath of which some employers tried to cut the pay of factory committee members to reflect the fact that they were not engaged in productive work.[13]

INDUSTRIAL CRISIS

As Steve Smith has commented, 'the revolutionary process of 1917 can only be understood in the context of a growing crisis of the economy [...] a crisis in the economy underpinned the crisis in politics'. By September the output of manufactured goods throughout Russia had fallen by 40 per cent since the start of the year, and for many employers closing factories seemed the only option: between March and July, 568 textile and food-processing plants closed. Skilled workers in war-related industries had more success in defending their jobs; only 3 per cent of metal workers were unemployed in October.[14] During the first three months of revolution, price rises of over 40 per cent were matched by wage increases of over 50 per cent; but from July onwards, even though nominal wages continued to rise dramatically, their real value began to decline significantly as inflation took hold.[15] By the autumn, the supply situation was again acute. In February the government had set the bread ration at 500 grams per day; by October it had been reduced to 300 grams. During those months the state price for bread rose 230 per cent, while black-market prices skyrocketed. The black market, however, meant avoiding the daily bread queue, which could take 4–5 hours a day. In this rapidly worsening situation it was often the intervention of the factory committees that restored an element of stability. At the end of August, the management of the Putilov Works called for 10,000 redundancies: the factory committee demanded talks and reduced the redundancies to 3,200 by agreeing to accept a reduced level of redundancy pay and mediation from the Soviet; it was also agreed that all redundancies would be voluntary, after Bolshevik pressure put a stop to a move by some members of the factory committee to meet the redundancies by concentrating the dismissals on women. Nevertheless, as summer turned to autumn the Putilov Works was effectively operating at only one-third capacity and that was only maintained after another initiative by the factory committee – it was the factory committee which set about ensuring production by modifying the coke boilers so that they could use wood. Workers from the Pipe Factory, and from many other factories in the capital, were sent to southern Russia to scout for cargoes of coal stranded in railway sidings which could be brought to the capital.[16]

As the economic situation worsened, so the factory committees gained in influence. Although by the end of May the Bolsheviks had control of the Petrograd Trade Union Council, at the national level the trade unions were firmly under Menshevik control and unwilling to take up the radical demands emanating from the factory floor. The factory committees were not circumscribed in this way. The First Conference of Petrograd Factory Committees was held from 30 May to 3 June and asserted the right of factory committees to check company accounts. There was then a lull in activity until a second Conference was held on 7–12 August, a third Conference on 5–10 September and a fourth on 10 October; the First All-Russian Conference of Factory Committees was held on 17–22 October. The decisions taken at these conferences reflected the growing assertiveness of the factory committees in questions of production. If in March and April factory committees democratised factory life and took control of hiring and firing, in May and June they began to monitor raw materials and their efficient use. Then, in July and August the employers tried to limit the powers of factory committees, which had begun to establish various 'control commissions' to monitor production, orders and finance. By September and October, when many employers were trying to close production or leave Russia, factory committees were discussing taking control of the factories.[17] This process was typified by a resolution passed by the factory committee at the Respirator Factory at the end of August:

> We have made clear our position regarding the sabotage of our factory by the administration, which has gone away at this most pressing and critical moment. We consider this to be an act of desertion of the home

front. In order not to disrupt the front, and in order that the factory can work normally – in spite of the eight day absence of the administration – we unanimously resolve: as circumstances will not permit any delay, to demand the immediate appointment of a commissar to take care of the legal side of things and that he be someone neutral. The works committee and shop stewards committee take responsibility for production and maintaining output. [18]

These efforts by workers to remove the factory administration were not inspired by any syndicalist utopianism but the very practical and pragmatic desire to save jobs.

Whatever the motivation for demands for workers' control, Kerensky was not going to accept them. His government was wholly opposed to any degree of workers' control. Thus the Special Council on Defence made clear on 23 September that the following principles would operate in future in defence-related industries: 'the owner of the plant is always at the head of the factory and workers have no right to interfere with the actions of the plant administration, far less do they have the right to change them; in hiring and firing of workers, the existing statutes on this matter must be strictly adhered to'.[19] The factory committees would not accept this. As early as the Second Conference of Petrograd Factory Committees in early August, resolutions were being passed which echoed Bolshevik rhetoric. Thus 'the crisis, worsening with every passing day, is being exacerbated by the policies of the bourgeoisie, which fears losing not only its political power but also its power over organised production'; the bourgeoisie was not only failing to organise production but 'waging a policy of sabotage, resorting to hidden lockouts'. Thus 'regulation [of production] in Russia can be implemented only by an organisation controlled by the proletariat and the strata of the peasantry which support it [and] this requires that they take control of state power'. This resolution was proposed by Vladimir Milyutin, a labour activist of long standing who had been an active trade unionist in Moscow after the 1905 Revolution and a worker delegate in 1910 to the Anti-Alcohol Congress.[20]

Rumours of the evacuation of key defence industries from Petrograd after the Germans captured Riga on 21 August were also at the forefront of factory committee concerns. In September, the administration of the Putilov Works attempted to send machinery by canal to Saratov, but the factory committee held up the barge for a month until the administration had proved to their satisfaction that the machinery was not needed in Petrograd. At the Pipe Works, management planned to remove operations to Penza, Voronoezh and Ekaterinoslav, transferring 4,000 machines and 20,000 workers, but when the factory committee visited these towns it became clear that there were no plans to receive the evacuated labour force and that in reality fewer than 1,300 workers would be transferred. Evacuation plans were also obstructed at the Okhta Explosives Works, the Okhta Powder Works, the Arsenal and the Optics Factory on the grounds that the evacuation plans were inadequately prepared. The Third Conference of Petrograd Factory Committees in early September condemned evacuation, except for the partial evacuation of single enterprises carried out under strict working-class supervision.[21] Evacuation could simply mean closure under a different name, and workers' control was first and foremost an attempt by factory committees to stem the tide of industrial chaos, which led them almost naturally to back Bolshevik demands.

WOMEN WORKERS

During the redundancy crisis at the Putilov Works in September, some of the factory committee had pushed for redundancies to be targeted at female labour on the grounds that women had only recently joined the workforce as men were drafted into the army; the Bolsheviks determinedly resisted such a response.[22] For the Bolsheviks, women were to be encouraged as active participants in the revolutionary process. The Provisional Government had conceded under pressure that all women would have the vote in local and national elections, and on 10 March the Bolshevik St Petersburg Committee committed itself to the task of organising among women for those elections; on 15 March it resolved to form a Women's Bureau and to relaunch the 1914 women's newspaper *Rabotnitsa*. When the women's activist Alexandra Kollontai returned to Russia on 19 March, she immediately wrote in *Pravda* about the need to prepare working women for the planned elections to the Constituent Assembly and proposed that a founding meeting of the Women's Bureau should be held at once. Kollontai had helped organise a delegation of textile workers to the Women's Congress in 1908 and back then she had faced opposition from those Bolsheviks who were suspicious of any separate organisation being established for women. Now the same thing happened again. Lenin returned on 3 April accompanied by his wife Nadezhda Krupskaya, who had always opposed Kollontai on the idea of a separate Women's Bureau. The initiative stalled and when Kollontai raised the issue of the Women's Bureau at the Petrograd Party Conference at the end of April, the proposal was withdrawn on the instructions of the chairman, an intervention from on high which infuriated that firebrand underground veteran Bagdatiev, who had been a member of the St Petersburg Committee at the time of the Women's Congress.[23]

Despite these organisational setbacks for Kollontai, Bolshevik women activists concentrated their efforts in 1917 on two specific groups of women: soldiers' wives and laundresses. Ever since 1912, soldiers' wives had been eligible for limited financial support. However, the legislation excluded common-law wives, and in the Russian Empire this category included a large number of women who considered themselves to be in a recognised and permanent relationship. For the Christian subjects of the Tsar, Imperial Russia only recognised those who married within the Orthodox Church, but there were vast numbers of women in communities of Old Believers and other religious sects who considered themselves married according to their traditions, but were considered common-law wives under the law.[24] One of the first acts of the Provisional Government had been to end such religious discrimination, but the financial consequences of this decision had not been thought through, especially since the real value of these benefits had been eaten away by inflation. On 11 April, 15,000 soldiers' wives marched to the Soviet to demand an increase in benefits. Met by its chairman, they were told that the exchequer was empty. When Kollontai tried to protest, she was refused the floor and so she organised an impromptu meeting at the gates of the Tauride Palace. She called on the women to form an organisation of their own, from which they could gain representation on the Soviet, a policy the Bolsheviks supported. By mid-April an all-city committee of soldiers' wives had been set up, involving Kollontai and some other members of the Soviet; by June this had become a Union of Soldiers' Wives, which the Bolsheviks soon dominated.[25] Under this pressure, the First Coalition Government made some concessions: the eligibility criteria were expanded to common-law wives, foster children and step-parents. This decision, however, put an enormous burden on the state: the cost of the benefit went up from 25 million roubles in 1916 to 36 million by September 1917, or 11 per cent of military expenditure.[26]

The Bolsheviks also were active in the Union of Laundresses, formed in late April. The laundresses demanded an eight-hour day to bring them into line with other workers in Petrograd. When the employers refused, they called a strike which started on 1 May. The Union of Laundresses was led by a Bolshevik, and Kollontai wrote up the campaign in detail in a series of articles for *Pravda*. On 8 May the Soviet agreed to back the strike, which continued throughout the month until the laundresses achieved victory, although that victory was only partial because some employers reneged on the deal and others closed their laundries because bankruptcy threatened. During the laundresses' strike, on 10 May, the Bolshevik Party produced the first edition of the long promised weekly women's newspaper *Rabotnitsa*. Then, during May and June, the Bolsheviks used a series of public meetings organised by the editorial board of *Rabotnitsa* to develop a school of agitators attached to the newspaper; their target was the upcoming municipal *duma* elections fought on the slogan 'Against War and High Prices'; several mass open air meetings of women's workers were held in June.[27]

The July Days impacted badly on *Rabotnitsa*. Kollontai was arrested and some Bolshevik women activists were roughed up. A whole month passed before another public meeting could be held, on 30 July, and the Bolsheviks were disappointed when only 700 people turned up. Then the situation began to improve. On 1 August a meeting of domestic servants attracted over 1,000 women who protested at Kollontai's arrest and denounced what they called the slanderous attacks on the Bolsheviks; the next *Rabotnitsa*-sponsored meeting attracted 5,000 people and again demanded that the arrested Bolsheviks be freed; when Kollontai was eventually released after Kornilov's failed military coup, she was carried out of the next *Rabotnitsa* meeting shoulder high. Early in October, an Initiative Group for Women Workers was set up to prepare for a Petrograd Conference of Working Women which would in turn be given the task of organising the female vote in the elections to the Constituent Assembly; some 70 preparatory meetings were planned.[28]

LAND COMMITTEES AND THEIR OPERATION

The February Revolution had begun in the capital and had been the achievement of workers and soldiers. As the year developed, however, the peasants became ever more actively involved in revolutionary struggle. The overthrow of the Tsar was interpreted in the villages as signifying an end to an unjust system of land tenure, and the peasants expected that the departure of the most prominent landowner in the country, the Tsar, would presage a similar fate for the rest of the land-owning nobility that had been the mainstay of his regime. Numerous peasant resolutions passed at this time assumed that the land currently held in private noble hands would soon be expropriated and passed over to the peasants. Throughout the country, in early March, peasant committees were elected at village and parish level, usually by general meetings of the peasants; those elected as peasant representatives were a mix of traditional local leaders and SR activists.[29] In the immediate aftermath of the February Revolution, peasants showed their support for the new order by donating increased supplies of grain to the authorities to help meet the immediate supply crisis.[30] However, as with the workers, peasant support was not uncritical: one village committee near Kostroma resolved on 30 March to support the Provisional Government 'so long as' it moved quickly to call a Constituent Assembly.

Peasants were also keen to see the establishment of new democratic authorities at local level and to get rid of the old land captains and dignitaries who had dominated rural affairs. These elections did not take place until August and September, however, and in the interim the previously existing *zemstvo* boards and their noble leaders continued to operate, much to the disappointment of the peasants.[31] *Zemstvo* chairmen were usually nominated as the new provincial commissars and they were advised by the Provisional Government to bring into their work 'local landowners and all the intellectual forces of the countryside'; peasants were not referred to. This advice seemed to contradict the undertaking given in the Provisional Government's declaration of 7 March that the local administration would be popularly elected. The decision three weeks later to advise provincial commissars on how to summon troops in the case of possible rural disorder did not suggest that these new authorities had a peasant-centred approach. As Graham Gill has commented, 'the government appeared to be doing little more than renaming the old oppressive power structure while retaining it intact'.[32]

The Tsar had been brought down by food shortages, so it is hardly surprising that the first forays of the Provisional Government into the area of agrarian policy were directed at securing supplies. On 5 March provincial *zemstvos* were given the power to requisition grain, and on 9 March a special Supply Committee was established within the Ministry of Agriculture. On 25 March the Provisional Government took its most radical decision yet and declared a state monopoly over the buying and selling of grain: noble and peasant farmers were equally obliged to offer their entire crop to the state at fixed prices, apart from the minimum needed for their own subsistence. To enforce this system, a hierarchy of supply committees was established the same day. In an attempt to increase productivity, the Provisional Government also decreed that any agricultural machinery which was left unused could be confiscated and allocated to those farmers who were prepared to make use of it.[33]

Then, on 11 April, the Provisional Government moved to put all sown land under state protection until it could be safely brought to harvest; it became an offence to damage sown land in any way. In a parallel move, the Provisional Government also endeavoured to extend the area under cultivation. Many of the large estates were run by absentee landlords, noble families who were resident in the cities. Their estates were run by stewards, who found that the war had deprived them of both labourers and horses, and so they had little choice but to reduce the area under cultivation. In some highly productive areas in the Black Earth belt, like the province of Saratov on the river Volga, the area under cultivation had fallen by as much as 50 per cent, although in the country as a whole the figure was only 10 per cent. To ensure that as much land was cultivated as possible, the supply committees were empowered to take charge of any land left uncultivated and arrange for it to be leased to those willing to farm it.[34]

The Provisional Government showed far less energy when it came to the question of land reform. The liberal minister of agriculture announced on 19 March that land reform would come through 'legal means and not by violence' and condemned any move by peasants to seize land before the Constituent Assembly had had a chance to legislate. The only reform undertaken at this stage was for the state to take over the former royal estates. The minister of agriculture did, however, establish a hierarchy of land committees which were to audit the country's land stock and register all land holdings in anticipation that the Constituent Assembly, when it met, would want to address the issue of land reform. The Main Land Committee, at the apex of the hierarchy of land committees, was established on 21 April. It was empowered solely with providing information to the Provisional Government and was in no hurry to assemble; the Main Land Committee had its first full meeting on 20 May and it too urged moderation, calling for no illegal actions while it undertook the work it would present to the Constituent Assembly.

The agenda of the local land committees was rather different: the local land committees were empowered not only to register land ownership but 'to preserve the land stock'. This meant that their powers seemed to rival and even exceed those of the local supply committees.[35] Local land committees had the authority to expel from their land those proprietors who 'depreciated the national land fund'. This provision could be interpreted to mean that any landowner who did not farm sufficiently intensively could be deprived of his land. Once the First Coalition Government was formed, and the SR leader Victor Chernov took over as minister of agriculture, the ambiguity in the powers of these local land committees began to be used to introduce the piecemeal reallocation of land, a process which accelerated when the All-Russian Congress of Peasant Soviets met from 4 to 28 May.

Just under half the delegates to the congress were SRs, and although some SR activists were keen to revive the Peasant Union which had been formed in 1905, most SRs preferred to use the term 'soviet' to describe the structures they were establishing, which was in effect a hierarchy of peasant councils from parish to nation level. After being addressed by Chernov on 24 May, the congress voted on the next day for the transfer of all land to the peasants. How this would happen was made clear in an appeal which was published on the 26th: peasants were to form land committees, which would prepare for a land reform based on 'the equal distribution to all toiling people' of all land. As an immediate, but interim, measure, until the Constituent Assembly met to finalise arrangements, all land was to be put at the disposal of land committees, which would determine the appropriate manner of sowing and harvesting and would then sequester the necessary machinery. Any land confiscations which took place outside the oversight of the land committees were condemned as 'arbitrary'.[36]

After the congress, wherever the SRs won control of a local land committee, they would declare that 'the national land fund was being depreciated' and at the same time sequester the local noble's land, allocating farm machinery to those peasant farmers able to make use of it. In doing this they followed the so-called Peasant Mandate on the Land, also adopted by the All-Russian Congress of Peasant Soviets, which made clear that private landownership was to end and all land to be expropriated without compensation and transferred to the ownership of the whole people, passing 'into the use of all those who cultivate it'; land tenure would then be equal, taking into consideration local conditions, and land cultivation would be permitted on both an individual or co-operative basis, although 'the employment of hired labour is not permitted'. The only exceptions to this last point were certain 'orchards, plantations, nurseries' cultivated 'by highly developed techniques' which would become model farms run by the state.[37] Thus the SRs were beginning to implement the policies they had been advocating since the party was founded in 1901. For liberals, however, the decisions of the peasant congress simply endorsed violent action by land committees, and Chernov's fellow ministers were soon concerned that the whole Ministry of Agriculture in practice favoured granting land committees full rights over the land.[38]

The Third SR Congress took place as the peasant congress closed, on 25 May to 4 June. It adopted a similarly contradictory stance. The congress accepted that only the Constituent Assembly could implement full land reform, but it also resolved that, as an interim measure, all land should be placed under the management of democratised land committees and that 'all productive elements and livestock be distributed to the best possible advantage'. Chernov, like all SRs, believed that peasant land ownership would prove to be more productive than noble land ownership, and so he was happy to encourage the use of the government's legislation to cultivate uncultivated land as a way of allowing peasants to acquire more land straight away, even before the Constituent Assembly met. The liberal ministers in the Coalition saw this as the worst kind of deviousness, but, under Chernov's watch, 'back door' land seizures multiplied. Peasants would use the decree on the need to ensure cultivation to confiscate farm machinery from their noble landlord, and then, since the noble could not cultivate the land without the machinery, the peasants would claim that the land was now uncultivated and therefore subject to redistribution. Other peasants would refuse to work for their noble landlord, force him to the verge of bankruptcy and then demand to acquire the uncultivated land; if the noble responded – as some did – by bringing in 'Chinese' labour, these migrants would be driven from the village by an angry mob. Chernov connived at such measures because he was clear that, ultimately, the Constituent Assembly would be dominated by the SRs when it met, and would therefore implement an SR land reform; the Constituent Assembly would eventually simply ratify retrospectively the changes that he was encouraging.[39] He told the Third SR Congress that 'since the Constituent Assembly would work on the basis of land being placed in the hands of those who worked it, the passing of that land to land committees would not usurp the Constituent Assembly but implement the decision it was yet to reach'.[40]

When the second full meeting of the Main Land Committee met from 1 to 6 July, Chernov used the occasion to criticise his fellow liberal ministers and to introduce a resolution in line with Peasant Soviet and SR policy. He also prompted some committee members to resign in protest when he insisted that 12 representatives from the Peasant Soviet join the Main Land Committee. Then, on 16 July, when Chernov feared that the negotiations over the formation of a second Coalition Government would result in his dismissal, he sent a circular to land committees and supply committees, without the agreement of his fellow ministers. This circular fixed rents and systematised backstairs land seizures by expanding the power of the committees. Since the committees were responsible for the correct exploitation of all arable and grazing land, they should prepare to harvest any land that noble landlords were unable to harvest; any unharvested land or harvesting machinery was to be taken under the control of the committees. The circular concluded that 'land committees must look on themselves as organisations of state power [...] committees can go a long way in satisfying the just demands of the working peasantry, but under the absolute condition that this does not lead to the disintegration of the national economy and the dissipation of productive forces'. Chernov was effectively sanctioning what peasants were doing and calling for more. His fellow ministers were appalled.[41]

LAND SEIZURES BEGIN

The day after Chernov issued his circular calling on land committees to act as organs of state power, his fellow minister Tsereteli, still acting as minister of the interior despite the formal resignation of Kerensky's interim administration, responded by instructing the provincial commissars to take a firm line against illegal land seizures. On 18 July the minister of supply offered his support to the minister of the interior and instructed supply committees to cease acting illegally; his circular to all supply committees called for a ban on surreptitious land seizures on pain of dismissal or criminal proceedings.[42] Even though Chernov stayed in his post once the composition of the Second Coalition Government had been finalised, these moves by his fellow ministers showed how his position was gradually being undermined, and by the end of August he had decided to resign. The marginalisation of Chernov became particularly clear on the vexed question of land sales. Peasants had always argued that with the establishment of the Main Land Committee there should be a moratorium on land sales, if the Main Land Committee was trying to establish a definitive audit of land before it was expropriated and redistributed, so the nobles should not be able to sell off piecemeal plots of land which they would soon lose through expropriation without compensation. In the First Coalition Government the SR minister of justice had tried to outlaw land sales, but the liberal ministers had got this rescinded on 23 June. On 12 July, during the interregnum between the First and Second Coalition Governments, Chernov had taken advantage of the absence of any liberal ministers to restrict land transactions once again. This was rescinded in turn on 22 July when the Second Coalition Government passed a law allowing land sales, if the provincial land committee agreed to the sale and the Ministry of Agriculture confirmed it.[43]

To peasants, it seemed unjust that it was legal for nobles to sell land, but not for peasants to acquire it. On 14 August the Executive of the Peasant Soviet complained to the Second Coalition

Government that many of the local chairmen of peasant soviets were being arrested on charges of having been involved in the very sort of land seizures that Chernov had encouraged them to undertake. The government did not back down; indeed the minister of supply took the power on 24 August to dissolve what he termed 'disobedient' land committees. Yet land committees continued in their disobedience, since they no longer trusted the government. The decision, on 9 August, to delay the elections to the Constituent Assembly from mid-September to mid-November did not encourage peasants in the belief that their demand for land reform would be met any time soon.

The government was quite effective at retaining control of land committees from provincial down to district level. However, at parish (*volost'*) level, the overwhelming desire for peasants to govern themselves rather than be governed was impossible to resist. From a government perspective, the parish committee, often rebranded as a parish soviet, was the base unit of its administration, responsible for ensuring law and order and guaranteeing the food supply. In practice, the parish level of administration was an entirely peasant affair, responsible for organising unrest as often as order – if unrest occurred, it was always organised at a parish level. The parish supply committees proved a particular thorn in the side of the government. Whatever their supposed purpose, they were usually merged with the parish soviet and took no notice of the instructions coming from above; they were, in the words of Gill, 'more responsive to impulses from below than directives from above'. It was the same with the parish land committees: they too were effectively swallowed up by the parish soviet since there was no clear delineation of the difference between them and the supply committees. The gap between the government and the villages was becoming unbridgeable. At parish level, peasant wishes held sway and the peasants wanted land. For them it was simple: 'land was a blessing created by nature to be used by all who wished to work it with their own personal strength'.[44]

When the state monopoly of grain had been established by the Provisional Government, the fixed price paid to the peasants had been a 60 per cent increase on what the Tsar had previously paid. Rampant inflation soon made this increase worthless. Peasants began to hold back on grain deliveries to the state in order to try to force up the price, and would sometimes even seize noble land simply to prevent the nobles undercutting them by making their deliveries to the state. In a desperate effort to end this policy of non-co-operation, the government suddenly doubled the delivery price for grain on 27 August, having repeatedly stated that this was a concession that would never be made.[45] The price increase was part of a carrot-and-stick approach on the part of the authorities, who were ready to use force. Between March and August there were only 56 incidents of force being used against peasants; in September and October the figure was 105. On 8 September, as Kerensky tried to restore his authority in the aftermath of the Kornilov rebellion, he gave provincial commissars the right to use force against the peasants whenever necessary; by October he had given them 'special powers' to cope with rural unrest, including the right to hold reserve cavalry units at their disposal. In practice, however, on many occasions when these troops were brought to confront the peasants, they refused to use force against them.[46]

By September, peasant unrest was endemic, with the grain-rich Central Black Earth and Middle Volga regions the worst affected. Tambov province was the very worst, with 105 estates destroyed in September, 24 in one particularly brutal three-day period in Kozlov District. On 15 September, troops were sent from Moscow to restore order, but significantly order was only restored after, in defiance of government policy, the local land committee had taken all local land into its management; that committee then expropriated the land from the noble landowners and divided it up among the peasantry.[47] In his tour of the Volga region in September 1917, the *Guardian* journalist Morgan Philips Price described the 'temporary land socialisation scheme' that the local soviets had put in place there: 'the expropriation of the landlords and the division of the land on a communal basis has been accomplished and only awaits legal sanction'. Indeed, Philips Price found that ever since the summer the Samara Provincial Land Committee had banned all land sales and taken over the management of any land not worked by the peasants; nobles had only been allowed to retain that land which could be worked by their own physical labour without employing the labour of others. The land fund created in this way was then distributed to the peasants who paid no rent for it. Other regions were following suit by moving to establish provincial land funds. Thus, in the villages the SR policy of an interim land reform before the Constituent Assembly met was already underway, despite the efforts of Kerensky's provincial commissars.[48]

SOLDIERS AND THE RESTORATION OF DISCIPLINE

After six months of revolution, workers and peasants were clearly intensely frustrated by the failure of the Provisional Government and the two Coalition Governments to address the social issues of the day. Both were already taking matters into their own hands, by taking over the factories and seizing land. What was the attitude of soldiers? Garrison troops reacted to the overthrow of the Tsar at once. The establishment of soldiers' committees was almost instantaneous, with Order Number One often simply formalising what had already been established. Soldiers would often demand the election of officers, but settle for the dismissal of unpopular ones.[49] As to the front, there was not a single sector of its 2,000 miles that was not affected by Order Number One. Soldiers at once ceased to salute or stand to attention; they addressed their officers as 'Mister Lieutenant' rather than 'Your Excellency', and insisted on being addressed respectfully by the formal 'you' rather than the demeaning 'thou'. Committees soon presented officers with demands, requested explanations, countermanded orders and instituted controls over arms and ammunition. All attempts by officers to explain that Order Number One had no official standing failed, and all the Provisional Government could do was to persuade the Soviet on 5 March to issue Order Number Two, which made clear that officers were not to be elected and that there was to be no interference by committees in matters of military strategy. However, Order Number Two also stated that those officers already elected should remain in post and hinted that the concept of elected officers might yet be established, once an appropriate mechanism had been devised. Essentially, as Allan Wildman noted, Order Number One 'institutionalised the trench soldier's inner liberation from the yoke of officer and military discipline'.[50]

Lynchings of officers did occur, but mostly in the rear rather than at the front, with the highest number of incidents taking place in Petrograd and the Baltic Fleet. In practice, most of the 'counter-revolutionary' officers who were detained by committees were quickly and quietly released shortly afterwards. In frontal towns like Pskov, Dvinsk (Daugavpils), Minsk and Kamenets-Podolsk, local commanders organised triumphal celebrations to mark Russia's transformation into a democratic state, celebrations often attended by newly appointed commissars from the Provisional Government. As March progressed, the committee structure became more formalised. Spontaneous grass-roots rallies were replaced by a hierarchical network of committees; thus, 'by the end of March the committee structure from company to army level was virtually complete and enjoyed the active or passive co-operation of the unit commanders'. Amongst the first army committees was that for the Twelfth Army, quickly followed by the First and Fifth Armies. All of these were on the Northern Front; on other fronts the process took longer, but it was only the Eighth Army which resisted the process with any determination, and eventually the Eighth Army commander was advised that a committee would be 'useful' if discipline were to be restored.[51]

Desertion was a problem, but not an insurmountable one. At first, rumours of land reform being implemented at once led to a desertion rate of 1–2 per cent, but many of these deserters returned to their units once they had established that their family was well and that land reform was in fact far from imminent. An amnesty for all deserters who returned by 15 April effectively kept the problem within manageable proportions.[52] Preparations for the June Offensive then prompted more instances of desertion and protest. Often leave that had been carefully negotiated to coincide with essential work on the family farm was cancelled at short notice, to the fury of those affected. The offensive also led to the recall of the recovering wounded and soldiers aged over 40 who had been released for field work. Around the time of the July Days, several units in the Moscow Military District mutinied rather than face redeployment to the front, while there were similar mutinies in Tsaritsyn and Nizhnii Novgorod.[53]

After the July Days, the renewed campaign to restore discipline with the threat of the death penalty was resisted in the rear garrisons, while at the front the discipline campaign saw some armed clashes and arrests.[54] In the Moscow Military District, for example, the Bolsheviks were able to capitalise after the July Days on the attempts by the authorities to restore military discipline, officer authority and regular training duties. Until July, most soldiers' soviets were under the secure control of reformist SRs, but as a direct result of unrest during the discipline campaign, which included punitive expeditions against recalcitrant reserve regiments which did not want to be transferred to the front, the soldiers began to transfer their allegiance to the Bolsheviks.[55] The soldiers' gradual turn away from the SRs and towards the Bolsheviks was also fuelled by the SRs' apparent acquiescence to propaganda associated with the discipline campaign, not to mention Kerensky's enthusiastic backing of it.

In the build-up to Kornilov's failed military coup, it was politically important for the Commander-in-Chief to create a sense of crisis in order to justify the reintroduction of the death penalty. As a result, the military high command issued reports which maligned the fighting ability of rank-and-file soldiers. Although the Soviet press sometimes took General Staff Headquarters to task for this, Kerensky had shown his sympathies towards Kornilov with his speech to the Moscow State Conference. In the end, the criticism of the rank-and-file soldier during the discipline campaign was too much for the SRs. On 25 August, the SR newspaper *Delo naroda* challenged official reports of a regiment having fled the battlefield in disarray: Soviet investigations had revealed that the regiment concerned had suffered 75 per cent casualties before it took the entirely reasonable decision to withdraw; another unit accused of cowardice, it was later established, had withdrawn because its 16 guns were no match for the enemy's 200 guns. According to the pro-government press, the fall of Riga on 21 August was similarly due to units 'wilfully leaving their positions'; however, the assistant commissar of the Northern Front had written a report which showed that nothing of the sort had happened.[56] The chairman of the Soldiers' Soviet of the Twelfth Army was equally forthright: in Riga the army had retreated 'only after suffering enormous losses and failing to receive reinforcements'; despite their retreat, they had launched frequent counter-attacks; in sum, this was no chaotic disorderly flight but a disciplined and managed retreat.

Growing hostility among rank-and-file soldiers to the policies of both Kerensky and Kornilov meant that during the Kornilov rebellion the vast majority of soldiers opposed the coup attempt. A plethora of extraordinary committees were set up by rear-garrison soldiers to resist Kornilov's counter-revolution; in the Moscow

Military District at least 81 such committees were active between 28 August and 1 September. These committees took the lead in arresting suspicious officers and distributing weapons to the Red Guards, and, at their assemblies, they would frequently demand the dissolution of the counter-revolutionary Union of Officers which had supported Kornilov's adventure. Often, these ad hoc committees did not disband once the Kornilov danger had passed, but helped the Bolsheviks secure impressive victories as the army committees of the rear came up for re-election. It was to the rear garrisons that the provincial commissars turned when they wanted to use troops against peasant disturbances. Given this growing oppositional mood among garrison soldiers, it was not surprising that they so frequently refused to participate in operations to combat rural disorder.[57]

After six months of revolution, soldiers in the rear, if not those at the front, were beginning to question the policies of the authorities. In February, Kerensky had embraced the mutinous soldiers and forced the Duma liberals to depose the Tsar. By September, workers were taking control of the factories and peasants were seizing land, and soldiers were not prepared to put a stop to either process. Workers, peasants and soldiers were equally frustrated at the lack of social progress since February. Kerensky's government had simply failed to live up to what were perceived as minimal demands of the revolution and the Bolsheviks were able to reap the organisational benefits.

6

INSURRECTION

Once Kornilov's attempted military coup had failed, Kerensky was determined to establish a third Coalition Government. This proved more problematic than establishing the Second Coalition Government, because in the post-Kornilov mood, with the Bolsheviks 'blossoming', the alternative call for a Soviet Government was increasingly heard. The struggle against a third Coalition and for a Soviet Government was a struggle to restore the revolutionary tradition of Russian labour which since 1905 had been suspicious of political agreements with liberals. When Kerensky called for yet another coalition, his days were numbered, and the Bolsheviks, who had been calling for a Soviet Government since February, were the inevitable beneficiaries. On his return to Russia, Lenin had told his comrades that the time would come when the Bolsheviks had a majority in the Soviet. Immediately after the failure of Kornilov's military coup, the Bolsheviks won that majority. However, if the Bolsheviks were agreed that the time for a Soviet Government had come, and the vast majority of workers, soldiers and peasants thought the same way, there were tactical disagreements within the Bolshevik Party about how best to establish such a government, whether through democratic processes or insurrection. These rows were bitterly fought because behind them lay important issues of ideology and the future revolutionary path to be followed.

Geoffrey Swain

A SOVIET GOVERNMENT

On 1 September, once it became clear that Kornilov's political ambitions had failed, the daily paper of the SR Party, *Delo naroda*, published an editorial which must have seemed as contradictory to the contemporary reader in 1917 as it does to the historian today. *Delo naroda* declared that 'the social character' of the Russian Revolution had been bound to push landowners and industrialists into the camp of counter-revolution, and now this had happened, the almost bloodless liquidation of the Kornilov conspiracy showed that the danger of counter-revolution could be reduced 'to a handful of generals'; even the soldiers sent by Kornilov to Petrograd to overthrow Kerensky had ended up defending the revolution, once they had understood that what they were engaged in was an armed attack on that revolution. It was 'only the mass of toiling workers, soldiers and peasants who were on the side of revolution', while the liberals had revealed their counter-revolutionary character. 'Should not the Provisional Revolutionary Government consist only of representatives of the toiling masses?' the paper asked, since the liberals had shown themselves to be mired in Kornilov's counter-revolution? 'No public leader, loyal to the revolution and furthermore to socialism, could or should participate with the Kadets in the exercise of government authority,' the editorial went on. And yet, in spite of this clear statement that what was needed was a government of the toiling masses, the editorial concluded with these words: 'In spite of this, we express ourselves in favour of coalition government. We think that the Russian Revolution did not eliminate the possibilities of capitalist development and that until a socialist revolution occurs in Western Europe, there can be no question of overthrowing the capitalist regime.'[1]

What were readers supposed to think? The whole logic of the SR daily's analysis of post-Kornilov Russia suggested the need for a 'government of the toiling masses', in other words a government composed of the parties represented in the Soviet, a Soviet Government, yet an abstract doctrinal belief that Russian capitalism needed to be allowed to develop further convinced the editorial writers that a further coalition with industrialists and landowners was required. This coalition, however, could not be with the Kadets, now branded as those who had betrayed the revolution – yet the

Kadets were the only party industrialists and landowners showed any interest in supporting. The SR stance seemed quite nonsensical. What made more sense to many were the rumours circulating on the very day on which this editorial was produced to the effect that Chernov was to try to form a new revolutionary government, based on the Soviet, in which the Bolsheviks would be represented. And Lenin's mind was working in the same direction. He was willing to support such a government, as he made clear in the article 'On Compromises', also written on 1 September. In this essay, Lenin suggested that the post-Kornilov moment had produced a unique set of circumstances, perhaps valid only for 'a few days', which enabled the formation of 'a government of SRs and Mensheviks responsible to the Soviet' which could 'secure the peaceful advance of the whole Russian revolution'. The Bolsheviks would not join such a government, but would support it until the SRs and Mensheviks convened the Constituent Assembly 'without further delays or at an earlier date'.[2] Lenin felt as early as 3 September that this unique moment had already passed, and, of course, no Chernov government was ever formed. Instead, Kerensky made clear that he would use the emergency powers he had been granted during the Kornilov crisis to form a third Coalition Government.[3]

The call for a Soviet Government was far from new: it had been heard among Bolsheviks even as the Tsar was being overthrown. The reasons for rejecting the idea then were summed up in a speech made by Yurii Steklov, one of the founders of the Soviet, on 30 March. He explained that 'an attempt on the part of the extreme revolutionary democratic forces [in the Soviet] to take power into their hands can have a historical basis [...] only in the event that moderate liberalism has become bankrupt and incapable of realising the demands of the working masses; then we may be confronted with the question of revolutionary democratic forces seizing power against the bourgeoisie'.[4] *Delo naroda* thought on 1 September that there was still the need for capitalist economic development in Russia, but if Steklov's premises were accepted, it was quite easy to show that both capitalist politicians, and the Kadet liberals, were 'bankrupt and incapable of realising the demands of the working masses'. Thus, following Steklov's logic of March, by September the time for a Soviet Government had come. Workers had recognised this as early as the July Days when the Soviet's Workers' Section had first voted in favour of a Bolshevik call for a Soviet Government; it took Kornilov's adventure to radicalise the Soldiers' Section of the Soviet. On the night of 31 August to 1 September the Petrograd Soviet first voted for a Bolshevik resolution calling for a Soviet Government. The victory on that occasion was a narrow one, and both the Bolsheviks and their opponents prepared for a second and decisive vote on 9 September: after an address from Trotsky, the demand for a Soviet Government was passed decisively once again and the Bolsheviks had control of the Petrograd Soviet.

Before this happened, the Soviet Executive had decided to summon what it called a Democratic Conference, and this took place from 14 to 22 September. Representatives of the soviets, the trade unions and the recently democratised local *dumas* and *zemstvos* met to assess the way forward for the revolution and to set the date for a second Congress of Soviets on 20 October. At the Democratic Conference, the Bolshevik Lev Kamenev took up the theme of Lenin's 'On Compromises' and suggested that state power be transferred there and then to the Democratic Conference, 'to democracy represented here today': the Bolsheviks, he said, initially following Lenin, would support but not join such a government; however, he added, going much further than Lenin, the Bolsheviks would reassess that decision when the Second Congress of Soviets had met. The Democratic Conference ignored Kamenev's offer and in a series of confusing votes, interspersed by much wrangling behind the scenes, voted first for the principle of coalition, then for an amendment to exclude from the coalition the Kadets and any other liberals who had openly sided with Kornilov.

Many delegates to the Democratic Conference had wanted this Third Coalition Government to be made responsible to the Democratic Conference, but Kerensky insisted that an alternative be found, since the property-owning classes were not represented in the Democratic Conference. In the end it was agreed to summon a new body, a 'Pre-parliament', representing all strata of society. On Kerensky's insistence, the Third Coalition Government would not be responsible to the Pre-parliament, but would need to have its confidence.[5] When, on 24 September, two days after the Democratic Conference had closed, the SR Central Committee also decided to back Kerensky, Chernov, the party's leader, announced that he would boycott all future Central Committee meetings. The membership of the Third Coalition Government was finally established on 25 September: it included four Kadet ministers and one former Kadet, all deemed unsullied by Kornilov's adventure; the minister of labour was Gvozdev, whose reformist policies workers had first rejected back in 1911.

In the spirit of Lenin's 'On Compromises', the Bolshevik Central Committee voted on 21 September to take part in the Pre-parliament, but this decision was very close, just nine votes to eight, and so it was decided to debate the issue again on 23 September when the Central Committee could meet jointly with the Bolshevik delegation to the Democratic Conference; this much larger meeting also voted, 77–50, to take part in the Pre-parliament; at this meeting there was even renewed discussion of forming 'a ministry of similar parties', in other words a coalition of socialist parties. Lenin was furious. If on 3 September he was already wondering if compromise was the right tactic, by 12 September he had completely rejected the idea of compromise and was writing to the Bolshevik Central Committee insisting that 'the Bolsheviks must assume power'. The large number of Bolsheviks attending the Democratic Conference would be a de facto Bolshevik congress and they needed to be clear that 'the present task must be an armed uprising in Petrograd'. The next day he stressed that, whereas seizing power in July would have been Blanquism because 'we still did not have a majority among the workers and soldiers of Petrograd', now the Bolsheviks did; 'we have the following of the majority of the people' he asserted, so insurrection, far from being Blanquism, was the order of the day.[6]

Over a week later, Lenin was concerned that his views had still not been taken on board. On 22 September he wrote about 'the mistakes of our party': it had been a mistake, he now suggested, to take part in the Democratic Conference, and to correct that mistake 'we must boycott the Pre-parliament' and instead 'go to the soviets' and call on the masses to struggle. As a result of these interventions, on 24 September, the Bolshevik Party bowed to Lenin's wishes and decided that the activities of the Pre-parliament would be 'merely auxiliary and completely subordinated to the tasks associated with mass struggle' and the 'transfer of power to the Second Congress of Soviets'. By 5 October, the Bolsheviks had come over fully to Lenin's point of view and voted to boycott the Pre-parliament. When it opened on 7 October, Trotsky led the Bolsheviks in a dramatically staged walkout.[7] Given permission to make a special announcement during the opening ceremony, Trotsky denounced the assembly, formally designated the Council of the Republic rather than the Pre-parliament, as 'the council of counter-revolutionary connivance' in cahoots with 'this government of treason to the people'. His peroration ended:

> The revolution and the people are in danger. The government is intensifying this danger, and the ruling parties are helping it. Only the people can save themselves and the country. We address the people: Long live an immediate, honest, democratic peace. All power to the soviets, all land to the people. Long live the Constituent Assembly.[8]

Why had Lenin moved so quickly from suggesting that the Bolsheviks could support a coalition government of Mensheviks and SRs to insisting that the Bolsheviks should assume power through the means of an insurrection? The explanation lies in the distinction he had drawn in the April Theses between the 1905 proposal for a 'democratic dictatorship of the proletariat and peasantry' and the 1917 demand for a 'democratic dictatorship of the proletariat and *poorest* peasantry'. In his view the bourgeois democratic phase of the Russian revolution had been over as soon as it had begun, for even in March the Soviet had de facto control of the government. The revolution was entering its socialist phase, and that called for the most extreme care. All socialists were haunted by the 1848 Revolution in France when peasants had been granted the vote and had immediately voted the socialist sympathising provisional government out of office and replaced it with a counter-revolutionary one. The revolution would not enter its socialist phase if the working-class vote was swamped by peasant small proprietors. The revolution needed to be led by the working class, and for that to happen the peasant vote had to be split by encouraging an alliance between the workers and the poor peasantry. If the balance in a socialist coalition government were wrong, if the peasant-supporting SRs had too much power, such a coalition could quickly degenerate and certainly never introduce socialism. In 'On Compromises' Lenin had envisaged the Bolsheviks using their power in the Soviet to destabilise a Chernov-led government and force it to adopt a radical land reform which would almost certainly split the SR Party, but the *Delo naroda* editorial suggests that that moment had not yet come. On reflection, Lenin believed it was much safer for the Bolsheviks to take a lead, seize power and then work towards splitting the peasant vote. The other support the Bolsheviks could look to as the revolution entered its socialist phase was the prospect of a European revolution, as Lenin had made clear in the April Theses, but his control over the European revolution was minimal, unlike his influence over the peasant revolution.

DEBATING INSURRECTION

The Bolshevik walkout from the Pre-parliament, coupled with their control of the Petrograd Soviet, meant that the question on everybody's lips was what were the Bolsheviks planning? Lenin was firmly convinced that for 'a transfer of power at the Second Congress of Soviets' to take place, an insurrection was essential before the congress assembled. In a letter of 29 September he denounced the tendency in the party which favoured waiting for the Second Congress of Soviets to assemble and called for immediate insurrection:

> We must *aussprechen was ist*, state the facts, admit the truth that there is a tendency, or an opinion, in our Central Committee and among the leaders of our party which favours waiting for the Congress of Soviets, and is opposed to taking power immediately, is opposed to an immediate insurrection. That tendency, or opinion, must be overcome [...] To 'wait' for the Congress of Soviets would be utter idiocy, sheer treachery.'[9]

Lenin was so furious that he resigned from the Central Committee to underline his 'profound conviction that if we "wait" for the Congress of Soviets and let the present moment pass, we shall ruin the revolution'.[10]

What form would Lenin's insurrection take? Writing on 8 October for the benefit of Bolshevik delegates to the upcoming Congress of Northern Soviets, he called for troops loyal to the Bolsheviks to prepare for 'a simultaneous offensive on Petrograd, as sudden and as rapid as possible', which would aim 'to encircle and cut off Petrograd; to seize it by a combined attack of the sailors, the workers and the troops'.

'The success of both the Russian and the World Revolution,' he concluded, 'depends on two or three days' fighting.' A second letter written on the 8th made clear that 'the fleet, Kronstadt, Vyborg and Revel (Tallinn) can and must advance on Petrograd'. The decision to launch this offensive would, Lenin hoped, be made at the Congress of Northern Soviets, which had been due to open on 8 October but was postponed until 11–13 October.[11]

Lenin returned to Petrograd in disguise on 10 October for a key meeting of the Central Committee which he hoped would support his call for an immediate insurrection, but which in fact scuppered his plans. Lenin put his case for an immediate uprising using the military forces referred to in his advice to delegates to the Congress of Northern Soviets. However, as Trotsky noted, 'the task of insurrection he presented directly as the task of the party; the difficult question of bringing its preparation into accord with the soviets is as yet not touched upon; the Second Congress of Soviets did not get a word'.[12] Kamenev, supported by Grigorii Zinoviev, until then one of Lenin's most loyal supporters, objected to more than the timing of the insurrection. They put the case against the need for an insurrection at all, the case Kamenev had been arguing since the Democratic Conference: events were moving in the Bolsheviks' favour; they would secure a majority at the Second Congress of Soviets; they could win one-third of the seats in the Constituent Assembly when those elections were held in mid-November; and the growing division between left-wing and right-wing SRs meant that the Bolsheviks would have widespread support beyond their own party when the Constituent Assembly met. Seizing power was an unnecessary gamble when power was slowly but surely falling into their hands. The parties representing the peasants had moved towards the Bolsheviks at the time of Kornilov's failed military coup, but just 'one careless step, one ill-considered move' and, just like in France in 1848, they could move over to counter-revolution. Kamenev and Zinoviev conceded that 'attempts at a new Kornilov revolt would, of course, leave us no choice', but as long as that did not happen 'we can and must confine ourselves now to a defensive position'.[13]

The Central Committee meeting of 10 October ended by adopting a resolution which 'put an armed rising on the order of the day' since 'its time had come' and 'suggested that all party organisations be

Fig. 10: Lenin, disguised as a worker so that he could return to Petrograd for the
Bolshevik Central Committee meeting on 10 October 1917

guided by this'.[14] However, while this represented a shift in formal
policy, it did not commit the party to a seizure of power before the
Congress of Soviets or at any other specific time.[15] Had Lenin's policy
triumphed? Trotsky later recalled that, whatever the resolution said,
it had been informally understood that, as a guide date, something
should happen by 15 October, in other words an insurrection should

build on the Congress of Northern Soviets now scheduled for 11–13 October.[16] Trotsky's recollection is perhaps confirmed by Kamenev, who later commented that it was said that the insurrection must be 'before the 20th', in other words before the planned opening of the Second Congress of Soviets – what Lenin had been calling for.[17] However, if the written record is to be believed, Lenin failed to convince his comrades that the insurrection should be staged before the Congress of Soviets met.

When Trotsky attended the Congress of Northern Soviets he persuaded delegates to pass a resolution which was 'an almost undisguised summons to insurrection'; however, this was a summons to an insurrection to take place on 20 October, that is, the day when the Second Congress of Soviets was due to open, not to an insurrection before the congress opened, as Lenin had been calling for. At the Congress of Northern Soviets, the Latvian Riflemen rallied to Trotsky's call. They made clear they would 'defend the Congress of Soviets', but they said nothing about supporting a Bolshevik coup before it took place. Trotsky had co-opted the leaders of the Congress of Northern Soviets to *his* policy, rather than to Lenin's. Significantly, in his speech on this occasion Trotsky referred to Kerensky's plans to withdraw two-thirds of the Petrograd garrison from the capital, and he must have appreciated the implications of a report from the Finnish regional committee of soviets which described how it had been established that 'not a single order of the Provisional Government is carried out in Finland unless it is signed by the commissar of the regional committee'.[18]

Would there be a Bolshevik insurrection before the Second Congress of Soviets as Lenin so fervently hoped? At a meeting of the St Petersburg Committee on 15 October, speaker after speaker reported doubts that the workers and soldiers would come out in support of any Bolshevik attempt to seize power, especially one staged before the Congress of Soviets. On the other hand, those present made clear that workers would rally to defend the Petrograd Soviet and frustrate any attempt to prevent the Second Congress of Soviets from taking place.[19] When the Bolshevik Central Committee met the next day, 16 October, the debate on the insurrection resumed. This was an expanded meeting of the Central Committee, attended by representatives from the St Petersburg Committee, the Military Organisation and leading Bolshevik members of the Soviet.

Its purpose was to reach a consensus on the issue of the insurrection, and the reports from the districts were not good news for Lenin: on Vasilevskii Island 'the mood is not militant'; in the First City District 'the mood is difficult to assess'; in Moscow District the workers 'will come out if the Soviet calls but not the party'; in Narva District the workers 'were not eager for action'; in the Neva District 'everyone will follow the Soviet'; and in the garrisons 'comrades working in the districts [...] say that they would have to be positively stung by something for a rising, that is the withdrawal of troops'. Other key reports also favoured caution and questioned Lenin's policy. From the Petrograd Soviet it was reported that 'no one is ready to rush out on the streets, but everyone will come if the Soviet calls', concluding that the moment had not yet arrived. Shlyapnikov commented that Bolshevik influence predominated in the Metal Workers' Union, 'but a Bolshevik rising is not popular'. Milyutin suggested that 'we are not ready to strike the first blow'. [20]

Kamenev could rightly point out that almost a week had passed since the resolution of 10 October in favour of insurrection had been passed and nothing had been done. There was no apparatus for an insurrection; all the resolution had done was to warn Kerensky what was afoot and give the government time to prepare a crackdown on the Bolshevik Party. Once again Kamenev and Zinoviev called for the policy of insurrection to be dropped. Zinoviev was clear: 'if the insurrection is tabled as a long-term prospect, there can be no objection, but if it is on the order for tomorrow or the day after, then this is adventurism'. Once again Lenin demanded an immediate insurrection. The target of his anger, therefore, was as much Trotsky as Kamenev and Zinoviev, for Lenin interpreted as shilly-shallying on Trotsky's part the statement made by his representative at the meeting. Trotsky's spokesman made clear that insurrection should remain on the agenda, but that no precise date should be set: 'our task is to bring armed force to support an insurrection if one flares up anywhere'. It was likely that the planned attempt by the government to remove troops from the capital would spark the sort of crisis needed for an insurrection, and in the elliptical phrase recorded in the Central Committee minutes, Trotsky's view was that 'there is no point worrying about who is to begin, since a beginning already exists'. In the end the Bolshevik Central Committee meeting of 16 October 'endorsed' the decision of the 10th, but again set no date and drew up no plans. As one participant summed it up, 'the spirit of the resolution is the need to use the first suitable occasion to seize power'.[21]

After the Central Committee meeting of 16 October, Kamenev resigned from the Central Committee and on the following day published an article outlining his views in the independent left socialist newspaper *Novaya zhizn*. This made clear that he and Zinoviev had written to major party organisations opposing an insurrection: 'not only Comrade Zinoviev and I but also a number of comrades with experience in the field consider it would be inadmissible, fatal for the proletariat and the revolution for us to initiate an armed insurrection'. Having made public that an insurrection had been discussed within the Bolshevik leadership, he also made clear that no decision had been taken by stating, 'I am not aware of any decisions by our party which fix a rising of any sort for this or any other date; the party has made no such decisions.'[22] By 18 October the press was full of comment on plans for a Bolshevik Party coup, to the extent that Trotsky felt it had to be denied. He later recalled how alarm 'penetrated even the workers' sections and still more the regiments; to them, too, it began to seem as though a coming-out were being prepared without them'.

So Trotsky resolved to make a statement to the Soviet in which he outlined what he saw as the strategy for revolution.

The decisions of the Petrograd Soviet are published for public information. The Soviet is an elective institution; every deputy is responsible to his electors. This revolutionary parliament cannot adopt decisions that would be withheld from the knowledge of all the workers and soldiers [...] If the Petrograd Soviet finds it necessary to call a demonstration, then it will do so, but I do not know where and when these demonstrations were decided on [...] Concerning the convocation of the Congress of Soviets, they want at this time to clear Petrograd of its garrison. This is perfectly understandable, because they know that the Congress of Soviets will definitely pass a resolution transferring power to the Congress, for an immediate conclusion of truces on all fronts, and for the transfer of land to the peasants. The bourgeoisie knows this and, therefore, wants to arm all the forces that are subordinate to it against us. This lie and slander is, in fact, the preparation for an attack against the Congress. It is known to all honest people that the Petrograd Soviet has not set a date for an armed demonstration, but if it does so, the entire Petrograd garrison and the proletariat will follow under its banner. At the same time, we declare to the workers and soldiers that the attack in the bourgeois press against the soviets is in preparation for a conflict, a mobilisation of all forces against the workers and soldiers. We have still not set a date for the attack. But the opposing side has, evidently, already set it. We will meet it, we will repel it duly, and we will declare that the first counter-revolutionary attempt to hamper the work of the Congress we will answer with a counter-offensive which will be ruthless and which we will carry out to the end.[23]

To Trotsky's fury, Kamenev, who was sitting next to him on the Soviet podium, immediately jumped to his feet and stated that he endorsed Trotsky's statement fully, implying that the statement was a rejection of the insurrection rather than a rather tortuous explanation of how the insurrection might evolve. Immediately after the incident, Trotsky met with Lenin and tried to reassure him that he was still committed to insurrection and that if they were patient, the opportunity to act would yet present itself.

Kamenev's action meant that when the Bolshevik Central Committee next met, on 20 October, it focused on internal disagreements rather than the implications of the decision made a couple of days earlier to postpone the opening of the Second Congress of Soviets from 20 to 25 October. Trotsky was still smarting from the way Kamenev had outmanoeuvred him at the Soviet meeting on the 18th; he insisted on clarifying the meaning of his statement and demanded that Kamenev's behaviour be put before a party court. Lenin had written a long and vitriolic letter to the Central Committee calling Kamenev and Zinoviev 'strike-breakers' for 'betraying' to Kerensky the decision about an armed uprising; he therefore demanded their expulsion from the party. The Central Committee resolved at once that it did not have the authority to expel anyone, but Kamenev had submitted his resignation from the Central Committee and this would be accepted. Stalin, who had agreed to a statement by Zinoviev being published in *Pravda* and had tried to smooth over the disagreement between Lenin and his comrades, felt that he too should offer his resignation; but his resignation was not accepted by the Central Committee. It was only on 21 October that the Central Committee put the past behind it and again focused on the future. It was decided not to publish as a brochure Lenin's attack on the 'two sad pessimists' Kamenev and Zinoviev and to concentrate instead on how to ensure Bolshevik dominance at the Second Congress of Soviets.[24]

THE MILITARY REVOLUTIONARY COMMITTEE

Trotsky had been right to suggest that Kerensky's plans to move garrison troops to the front would provide a spark for insurrection. There would have been no Bolshevik insurrection if Kerensky had not behaved in the way he did; it was he who unexpectedly handed Lenin his opportunity to seize power before, but only just before, the Congress of Soviets opened.[25] On 6 October the Commander of the Petrograd Military District was told to prepare to move garrison troops to the front. On 9 October the Soviet responded by proposing to set up a Committee for Revolutionary Defence. Three days later, on 12 October, Trotsky, as Soviet chairman, set about implementing this proposal, renaming the committee the Military Revolutionary Committee (MRC). Following from this initiative, the Bolsheviks organised a conference of the Petrograd garrison from 18 to 21 October, during which, on 20 October, the MRC held its first formal session. It was incontestable that the German Army was advancing slowly but surely towards Petrograd, but did Kerensky have another purpose in wanting to move those troops seen as the guardians of the revolution? Did Kerensky and those close to him want to stage 'a second Kornilov movement' and engineer a military coup once Petrograd's revolutionary troops had been sent to the front? This is what the MRC feared, and to prevent such a scenario developing, from 21 to 23 October it started to send out commissars to the Petrograd garrison and took other measures aimed at overseeing all decisions taken concerning troop movements.

Until 23 October, the moves taken by the MRC were essentially defensive, indeed attempts were still being made to negotiate an understanding between the Petrograd Military District and the 'mutinous' MRC commissars, despite very angry words being exchanged. When on 21 October the MRC delegation informed General G. P. Polkovnikov, the commander of the Petrograd Military District, that henceforth his orders would only be valid if countersigned by the MRC, he, of course, rejected the ultimatum point blank.[26] However, during 22 October the MRC was approached by representatives of the Petrograd Military District to see if some sort of compromise were not possible. As Trotsky later explained, these compromise proposals were only discussed by the MRC on the 23rd, and by then the moment had passed: 'On Saturday [21st] those conditions of semi-honourable capitulation would have been accepted; today, on Monday [23rd], they were already too late.' Sunday, 22 October had been designated 'Soviet Day', a day of peaceful meetings and rallies in support of the Soviet and to welcome the Second Congress of Soviets. Trotsky spent the day addressing public meeting after public meeting, concentrating his efforts on those garrison troops that were wavering in support for the MRC. This agitation proved so successful that on 23 October the MRC could announce that commissars were in place throughout the capital and only orders confirmed by the MRC were to be obeyed, although in truth it was only on the afternoon of the 23rd that Trotsky won over the support of the troops garrisoned in the Peter-Paul Fortress, at the very heart of the capital. Trotsky later recalled that 'the word insurrection was not spoken by any one of the leaders' as the MRC took control of the garrisons; when he reported on the MRC's work to the Soviet on the evening of the 23rd, his measures were accepted as being taken to defend the Congress of Soviets, not as part of preparations to seize power.[27]

Kerensky was fully aware of what the posting of MRC commissars signified. During the night of 23–24 October he wanted to arrest the whole MRC, but his ministers would agree only to him arresting certain MRC members and closing the Bolshevik press.[28] However, by moving against the Bolshevik press and the MRC commissars, Kerensky laid himself open to the Bolshevik charge of acting like a second Kornilov. He took this gamble because the system of power he had established with the formation of the Third Coalition Government was proving increasingly unstable. Indeed, the Pre-parliament set up to support his government seemed to be turning against him.

THE DISINTEGRATION OF THE PRE-PARLIAMENT

For the Pre-parliament to continue to support Kerensky there had to be a degree of agreement between the left wing of the Kadet Party and the right wing of the SR Party. Pivotal in this relationship were two small political groups which stood to the right of the SRs and therefore to the left of the Kadets: the Popular Socialist Party and the delegates from Russia's thriving co-operative movement;

it was the co-operative movement which had swung the vote in favour of forming a third Coalition Government at the Democratic Conference.[29] The Kadets took the Pre-parliament more seriously than other political parties, hoping to turn it into a sort of last redoubt against Bolshevism. They held daily strategy meetings and devoted considerable efforts to drafting various statutes, but their problem was that the Popular Socialist Party and its co-operative allies were luke-warm partners. Even before the Pre-parliament had opened, the Popular Socialist Party decided at its conference on 26 September that, in the campaign for the Constituent Assembly elections then underway, it would have nothing to do with the Kadets; electoral agreements could only be forged with other socialist parties. Of even more concern for the Kadets was the decision of an emergency co-operative congress on 4 October that there should be no joint initiatives with non-socialist groups.[30]

These decisions hardly augured well for the smooth running of the Pre-parliament. What saved the day for Kerensky, at least in the short term, was the resolution passed at a second Meeting of Public Figures, held on 13–14 October, which instructed the Kadets in the Pre-parliament to work together with the Popular Socialists; the 10th Kadet Congress came to a similar decision on working to foster support for the Coalition.[31] However, moving from abstract statements of commitment to practical politics proved difficult. The co-operatives took the initiative on 18 October in drafting a programme in support of the Third Coalition Government. At first the parties supporting Kerensky appeared to hold together: the Popular Socialists, co-operatives and Kadets all voted as a bloc and defeated the Mensheviks and SRs who now opposed Kerensky by five votes. However, that victory was achieved through a show of hands. The opposition demanded a balloted recount, and this went against Kerensky, depriving him of his first and only triumph in the Pre-parliament.[32]

Indeed, support for the coalition was soon disintegrating. The key figure in this process was Kerensky's new defence minister, General A. I. Verkhovskii, a man whose political views were close to those of the Popular Socialists. To the growing anger of the Kadets, and the increasing alarm of Kerensky himself, Verkhovskii had come to favour a form of 'shock therapy'. He argued that the only way forward for Russia was to come to terms with the opposition in the Pre-parliament and recognise some of its key demands. Most important of all was the issue of peace. Verkhovskii was convinced that the only way the Russian masses could be persuaded to fight on in World War I was for the Allies to advance a peace proposal and for the Central Powers to reject it: this would provoke a huge public outcry and 'only then would we create a volunteer army truly up to the task', he wrote. Verkhovskii succeeded in persuading the socialist members of the Third Coalition Government to agree that this dramatic proposal should be put to the Inter-Allied Conference, due to be held in Paris at the end of October. However, the Kadet foreign minister, who was to represent Russia at this conference, could not be persuaded, and neither could the Kadet Party. As a consequence of this fundamental disagreement within the government, Verkhovskii resigned on 19 October.[33]

When Kerensky decided during the night of 23–24 October to close the Bolshevik press and arrest the MRC commissars, he hoped to get the support of the Pre-parliament for his actions. The Pre-parliament assembled as usual on 24 October, opening its debates about midday, and Kerensky made a lengthy speech in which he attacked Lenin and Trotsky by name for planning an uprising and noted that 'after preparations of this kind and propaganda for an uprising the group that calls itself Bolsheviks has come to the point of carrying it out'. He made clear that he had not rushed to challenge the MRC in appointing commissars, so as to leave time for soldiers 'to realise their own intentional or unintentional mistake'; but now that it was clear that an insurrection had begun, 'arrests had been ordered' for 'when the state is imperilled by deliberate or unwilling betrayal and is at the brink of ruin, the Provisional Government, myself included, prefers to be killed and destroyed rather than betray the life, honour and independence of the state'. During this speech Kerensky was passed a note which stated that the MRC had ordered all regiments to stand by for action. Kerensky denounced 'this attempt to incite the rabble against the existing order' and he justified the use of the term 'rabble' by explaining how, 'just as in the month of July, [the insurrection] could serve as a signal for the Germans at the front to deliver a new blow on our borders'. He ended his final appeal with these words: 'I demand that this very day, at this afternoon's session, the Provisional Government receive your answer as to whether or not it can fulfil its duty with the assurance of support from this exalted gathering.'[34] Preparing to reply to Kerensky's speech, the Kadets again took the lead in gathering support for the government, but when the Pre-parliament reconvened, a resolution demanding support for Kerensky and expressing 'confidence' in his government's decisive measures was defeated.[35] During the afternoon the Kadets had met with stubborn resistance from the co-operative leaders, many of whom decided to abstain rather than offer their support to Kerensky; it was the co-operative abstentions which lost Kerensky his vote of confidence.[36]

It was symptomatic of Kerensky's ever growing isolation that throughout the short life of the Pre-parliament the Mensheviks and SRs, once Kerensky's government bedfellows, acted as the opposition. The Democratic Conference had insisted that 'power must belong to a government which had the trust of the Pre-parliament'; by the early evening of 24 October, Kerensky no longer had that trust. In the resolution effectively dismissing Kerensky's government, the Pre-parliament called for immediate peace talks with the Allies and the transfer of all land to the land committees. Although some SRs on the left of the party suggested expelling the Kadets from the Pre-parliament and establishing a Revolutionary Convention, most of the SR and Menshevik opposition within the Pre-parliament saw no reason for its continued existence and joined the voices calling for a Soviet Government. Later on the 24th, the Menshevik delegates to the Second Congress of Soviets voted in favour of forming a coalition government of soviet parties, a call echoed still later in the day by the SR-controlled Petrograd Duma. When even the Popular Socialists and the co-operatives turned against the Coalition Government, Kerensky's fate was sealed.[37]

STAGING THE INSURRECTION

As Kerensky acted to arrest the MRC commissars and close down the Bolshevik press, so Trotsky and the MRC moved to resist both moves. The Soviet and one of its committees was under attack, and so the Soviet resisted. It seemed entirely logical, however, as Trotsky had planned and others quickly came to understand, that as the Bolsheviks led Soviet resistance to Kerensky's Kornilov-like act, they were steadily acquiring control over the state; defending the Soviet and staging a Bolshevik insurrection became part of the same process. For as long as was conceivably possible, Trotsky talked

Fig. 11: Soldiers and red guards ready for action

of defence rather than attack. This was because things stood on a knife edge. During the morning of the 24th, news reached Trotsky that the Bicycle Battalion of the Peter-Paul Fortress was still loyal to Kerensky. The MRC at once cut the telephone connection to the battalion and at 4 pm in the afternoon Trotsky dashed to a meeting with them and persuaded them to back the MRC. His speech to an extraordinary session of the Petrograd Soviet shortly afterwards was full of ambiguity. The MRC was defending the revolution, but it was not afraid of shouldering responsibility for order. He was clear that the Second Congress of Soviets should transfer power to the soviets and when this happened there might be an insurrection or there might not, depending 'on those who, in defiance of the people's unanimous will, still hold governmental power'. Yet he also said that it was the task of the MRC 'to carry [the power it had acquired], undiminished and unimpaired, to the congress'; here he seemed to be saying that the MRC already had seized power which it would offer to the Second Congress of Soviets. His final words summed up what was actually happening: 'if the illusory government makes a hazardous attempt to revive its own corpse, the popular masses will strike a decisive counter-blow'.[38]

During the 24th, Kerensky was not inactive. He ordered that the railway stations be occupied by loyal troops, that checkpoints be established at major road intersections and that the bridges across the river Neva be raised. The MRC responded to the last of these moves by asking the crew of the cruiser *Aurora* to restore movement on the Nikolaevskii bridge, thus re-establishing the link between the city centre and the northern suburbs. The captain of the warship refused to implement the order, but agreed that he could be 'arrested', and, once under arrest, dutifully brought the cruiser towards the bridge, prompting Kerensky's guards to flee; the sailors then lowered the bridge. At about the same time, MRC commissars gained access to the telephone exchange and restored the telephone connection to the Soviet building which Kerensky had cut. Yet, in Trotsky's words, 'right up to the evening of the 24th, the umbilical cord of "legality" was not conclusively severed'. This could still be considered a defensive action rather than an offensive one because the MRC had frustrated Kerensky's actions and had restored the situation to that which had existed before Kerensky's action had begun, but it had done nothing more.[39]

When the Bolshevik Central Committee met on the 24th it too was unclear whether or not an insurrection had begun. It heard a report on the attempt to negotiate a compromise between the Petrograd Military District and the MRC, an issue now effectively overtaken by events; it took decisive measures to reopen the newspapers Kerensky had closed, but its moves 'to organise observation of the Provisional Government and the orders it issues' did not suggest that Kerensky's overthrow was imminent.[40] Trotsky remained enigmatic when he addressed the Bolshevik delegates gathering for the opening of the Second Congress of Soviets, recalling in later years that 'it was still impossible to throw off the defensive envelope of the attack without creating confusion in the minds of certain units of the garrison'. When a delegation from the Petrograd City Duma approached the Petrograd Soviet on the afternoon of the 24th for an explanation as to what was going on, Trotsky reassured them that 'the question of power is to be decided by the Congress of Soviets'.[41]

Around 6 pm on the evening of the 24th, Lenin wrote to the Central Committee urging the party to end the ambiguity and seize power. In this letter, Lenin made clear that it no longer mattered if power were taken by 'some other institution', that is, the Bolshevik

Party, or by the MRC; the important thing was to seize the moment: 'we must not wait! We may lose everything!' For him it was clear that 'under no circumstances should power be left in the hands of Kerensky and Co. until the 25th'.

> History will not forgive revolutionaries for procrastinating when they could be victorious today (and they certainly will be victorious today), while they risk losing much tomorrow, in fact, they risk losing everything. If we seize power today, we seize it not in opposition to the Soviets but on their behalf. Seizure of power is the business of the uprising; its political purpose will become clear after the seizure.[42]

Thus it would be 'a sheer formality to await the wavering vote' of the Second Congress of Soviets when it opened on 25 October. The Second Congress of Soviets was due to debate the formation of a Soviet Government, and there was a clear majority of delegates in favour of forming a Soviet Government, but Lenin could point to the confused voting at the Democratic Conference and preferred to present congress delegates with a fait accompli. 'The government is tottering. It must be given the death blow at all costs. To delay is fatal,' he wrote.[43] Fearing that this, like other letters, would be ignored by his Central Committee, he decided not to send it but to go in person and make his views clear, arriving at the Soviet building about midnight.[44]

7

A SOVIET GOVERNMENT

The ideological dispute within the Bolshevik Party latent in the disagreement over tactics concerning the seizure of power became overt on the question of the composition of a Soviet Government. Thus far, the focus of this Short History has been to trace the way the revolutionary tradition of Russian labour, first established in 1905, steadily reasserted itself, with Bolshevik support, during the months between February and October 1917. In overthrowing Kerensky, that revolution first envisaged in 1905 was completed. Yet as workers and Red Guards moved to overthrow Kerensky in the early hours of 25 October, a second and far weaker tradition of Russian labour came to the fore, one which concerned issues of Bolshevik ideology and theories of organisation about which the vast majority of those engaged in overthrowing Kerensky were completely ignorant. Already in the Bolshevik Party's debates about the timing of Kerensky's overthrow, Lenin had made clear that the ideas he had outlined in the April Theses meant that the construction of socialism in Russia would only be possible if, once Kerensky was out of the way, the Bolsheviks were not 'swamped' by the peasants and the political parties which represented them. As the composition of a Soviet Government was debated, Lenin's initial instinct was to oppose any form of socialist coalition. This was despite the fact that Lenin's own April Theses talked of a possible alliance with 'the poor peasantry', and the split in the SR Party which occurred during

Kerensky's overthrow saw the emergence of the Left SRs as the political voice of the poor peasantry. As the issue of the composition of the Soviet Government tore the Bolshevik Party apart, Lenin drew on that second tradition of Bolshevism, the concept of party discipline, to bludgeon his way to victory. This was, however, a pyrrhic victory, since underlying political realities forced Lenin to agree to the formation of a socialist coalition government, but one the Bolsheviks could dominate.

DISCOVERING THE LEFT SRs

According to Trotsky's account, the overthrow of Kerensky began with small groups 'usually with a nucleus of armed workers or sailors under the leadership of a commissar' occupying strategic sites such as the railway stations, electricity plants, bridges, the State Bank, big printing firms and the telegraph office. Many were briefed by Trotsky himself, who informed them, 'if you fail to stop them with words, use arms'. Meanwhile, delegates to the Second Congress of Soviets were assembling in an emergency pre-congress session. At about 3 am on the morning of the 25th, Trotsky addressed that gathering and finally ended the ambiguity of the preceding 24 hours. He stated unequivocally that an insurrection was underway in which the Bolshevik Party was playing the lead, and, he insisted, 'the enemy is already capitulating' and the Soviet could soon 'assume the place of master of the Russian land'. Trotsky was exaggerating. As dawn broke on the 25th, the insurrection seemed to stall. By 7 am in the morning the Petrograd Military District Headquarters and the Third Coalition Government in the Winter Palace had no telephones, but they showed no sign of surrendering. Although at 10 am in the morning the Soviet announced that Kerensky's government had been overthrown, that too was not the case. By midday, the MRC had persuaded members of the Pre-parliament to disperse, but the government was still inside the Winter Palace.

In the early afternoon of 25 October, Trotsky told an emergency session of the Petrograd Soviet that Kerensky had been overthrown, but again this was only partially true because, although by then Kerensky had left Petrograd with the help of the US Embassy in search of loyal troops, the Winter Palace had still not been taken.[1]

As the Second Congress of Soviets held its formal opening session after 10 pm that evening, artillery fire from the Winter Palace could still be heard; it was only at 2 am on the morning of the 26th that the fighting stopped and at 3 am in the morning that the ministers of the Third Coalition Government were taken under guard to the Peter-Paul Fortress.[2] Thus, while the fighting for control of the Winter Palace was still underway, the first session of the Second Congress of Soviets began its debates after midnight on 25–6 October. With SRs and Mensheviks preparing to walk out in protest at Kerensky's overthrow, left-wing Mensheviks called for an end to the fighting and a negotiated settlement, a resolution that was passed unanimously.[3] Trotsky countered:

> Our insurrection has conquered, and now you propose to us: renounce your victory; make a compromise […] No, a compromise is no good here […] To all who made like proposals, we must say – 'you are pitiful, isolated individuals, you are bankrupts, your role is played out. Go where you belong from now on […] into the dustbin of history'.[4]

Yet Trotsky was followed to the podium by another Bolshevik who insisted that the Bolsheviks were, in fact, quite ready to compromise and co-operate with any other socialist party. At 2 am in the morning the congress decided to hold a half-hour recess before returning to the issue of forming a Soviet Government. During that recess, news of the surrender of the Winter Palace came through, and the congress then voted to establish 'a provisional workers' and peasants' government' to administer the country 'until the meeting of the Constituent Assembly'. The Second Congress of Soviets then adjourned, leaving the question of the composition of this new government until the next day.[5]

As the insurrection began, there was a brief meeting of the Bolshevik Central Committee to discuss what a future Soviet Government might look like. The only decision taken on that occasion was to instruct Kamenev 'to make contact with the Left SRs'.[6] Co-operation between the Bolsheviks and left-wing members of the SR Party had a long pedigree. Despite being perceived as primarily a peasant party, the SRs had been extremely active amongst St Petersburg workers during the 1905 Revolution, for a while threatening to secure more working-class support than the Social Democrats during the election campaign to the First State Duma in spring 1906.[7] Then, between 1909 and 1910, the SRs briefly won control of the St Petersburg Metal Workers' Union. Because they boycotted the elections to the Fourth State Duma, the SRs were unable to take part in the first stages of the social insurance campaign, but once factory-based elections began, by spring 1914, that changed and the SRs took an active part in the insurance council elections.[8] In fact, during the labour unrest of spring 1914, the Bolsheviks and SRs had issued several joint proclamations including a shared May Day appeal.[9] Then, in August 1915, the Bolsheviks and SRs in Petrograd held a joint conference to plan their approach to the election of worker delegates to the War Industries' Committee and the two parties subsequently co-operated in boycotting the second round of elections held after Gvozdev's intervention. Some six months later the two parties co-operated in smuggling anti-war literature into the country. The Bolshevik leader Shlyapnikov was relaxed about this because the Petrograd SRs 'had a majority of leftists'. In early February 1917, when labour militants were discussing how best to mark the reopening of the Fourth State Duma, Shlyapnikov held talks with the Petrograd SR leader and it was agreed not to organise a rally at the Duma building but to stage strikes instead.[10] Such co-operation continued after the overthrow of the Tsar. At the Conference of Soviets in March, Boris Kamkov, a left-wing SR, worked jointly with the Bolsheviks in sponsoring an anti-war resolution.[11]

The left wing of the SR Party became increasingly determined to oppose the SR leadership as the summer and autumn progressed. The influence of the left in the SR Party had been growing steadily in the capital. At the Third SR Congress in May roughly 40 per cent of delegates voted for one or other of the leftist resolutions, and during the congress the left established an 'organisational bureau' of its own. At the time of the formation of the First Coalition Government, the left-wing SRs voted against the proposal after a speech by Kamkov which asserted that 'only a government put forward by the Soviets' could successfully 'reorganise the country along democratic lines'. On 3 May the left-wing SRs called for a Soviet Government when they took part in the SR Petrograd City Conference. During the July Days, Kamkov addressed the Soviet's Central Executive Council and demanded the formation of a Soviet Government, and the SR Northern Regional Committee, under the control of the left, helped bring the Kronstadters to Petrograd.[12] As one of the leading left-wing

Fig. 12: Alexander Shlyapnikov, a leading Bolshevik activist in the underground years and a key figure in February 1917; commissar of labour in Lenin's first government

SRs Isaak Shteinberg recalled, 'during the July Days, the left-wing of the SR party worked closely with the Bolsheviks and in solidarity with them', although this solidarity did not prevent the occasional squabble, as when the Bolsheviks prevented the left-wing SR Maria Spiridonova from addressing the Kronstadt sailors. It was after the July Days that the leftist SRs began to publish their own official statements, but deliberately chose not to split away from the party completely. They won almost 50 per cent support in the votes for the SR Party council held from 6 to 10 August, and after Kornilov's failed military coup they won control of the Petrograd SR organisation, on 10 September.[13] Indeed the Bolshevik victory in the Petrograd Soviet at the start of September would not have been possible without the support of the left-wing SRs, for the key to that victory had been winning over the Soldiers' Section of the Soviet to the demand for a Soviet Government, and that was as much the work of the left-wing SRs as the Bolsheviks, since they were a major force in the Soldiers' Section. On 14 September the Petrograd SRs called for an end to the coalition and the formation of a Soviet Government. With control of the northern naval bases, including Kronstadt, and important cities like Kharkov, Kazan and Ufa, their strength was considerable. During the Democratic Conference, alongside the Bolsheviks, the left-wing SRs had worked hard to garner support for the idea of a socialist coalition government, a proposal which Kamenev had already supported. Among left-wing SRs there were none of the divisions which the idea provoked among the Bolsheviks, to quote Michael Melancon: 'an all-socialist government was a Left SR idée fixe'.[14]

The newly elected head of the Soldier's Section of the Petrograd Soviet was P. Lazimir, a left-wing SR who had played a major role in defeating Kornilov. He was the obvious choice to head the Military Revolutionary Committee of the Soviet when Trotsky set it up, and he was joined in the work of the MRC by Kamkov.[15] On the evening of 24 October, Kamkov stood up in the Pre-parliament to demand the resignation of Kerensky and the Provisional Government and the formation of a socialist coalition government in its place.[16] Although the Left SRs were resolved not to support the Bolsheviks if they staged their much talked about insurrection, they did respond to Kerensky's attack on the MRC commissars by instructing their militants on the night of 23–24 October to support the reopening of the Bolshevik press and the seizure of strategic buildings like the State Bank, on the grounds that the fate of the revolution seemed at stake.[17] Kamkov then withdrew from the MRC during the night of the 24–25 October when he became convinced that the committee was being used by Trotsky to push through a Bolshevik coup.[18] When the SR leadership decided to walk out of the Second Congress of Soviets in protest at the overthrow of Kerensky, the leftist SRs refused to leave and as a result were formally expelled from the party. Thus on the morning of 26 October, as the debate about the composition of the Soviet Government began, the Left SRs were reborn as a separate political party.

For all these reasons, then, the Left SRs seemed a possible partner in government for the Bolsheviks, hence the Bolshevik Central Committee's decision to ask Kamenev to sound them out. During the day on 26 October, Lenin and Trotsky called an informal meeting of those Central Committee members who happened to be around and resolved to form a government comprised solely of Bolsheviks. Despite this, later in the day, the Central Committee invited three Left SRs to a more formal meeting and proposed forming a coalition with them; the Left SRs declined to join such a government, arguing that attempts should be made to involve all the Soviet parties in a Soviet Government. Thus at 9 pm on the evening of the 26th, when Kamenev opened the second session of the Second Congress of Soviets, he preferred not to mention the membership of the proposed Soviet Government. He announced the end of the death penalty, the freeing of arrested members of land committees and the anticipated arrest of Kerensky. Lenin then introduced decrees on peace and land, committing the government to opening peace talks with both allies and enemies, and declaring the immediate transfer of land to the local land committees. It was only at 2.30 am on the morning of 27 October that Kamenev faced the issue of the composition of the new Soviet Government, the Council of People's Commissars, and announced that it would be composed purely of Bolsheviks.[19]

THE VIKZHEL NEGOTIATIONS

The Left SRs protested at once. They had turned down the proposal of joining the Bolsheviks in government because they wanted a broader socialist coalition than one made up of just the Bolsheviks and Left SRs; they certainly did not want to see the Bolsheviks holding power alone.[20] After Trotsky had defended the new purely Bolshevik government, a representative from the Railway Workers' Union (Vikzhel) insisted on addressing the delegates. The Left SRs controlled Vikzhel and the representative read out a telegram demanding what was effectively Left SR policy, the formation of a 'revolutionary socialist' government, not a Bolshevik Government, and insisting that until such a government was formed, Vikzhel would monitor all movement on the railway. Ignoring this intervention, congress delegates decided to approve the Bolshevik-only government and elected a new Soviet Executive, dominated by the Bolsheviks but with a substantial group of Left SRs on it as well. Kamenev was made its chairman.

The Left SRs' desire to form a broad coalition of socialist parties was frustrated not only by the Bolsheviks' determination to form a government alone, but also by the intransigence of the leaders of the Right SRs and the Mensheviks who had walked out of the Second Congress of Soviets during the night of 25–26 October. These two parties promptly established a Committee for the Salvation of the Revolution and the Motherland (CSRM) with the aim of driving the Bolsheviks from power. It was to stop this nascent civil war between the Bolsheviks and their moderate socialist opponents that Vikzhel decided to intervene. In its address to the Second Congress of Soviets, Vikzhel had accused the Bolsheviks of splitting the democratic front by taking power in the name of a soviet of workers and soldiers' deputies which, by definition, could not represent all elements of democratic society; not only were hardly any peasants represented at the Second Congress of Soviets, but many non-industrial workers were excluded as well. Vikzhel demanded the formation of an expanded Soviet Executive, to involve all 'revolutionary democracy' in the political process, and argued that such a body would produce a broad-based socialist administration, a coalition of Soviet parties. After initial talks with both the Bolsheviks and the CSRM, on 28 October Vikzhel summed up its demands as the formation of a coalition socialist administration, to be responsible to a new 'legislative organ of revolutionary democracy' which would hold power until the Constituent Assembly met; any use of force to go against this decision would be met by a strike of railway workers and the paralysis of government.[21]

On the Bolshevik side, it was those Bolsheviks who had opposed Lenin on the issue of insurrection who responded first to the Vikzhel demand. The trade union leader David Ryazanov acted as a go-between during the talks of 28 October, liaising between Kamenev, the MRC and Vikzhel. It was the CSRM which was at first intransigent. The CSRM was immediately split by the same divisions which had hobbled the Third Coalition Government: should liberals be involved in its work? It was the liberals who had insisted that the word 'Motherland' be included in the name of the organisation, but the CSRM decided at once that liberals should not be included on the committee's executive; liberals delegated from the Petrograd Duma or the Pre-parliament could take part, but not the Kadet Party as such. Then, there was the question of whether the CSRM was trying to restore Kerensky to power, or to work for a socialist coalition but a coalition which would exclude the Bolsheviks. After the CSRM held talks with Vikzhel on 28 October, the supporters of Kerensky lost out; Kerensky 'would not form part of any combination of ministers proposed by us', Skobelev informed Vikzhel. The CSRM agreed with Vikzhel that a socialist coalition was needed, but not one which allowed the Bolsheviks to participate, even though it was accepted that this new government would pursue the 'Bolshevik' policy which the Second Congress of Soviets had just endorsed of giving land to the peasants and ending the war.

Kerensky had made his escape from the Winter Palace at 11 am on 25 October. He then went first to Pskov, the headquarters of the Northern Army, where he found a few troops prepared to support him, although the only unit which offered him unambiguous support was the Third Cavalry Corps, led by General Petr Krasnov; both Krasnov and the Third Cavalry Corps were supposed to have played a key role in Kornilov's military coup. Kerensky, Krasnov and the Third Cavalry Corps moved to Gatchina on 27 October and there they were joined by Kerensky's chief army commissar. He had been present at the first meeting of the CSRM on 26 October, at which plans had been drawn up for an anti-Bolshevik action to take place in the capital, timed to coincide with a military advance by Krasnov; the commissar was unaware of the divisions which had opened up in the CSRM after his departure and its decision no longer to campaign for the restoration of Kerensky's government. The SR Party's Military Commission, which was never fully under the control of the party's Central Committee, had made contact with the Officers' Training Corps in Petrograd, and when they learned, on 28 October, that Kerensky had arrived in Gatchina, they resolved to take action in his support. In the early hours of 29 October, Red Guards intercepted a courier carrying a message from these officers to Kerensky; realising that their plans were unravelling, the officers decided they had no choice but to take up arms against the Bolsheviks at once.[22] After some bitter fighting, the officers' action at dawn on the 29th was suppressed easily enough, but not before some 200 had been killed or injured. In response to the officers' action, later on the 29th the

MRC put Petrograd under martial law, appointing the Left SR Lt-Col. Mikhail Muraviev to lead the defence of Petrograd from Kerensky's attack.[23]

Vikzhel was infuriated by these developments, and understandably accused the CSRM of double-dealing. During the 29th it issued an ultimatum: a railway strike would take place unless meaningful talks resumed at once. The CSRM, however, continued in its intransigent stance, a leading SR declaring to Vikzhel on 29 October that 'even in the democratic camp there are moments when it is necessary to decide an argument with weapons'. Meeting on the afternoon of 29 October, on the other hand, the Bolshevik Central Committee was at its most amenable. It approved the principle of broadening the government by bringing in other parties, and it even hinted that Lenin and Trotsky might be deprived of their posts if that helped smooth an agreement. The Bolsheviks reminded Vikzhel that their party had called for a socialist administration back at the Democratic Conference, and that, whatever happened in the next few days, power would be transferred to the Constituent Assembly when it met. Later Kamenev made clear to the Soviet Executive that Lenin's position in government was not indispensable. The Vikzhel process seemed to be making progress and the talks went on for most of the night of 29–30 October.[24]

Meanwhile the forces assembled by Kerensky and Krasnov, led by the Third Cavalry Corps, had advanced to Pulkovo Heights, a small ridge of land in the otherwise flat countryside to the west of Petrograd. On 30 October, Muraviev hastily deployed a large force of lightly armed Red Guards to confront them. Krasnov was outnumbered, but his plan was to induce panic among the ill-trained Red Guards with a dramatic charge of his elite cavalry. Muraviev's plan was the very opposite: to prevent the cavalry charge having a devastating impact on morale by firing from some strategically placed machine-gun batteries. Muraviev's tactics proved superior: Krasnov's cavalry charge proved indecisive and the rest of the 30th was spent in rather desultory exchanges of fire; on 31 October a delegation of Baltic Sailors asked to talk to the Cossack cavalrymen and offered them safe passage back to their homes on the River Don, an offer that most of them accepted.[25]

While this fighting was underway, the Vikzhel talks made some tangible progress, not only because the fighting then taking place at Pulkovo made the threat of civil war seem very real, but also because the talks had been lobbied by a delegation of workers from the Obukhov Works: they demanded to know why an agreement had not been reached between what were, after all, fellow socialist parties, and they threatened 'to drop Lenin, Trotsky and Kerensky through the same hole in the ice if workers' blood was spilled'.[26] Under this twofold pressure, the CSRM began to shift its position. Although the SRs stated that they could not support a government 'which originated in a Bolshevik coup', a government 'of individuals', including Bolsheviks, could be formed. The Mensheviks were even more conciliatory; they would support a socialist coalition administration, even if they still had issues about taking part in such an administration.

At this time, the talks looked so promising that they moved on from general considerations of principle to specifics. The question of expanding the Soviet Executive was agreed quite quickly, establishing that the Soviet Executive needed to be broadened with additional representatives from the Peasant Soviet, those trade unions not represented in the Soviet, and representatives of the recently democratically elected Petrograd Duma. Personnel came next: Kamenev ruled out Kerensky, while the CSRM ruled out Lenin and Trotsky, but Chernov seemed the best candidate to head the administration with the Bolsheviks in charge of industry and the interior. On 31 October, the All-Army Committee, the apex of the hierarchy of soldiers' committees throughout the entire army, voted to back Vikzhel in the formation of a socialist coalition government. Even the British ambassador could report that 'it would appear that the [Vikzhel] proposal is favoured by the majority'.[27] On 1 November the Bolshevik-controlled newspaper of the Petrograd Soviet, *Rabochii i soldat*, informed its readers that agreement had been reached in the Vikzhel talks.[28]

OVERTURNING VIKZHEL

What the Vikzhel talks seemed to be proposing was the sort of Chernov-led government which Lenin had said he was prepared to tolerate on 1 September. Given that Lenin had decided as early as 3 September that such a compromise was unacceptable, it is not surprising that he was opposed to such a compromise when it was suggested by Vikzhel. Kamenev, who had welcomed the idea of a Chernov-led government in September and had suggested that the Bolsheviks might even join it, took the opposite view, urging support for the Vikzhel proposals; he could point out that since September the split in the SR Party and the formation of the Left SRs made virtually certain that the Bolsheviks, with the Left SRs as allies, would dominate such a government. Just as the Bolshevik Party had been divided on the issue of insurrection, so now it was divided on the question of the Vikzhel talks, and once again Lenin would threaten to resign when he seemed not to be getting his way.

Lenin had always insisted that the Bolsheviks could rule alone and, as soon as it became clear that Muraviev had driven Krasnov from the field of battle, he lost all interest in the Vikzhel talks; for him they had always been a mere stalling tactic, to try and wrong-foot the Bolsheviks' opponents until a military victory over Kerensky could be secured. Trotsky and the MRC had taken the same line, telling Vikzhel on 31 October that the talks 'cannot paralyse our struggle against the counter-revolutionary troops of Kerensky'. However, as Ryazanov made clear later in these discussions, the Bolshevik Central Committee had yet to make a decision on the question. Although no minutes of the meeting have survived, it is clear that the Central Committee met on 31 October and decided that the inclusion of Lenin and Trotsky in any government was non-negotiable; however, it did not oppose the Vikzhel talks in principle and accepted that the Soviet Executive could be expanded by adding extra representation from peasants and trade unions. As Kamenev made clear later, on 31 October 'the Central Committee was continuing to make a stand for going on with the negotiations'.[29]

Lenin's views were already very clear, however. On 1 November he announced to his opponents when attending a meeting of the St Petersburg Committee that if they got a majority in the Central Committee he would walk out and 'go to the sailors'.[30] When the Central Committee met later on 1 November, the Vikzhel talks dominated the agenda. The meeting was an expanded one, with representatives from the St Petersburg Committee, the Military Organisation and leading Bolsheviks from the Soviet Executive present. Kamenev explained what the Vikzhel offer was, and Trotsky immediately attacked it, asserting that 'the parties which took no part in the insurrection now wanted to grab power'; the Bolsheviks needed to have a majority in any government, he said, and Lenin had to head the government. Another supporter of Lenin added that on 31 October the Central Committee had decided to insist on Lenin and Trotsky's participation in the government, and Kamenev had failed to do this and, as a result, should be recalled from the talks. Kamenev insisted that his team had not discussed candidates for government posts, but had simply listened to and reported on the views of the others. One of those to support Kamenev was Aleksei Rykov. He insisted that 'Kamenev conducted the talks absolutely correctly'. In his view it was entirely acceptable to expand the Soviet Executive with peasants, other trade unionists and even members of the Petrograd Duma: this, he suggested, was merely 'confirmation of the decisions of the last Central Committee meeting'.

Ryazanov was the most forthright in his support for Kamenev: 'even in St Petersburg', he said, 'power is not in our hands but in the hands of the Soviet, and this has to be faced; if we abandon this course, we will be utterly and hopelessly alone [...] If we reject agreement today, we will be without the Left SRs, without anything, we will be left with the fact that we deceived the masses when we promised them a Soviet government.' Kamenev summed up the stance of those opposing Lenin: 'we can fight with Vikzhel, not against it'. Lenin was equally clear: 'Vikzhel is on the side of the Kornilovs.' The result of these heated exchanges was a partial victory for all. The Central Committee voted 10–4 against breaking off the Vikzhel talks immediately, as Lenin had proposed, but then decided, with no vote being recorded, to present the talks with an ultimatum; by five votes to four it was decided to allow only two hours before this ultimatum was accepted or rejected. Any government formed as a result of the ultimatum, the Central Committee resolved, would be responsible to the Soviet Executive, but a Soviet Executive 'which may be enlarged'.[31] After the meeting, a Bolshevik representative informed the Soviet Executive of the Central Committee's decision, adding rather confusingly that 'there is scarcely anyone who does not want an agreement'.[32]

The Bolshevik Central Committee met again on 2 November, but again no minutes have survived of this meeting. It is known that, by a one-vote margin, Lenin's resolution prevailed, but it only prevailed after two earlier votes had tied and after Lenin had contacted the St Petersburg Committee and instructed it to pass a resolution supporting his attitude towards the talks.[33] During the 2nd, Zinoviev held talks with the Bolshevik delegates to the Soviet Executive and persuaded them to soften the stance agreed, on Lenin's insistence, by the Central Committee; in order to win over the Left SRs, the Bolsheviks would demand only half the commissars in the new government, but both Lenin and Trotsky would be included. In this way, as Kamenev and Zinoviev later reported, 'by an incredible effort [on 2 November], we managed to get a revision of the Central Committee decision and a new resolution which could have become the basis for creating a Soviet Government'.[34] That new resolution was then endorsed by the Soviet Executive and taken, jointly by the Bolsheviks and the Left SRs, to the final session of the Vikzhel talks, which opened on 3 November. As that session opened, workers' delegations from the Putilov and Aleksandrovskii factories turned up and demanded that a coalition socialist administration be formed there and then. What the delegates to the Vikzhel talks had before them were two documents, different in points of detail but close enough to be reconciled if there was the political will: Vikhzhel proposed making the government responsible to an expanded Soviet Executive of 420 with representation for the Petrograd Duma, while the Soviet Executive wanted to expand its membership to 425 with only socialists from the Petrograd Duma being represented; that expanded Soviet Executive was committed to recognising the decrees on land and peace passed at the Second Congress of Soviets and to the principle of Soviet power.[35]

A deal on forming a coalition socialist government based on soviet power was there for the taking; workers were lobbying hard to bring it about, but Lenin would not back down. According to notes taken by Lenin, but preserved by no one else, late on 2 November the Central Committee reconvened to pass a resolution on 'the Opposition within the Central Committee'. This asserted that 'there can be no repudiation of the purely Bolshevik Government without betraying the slogan of Soviet power' and that the Central Committee would not give in to 'threats from the minority in the Soviets'. On the basis of this resolution, the Central Committee majority, supporting Lenin, sent an ultimatum to the Central Committee minority, supporting Kamenev, which asserted that at the Soviet Executive meeting on 2 November 'the Bolshevik Group, with Central Committee members belonging to the minority taking a direct part, openly voted against a Central Committee decision'. In Lenin's view, 'the opposition intends to take our party institutions by attrition' and sabotage its work; there was no other way forward than to demand that the minority agree in writing 'to submit to party discipline and carry out the policy formulated in comrade Lenin's resolution adopted by the Central Committee'. If the minority did not accept this ultimatum, then 'the party must emphatically suggest to the representatives of the opposition that they take their disorganising activities outside our party'. Lenin, Trotsky and Stalin led the signatories, and, on 3 November, Lenin began, in person, to interview every member of the Central Committee to insist that they give their signed support to his 'ultimatum of the majority to the minority'.[36]

When discussion at the Vikzhel talks resumed on 4 November, the Bolshevik delegation was no longer led by Kamenev but by Stalin, and it was clear from his stance that no progress would be made, although fruitless talks drifted on until 2 am in the morning.[37] Outside the talks, also on 4 November, Kamenev and Zinoviev, joined by Rykov, Milyutin and other supporters, resigned from the Central Committee in protest at Lenin's insistence on maintaining a purely Bolshevik administration in power. At the same time, Rykov resigned as commissar for internal affairs and Milyutin as commissar of agriculture: six other more junior members of the government also resigned; Ryazanov associated himself with the resignation statement; and Shlyapnikov, the commissar of labour, chose not to resign but issued a statement of protest that an agreement could have been reached on forming a coalition socialist administration.[38]

The statement issued by those who resigned made clear that a 'purely Bolshevik government has no choice but to maintain itself by political terror', and as if to prove them right, their statement was read out to the Soviet Executive while Lenin appeared before it to justify his government's decisions to close down the 'bourgeois' press and face the accusation that it had used martial law as a cover for arbitrary rule. Lenin was having none of this. He accepted that Muraviev had issued an order concerning martial law but it 'contained nothing contrary to the spirit of the new government', even if it had been 'phrased in such a way that undesirable misunderstandings could have resulted' – in fact Muraviev's order had led to widespread and purely arbitrary arrests of both real and imagined opponents of Bolshevik rule. For Lenin, however, those in the Soviet who criticised his government were simply 'apologists for parliamentary obstructionism'. The resolution Lenin proposed on this occasion made clear that the Soviet Executive was not a 'bourgeois' parliament, where procedural rules were used as 'a weapon of legislative obstruction'; the Bolshevik-run Soviet Government would report to the Soviet Executive, but would continue to rule by decree under only the shadiest of soviet scrutiny.[39]

Lenin's anger at his comrades' behaviour showed no sign of abating. After the resignations of 4 November, on 5 or 6 November, Lenin sent out a second ultimatum insisting that, since the 'minority' leaders had remained in the party while resigning from the Central Committee, they were still obliged to follow Central Committee resolutions. Yet 'in defiance of party discipline', he suggested, they continued to obstruct the work of the Central Committee and as a result the Central Committee had no choice but 'to raise the question of immediate expulsion from the party'. In his curt response, Kamenev insisted that 'nowhere outside the party have I spoken against Central Committee decisions, and at sessions of the Soviet Executive I voted according to what the majority of the group decided'. He too did not want to back down and accused Lenin of getting his spokesmen to introduce a resolution to break off the Vikzhel negotiations 'at a time when the Central Committee was continuing to make a stand for going on with the negotiations'.[40] On 7 November, Kamenev and Ryazanov wrote to the Central Committee denouncing 'the pogrom-style of the Central Committee's proclamation against us'. The next day, Lenin had Kamenev sacked as chairman of the Soviet Executive.[41]

PARTY DISCIPLINE AND THE WORKING CLASS

Solomon Lozovsky, the Bolshevik who had since June been the secretary of the Central Council of Trade Unions, responded to Lenin's ultimatum by writing a letter to the Bolshevik delegates to the Soviet Executive:

In view of the fact that the question of the day is group and party discipline, I deem it my duty to make the following statement:

I cannot in the name of party discipline remain silent when I feel with every fibre of my being that the Central Committee's tactics are leading to the isolation of the proletariat, civil war among working people, and to the defeat of the great revolution [...] I cannot, in the name of party discipline, remain silent when the MRC does as it pleases with the country, when it issues fantastic decrees about extraordinary tribunals [...] I cannot in the name of party discipline suppress the sullen discontent of the working masses, who fought for soviet power [only to discover] by some incomprehensible manoeuvre that power is wholly Bolshevik. I cannot, in the name of party discipline, become a hero-worshipper and insist that this or that person be a member of a government.[42]

Fig. 13: Solomon Lozovsky, a leading Bolshevik trade unionist and vocal critic of Lenin's decision to include only Bolsheviks in his first government

This impassioned plea was aimed at highlighting how Lenin's control of the Central Committee by just a couple of votes gave him the right to impose his views on the much larger Bolshevik delegation to the Soviet Executive, not to mention the rank-and-file labour activists who made up the core of the party. It raised an issue at the heart of Lenin's concept of the Bolshevik Party, an issue that had been thrashed out even before the 1905 Revolution, but an issue that most of those who came to support the Bolsheviks in 1917 knew very little about.

Since the Revolution of 1905, the main disagreement between Bolsheviks and Mensheviks had been that of reform or revolution, which crystallised into a disagreement about which social group was the more suitable ally for the working class. Mensheviks believed that ally should be Russia's bourgeoisie and that joint pressure from workers and liberal politicians could force the Tsar to cede power to parliament, introducing a prolonged period of constitutional democratic rule. The Bolsheviks emerged from 1905 convinced that their natural ally was the peasant, not the liberal, and that, together, workers and peasants could overthrow the monarchy and introduce revolutionary change. They therefore distanced themselves from the liberals and sought co-operation with the peasant party, the SRs. However, the original disagreement between the Bolsheviks and Mensheviks had concerned something quite different. Back in 1903, at the Second Congress of the Russian Social Democratic Labour Party, Bolsheviks and Mensheviks had split over the nature of the party they wanted to establish. Lenin had argued ever since his 1902 pamphlet *What is to be Done?* that it was the duty of the working-class party to lead the workers to revolution, and that for this to be effective, the party needed to be small, tight-knit and strictly disciplined.

This issue of discipline came to a head when the Second Congress debated the question of the party's rules, and in particular rule Number One, the definition of a party member. Lenin's proposal seemed uncontroversial enough: 'anyone who accepts the party's programme and supports it by personal participation in one of the party organisations is to be considered a member'. However, while this definition might make perfect sense in a state where political parties operated legally, in Russia Lenin's definition limited membership to a small elite of underground activists. Lenin's opponents wanted to extend membership to 'those who render [the party] regular personal assistance under the guidance of one of its organisations'. In practical terms, under Lenin's definition, the worker who stored political propaganda, circulated leaflets or even organised a strike would not qualify as a party member; only those directly involved in the work of the underground committee would be members. Under the Menshevik definition, these key activists would be considered party members.[43]

Behind these concerns lay disagreements about the nature of working-class consciousness. Lenin felt the working class needed to be led because he argued that, left to itself, it could only acquire trade union consciousness, it could learn to defend its immediate interests through strike action but not appreciate that only political revolution could fundamentally change its condition; political class consciousness had to be brought 'from without' the field of labour activism. His opponents argued that, through their own self-organisation, workers were quite capable of understanding that the only way to improve their lot was revolutionary change. Throughout the period 1905–17, Lenin made several attempts to assert this leadership role of the Bolshevik Party, but the opportunities for a foreign-based party elite to exercise leadership over the labour movement back home were limited. When such attempts were made, they were firmly rebuffed.

When the St Petersburg Soviet was established in October 1905, the Bolsheviks were initially rather cautious. On 29 October they tried to introduce a proposal that the Soviet should endorse the programme of the Social Democratic Party, but the majority of deputies would not agree and the idea was rejected out of hand.[44] During 1906, when the Tsar's provisional rules on freedom of association made possible the formation of trade unions, the Bolsheviks were slow off the mark; it was only at the end of the year and during the first half of 1907 that they threw their energies into the work of the trade unions, which until then they had left to the Mensheviks. When the Social Democratic Party held its Fifth Congress in London in May 1907 the Bolsheviks won a majority and a resolution was passed on trade union work. This made clear that members should encourage 'the recognition by the trade unions of the ideological leadership of the Social Democratic Party', and also seek to establish 'organisational links with the party'. It was the establishing of 'organisational links' that was to prove controversial.[45] In April 1908, when a group of worker delegates was sent to the Congress of Co-operative Societies, there was a disagreement between the Central Committee representative and the delegation at large. The disagreement concerned the rather technical issue of whether or not to allow co-operatives to offer goods on credit, but this was an issue on which the Social Democratic Party had a clear line and it was only after some patient negotiating by the Central Committee representative that a compromise was reached.[46]

There could be no easy compromise when the underground party committees started to tell labour activists that they should not take part in other legal congresses. Although the Bolsheviks had won a majority at the Fifth Party Congress, the Bolshevik faction had then split within itself about how best to respond to the dissolution of the Second State Duma and the summoning of a third State Duma with its greatly narrowed franchise, reducing Social Democrat representation by two-thirds. Left-wing Bolsheviks argued that the best response was to recall the deputies from the Duma in protest, and these Recallists also argued that workers should play no part in other 'sham' Tsarist concessions, like the trade unions and legal congresses. Lenin always opposed Recallism, but by summer 1908 the Recallists were so firmly in control of the St Petersburg Committee of the Social Democratic Party that its representative on the ruling board of the Metal Workers' Union kept trying to assert his imaginary power of party veto over decisions, while in the run-up to the Women's Congress of December 1908 the St Petersburg Committee was in a state of almost open warfare with Alexandra Kollontai as she tried to organise a delegation of working women to attend the congress. The St Petersburg Committee at first tried to prevent the delegation being formed, and then asserted it had the right to control its actions, which should be limited to unfurling red banners and staging a walkout. Kollontai's delegation took no notice of this instruction.[47]

By 1909 the underground apparatus of the Social Democratic Party had collapsed in Russia, while the legal labour movement was gaining in strength and authority. Abroad, Lenin was determined to rebuild his Bolshevik faction. In June 1909 he expelled the Recallists and then set about trying to re-establish the control over the party which the Bolsheviks had won at the Fifth Party Congress.

However, once it became clear to him that working within the existing party structures would end up with activists from the legal labour movement being involved in reconstructing the party, he changed tack again. He now resolved to form the Bolsheviks as a separate political party and insisted that legal labour groups could only be considered as belonging to the party if endorsed by 'a special decision taken by a congress or conference of illegal nuclei'.[48] These decisions were enshrined as party rules by the Prague Conference of January 1912, which formally established the Bolsheviks as a party separate from the Mensheviks.

Lenin continued to insist, despite the emergence in Russia of a powerful legal labour movement focused on the trade unions, that the small, underground hierarchy of Bolshevik committees, riddled as it was with police agents, was superior to the legal labour movement and had the right to lead it and give it directions in order to ensure that it took the right revolutionary road. In February and March 1914, for the first time since 1908, the Bolsheviks were in a position to try to impose some organisational links within the labour movement. As elections began to be held for working-class representation on the Insurance Council, the St Petersburg City Insurance Office and the St Petersburg Province Insurance Office, the Bolshevik Party tried to ensure its leading role by directing what should happen. *Pravda* suggested during the elections for the Insurance Council that those elected should 'bring all their activity into agreement with organised Marxists', in other words the Bolshevik Party. The Metal Workers' Union, however, despite the victory of Bolsheviks in the ruling board's election in 1913, proposed that those elected to the insurance bodies should be responsible not to 'organised Marxists' but a council of workers elected from the insurance funds. When this proposal was rejected, workers from the Putilov Works led the protests demanding that in future insurance elections there should be no attempt to tie workers to the guidance of 'Organised Marxists'.

During the elections to the St Petersburg City Insurance Office on 30 March, the Metal Workers' Union initially got its way and those elected were to be made responsible to an insurance council; however, a last-minute Bolshevik amendment changed the wording of the resolution so that those elected were responsible both to an elected insurance council and to Organised Marxists. This concept of dual responsibility was repeated during the election of workers to the St Petersburg Provincial Insurance Office, and although to some it seemed contradictory, there was a logic to it. It was in a way a happy compromise: the workers wanted party influence to be established not through the dictates of the Central Committee, but through the actions of local workers' representatives loyal to the principles of revolutionary change.[49] Reflecting this mood, it was during the insurance campaign that a group of dissident Bolsheviks emerged who were opposed to the decisions taken at the Prague Conference.[50] This Interdistrict Group would become one of the strongest and most militant underground groups during World War I and would, under Trotsky's leadership, merge back into the Bolshevik Party at the Sixth Party Congress in July 1917.

History repeated itself in October 1916 when social insurance council elections were held once again. The elections to the Petrograd City Insurance Board resulted in four Bolsheviks and one SR being elected. A fortnight later it was the turn of the Petrograd Provincial Insurance Board and on this occasion the Bolsheviks won three seats and the Mensheviks two. During both elections the electors were presented with two instructions, one drawn up by the Bolsheviks and one by the Mensheviks. Despite the Bolshevik victory in the two votes, it was the Menshevik instruction that was adopted because, while on the substantive issues of insurance the two instructions were identical, the Bolshevik instruction repeated the demand that the Labour Group on the insurance councils should be 'responsible to Organised Marxists', whereas the Menshevik instruction made them responsible to 'the collective of the funds', in other words the workers who had elected them.[51]

In 1908, 1914 and 1916 the number of workers involved in these tussles with the Bolshevik hierarchy about leadership and discipline were tiny, but the events of October–November 1917 suggest that the far larger number of workers responsible for the overthrow of Kerensky had similar concerns. When the Obukhov, Putilov and Aleksandrovskii workers lobbied the Vikzhel negotiations, they were repeating the stance taken by workers during the legal conferences of 1908 and the insurance campaign of 1914 and 1916. Party leadership should be asserted not through Lenin's wafer-thin control of the Central Committee but the actions of worker Bolsheviks elected to the Soviet Executive. This was the essence of Lozovsky's stance, and it was also the stance of Shlyapnikov. Shlyapnikov had returned to St Petersburg in April 1914 after an absence of six years and found work first in the New Lessner and then the Ericsson factories; in no time he had been co-opted onto the board of the Metal Workers' Union. Writing early in July 1914 he commented, 'I am in admiration of our proletariat. Since I last left St Petersburg it is as if it has been reborn. Real leaders have emerged from the deep cadres of the working class; despite exiles and arrests, the cause has moved forward.'[52]

These were the worker activists who had warned Kerensky back in February that revolution was coming. These worker activists did not see the need for Lenin or the Bolsheviks to lead them and give them directions. Shlyapnikov became aware of this again when he was back in Petrograd in October 1915 to re-establish the Russian Bureau of the Bolshevik Central Committee. Then he worked with activists from the insurance funds and by January 1916 he was supporting them in opposing 'guidance' being offered then by the Bolshevik St Petersburg Committee. In March 1916 he warned Zinoviev that 'terribly harmful tales about Ilych [Lenin] are circulating in Russia'. His rows with other Bolsheviks 'because of the smallest disagreement have made practical people shun us', and it was practical people like the insurance fund members who were to lead the February Revolution.[53] Shlyapnikov cannot therefore have been completely surprised when in November 1917 he once again found himself at odds with Lenin and the concept of party discipline.

8

THE BOLSHEVIK–LEFT SR COALITION

The row within the Bolshevik Central Committee about the composition of a Soviet Government ended up in an uncomfortable stalemate. Lenin had got his way by invoking party discipline, but several of his government commissars had resigned and there was no escaping the reality that the majority of Russia's peasant population was not represented in the Soviet Executive established by the Second Congress of Soviets. Although in the heat of his row with Kamenev, Lenin had stated that 'there can be no repudiation of the purely Bolshevik Government without betraying the slogan of Soviet power', his real concern was for the proletariat to lead the peasantry into the socialist revolution. A coalition of all soviet parties risked the Bolsheviks being swamped, but a coalition with the Left SRs alone, the political voice of the poor peasants, that was another matter, so long as the Bolsheviks had a majority of commissariats; such an arrangement would be fully in line with Lenin's April Theses. That is why the idea had been briefly considered on 25 October, and that is why, on 4 November, when the commissars of the Bolshevik 'minority' resigned in protest at Lenin's policies, the 'majority' Bolsheviks left in government tried to persuade the prominent Left SR Andrei Kalegaev to take up the portfolio of commissar of agriculture, a lone Left SR in an otherwise Bolshevik Government.[1] Once the dust in the Bolshevik Party had settled and the resignation crisis was over, the idea of a Bolshevik–Left SR coalition was revived.

Once such a government was formed, the key issue of which party would dominate the coalition remained.

NEGOTIATING THE NEW GOVERNMENT

Even at the height of the row about the Vikzhel negotiations, the Bolsheviks had always accepted that the Soviet Executive elected at the Second Congress of Soviets needed to be expanded, if for no other reason than so few peasants had been represented at it. After the Vikzhel talks had collapsed, this key issue remained under discussion within the Soviet Executive and progress began to be made as early as 11 November when the Extraordinary Congress of Peasant Soviets took place. This assembly gave a solid victory to the Left SRs, rather than the Right SRs, and proposed that its newly formed Peasant Soviet Executive and the Bolshevik-controlled Soviet Executive elected at the Second Congress of Soviets should merge on the basis of parity; a new government could then be formed by those parties which endorsed the programme accepted by both the Second Congress of Soviets and the Extraordinary Congress of Peasant Soviets, that is, the Bolsheviks and Left SRs. As a result, on the night of 14–15 November, the Bolshevik Central Committee and the leadership of the Left SRs in the Soviet Executive held talks and agreed that the Peasant Soviet Executive would indeed join the Soviet Executive, a merger implemented with some pomp and ceremony.[2]

During those talks of 14–15 November, the Left SRs first signalled that they were prepared to join the Bolsheviks in government, a step made public on 17 November in a speech to the Soviet Executive by their most charismatic leader, Maria Spiridonova. The only precondition advanced by the Left SRs was that the new coalition government really did have to be accountable to the expanded Soviet Executive. As Boris Kamkov assured the First Left SR Congress when it met from 19 to 28 November 1917, the Bolsheviks did accept during these discussions that 'not a single decree can be published unless it has been passed in advance by the Soviet Executive'.[3] Kamkov explained to congress delegates that the precise make-up of the Soviet Executive would only become clear 'once army delegates arrive from the front' – only then would the final representation within the Soviet Executive be agreed; as a consequence, it would only be then that the precise number of seats that the Left SRs would demand in government could be established. However, he added, 'we have decided to take part in exercising power' and therefore Kalegaev would be taking up the post of commissar of agriculture forthwith.[4]

The formation of the Bolshevik–Left SR Coalition Government was then put on hold. The Right SRs had always insisted that the Extraordinary Congress of Peasant Soviets had been organised in a rush and had been gerrymandered so as to give the Left SRs a majority. However, on 27 November a second Congress of Peasant Soviets assembled in Petrograd and, far from giving a majority to the Right SRs, the Left SRs once again emerged as the biggest single party: they had 350 delegates to the Right SRs' 305, with the Bolsheviks receiving 91.[5] Anticipating that the final shape of the Soviet Executive would give them parity with the Bolsheviks, the Left SRs initially proposed asking for five commissariats, but when the final composition of the Soviet Executive became known, the Bolsheviks had a slim majority, so the Left SRs agreed to take up only four commissariats, an arrangement that was agreed in principle on 7 December and finalised on 9 December.[6]

LAND REFORM

The Left SRs joined the Bolsheviks in government primarily because they saw it as an opportunity to introduce the land reform promised to the peasants in May at the First Congress of Peasant Soviets. Even before the Left SRs joined the government, the Bolsheviks had instructed district and parish land committees to start the process of confiscating privately owned estates and the Left SRs quickly used their power in the localities to organise this work. Often these estates were confiscated and inventories of their properties drawn up even before the new structure of parish soviets was completely formalised by March 1918; this was mostly an entirely peaceful process, with the recently established parish land committees, supply committees and *zemstvos* renaming themselves parish soviets. The work of land reform was carried out by two bodies: first the Peasant Section of the Soviet Executive, which was dominated by the Left SRs and which by early 1918 had sent nearly 50,000 agitators into the villages; and second, by the Commissariat of Agriculture, which was also dominated by the Left SRs, especially the Moscow Regional Commissariat of Agriculture which administered the 14 provinces in Russia's central heartland.

The confiscation of noble landed estates proved the easy part; moving towards equalised land redistribution proved much harder. By 11 April 1918 the Commissariat of Agriculture had issued provisional instructions which sought to meet the target of equality, but explained to peasants that reaching this target in full might take more time; since the spring sowing was imminent and the necessary statistical information might take many more months to collect, it was essential to get moving, if only on a provisional basis. In practice the period that this provisional redistribution was supposed to last varied tremendously: in some areas it was just a year, in others three years and in still others nine years; nine years would allow for the full rotation of the traditional three-field system. The announcement that the land redistribution was provisional also helped those Bolsheviks in the Commissariat of Agriculture who hoped that, at some later stage, collective farming might be introduced. In practice, as the country sank into civil war by summer 1918, the provisional land allocations of spring 1918 became permanent, at least in those areas of the country that remained under soviet control.

The extent of land redistribution reflected traditional areas of land shortage: thus land redivision was much more dramatic in the fertile black-earth provinces near the river Volga, where peasant holdings had traditionally been small, than it was in areas of Russia where the land was far less productive. The division of land was not always straightforward. In a very small number of cases, presumably under the political influence of Right SRs, peasants refused to divide the land 'without instructions from the Constituent Assembly'. More frequently, redivision did not take place where local parishes could not agree on a provisional redistribution because of conflicts over adjacent land; on these occasions representatives from the Peasant Section of the Soviet Executive or the Commissariat of Agriculture tried to adjudicate. By and large, however, land reform was a Left SR success story – a survey of provinces in spring 1918 showed that in 85 per cent of parishes the land reform had been implemented without any serious disagreement.[7]

THE CONSTITUENT ASSEMBLY

The Bolsheviks and the Left SRs were pretty much agreed on how they should begin to address the land question, and they were also to agree on how to face the first major problem of their new coalition administration: the future of the Constituent Assembly. Despite the resignations of 4 November, all Bolsheviks, even those most loyal to Lenin, made clear that although the Bolsheviks had taken power alone, 'power will not remain in our hands for long: we are not planning to delay the Constituent Assembly; we will assemble it immediately after the elections and transfer power to it'. The Bolsheviks had established a 'provisional workers' and peasants' government' pending the Constituent Assembly and in accordance with this, on 8 November, the Soviet Executive agreed to fund Lenin's Bolshevik-only government 'until the Constituent Assembly meets'; the same Soviet session announced that the elections to the Constituent Assembly would be held on schedule starting on 12 November. A couple of days earlier, on 6 November, the Soviet Executive had discussed the electoral prospects of the Left SRs. Because the Left SRs had only been formed as an entirely separate party during the Second Congress of Soviets, they had not been able to put up their own list of candidates in the Constituent Assembly elections. The Soviet Executive raised the possibility of delaying the elections so that separate lists could be drawn up, but the Left SRs were confident enough that they would win a substantial number of deputies and thus resisted any talk of delaying the elections.[8]

It was as the negotiations about a Bolshevik–Left SR coalition got underway on 14–15 November that the results of the Constituent Assembly elections began to come through. The Bolsheviks had hoped to win one-third of the seats and the Left SRs had talked of winning some hundred seats, but both predictions proved overoptimistic. The Constituent Assembly elections gave the Bolsheviks 23.7 per cent of the votes and the SRs 37.3 per cent; however, if the SRs' allies, such as the Ukrainian SRs, were included, the SR vote was just about 50 per cent: when transferred into seats, the Bolsheviks had 24 per cent of the seats and the SRs 54 per cent. The Bolsheviks had not achieved what they had hoped for, but they did control the industrial heartlands of Petrograd and the central industrial region surrounding Moscow. Unravelling the votes for Left SRs and Right SRs, however, proved impossible. All the Left SRs could do was to point out that in Petrograd, much of the Volga and much of Russia's south they now controlled the local party organisations, although those organisations would be represented in the Constituent Assembly by Right SRs because the party machine had ensured that Right SRs headed the electoral lists.[9]

The Left SRs were clear, therefore, that the results of the Constituent Assembly elections did not reflect the true strength of their party and should not mean that the revolutionary clock could be turned back. On 21 November, Kamkov told the First Left SR Congress that the soviets would remain legislative organs and the Constituent Assembly would not be allowed to crush the revolution; it had to be 'organically merged with the revolution'.[10] The same day both Lenin and the Left SR Vladimir Karelin addressed the Soviet Executive to explain that it was essential to introduce into the Constituent Assembly the soviet system of recall; like soviet deputies, members of the Constituent Assembly should be subject to recall if they no longer reflected the views of the electorate.[11] This would involve revising the electoral rules and would be difficult to manage because of the system of proportional representation used in the Constituent Assembly elections, but 'the people's revolutionary will' had to be exercised, Lenin insisted, and the SRs were 'a party which no longer exists'. The way forward, he suggested, was to give 'the right of recall to the soviets and in this way power can pass from one party to another by means of re-elections'. In other words, in areas where the Left SRs now controlled local party organisations, they could use their influence over the local soviets to have the local Constituent Assembly deputies recalled if they did not shift their support to the Left rather than the Right SRs. The Soviet Executive backed the principle of recall, leaving its technicalities to a commission.[12]

If the right of recall were to be exercised in a planned way, and if the soviets were to do the recalling, there was no way that the Constituent Assembly could open as planned on 28 November, and no way the Electoral Commission established by the Provisional Government could be left in charge of assembling the deputies. On 23 November the members of the Electoral Commission were arrested and on the 27th it was announced that the Constituent Assembly would not open until a quorum of 50 per cent, or 400 deputies, had arrived in Petrograd. On 29 November the Bolsheviks debated the issue of what to do next, and some proposed expelling the liberals from the Constituent Assembly and forming what they called a Revolutionary Convention. The Left SRs were happy to go along with this idea, suggesting that the Revolutionary Convention could be formed by merging the Constituent Assembly with a third Congress of Soviets. Thus although when the Soviet Executive met on 1 December the Left SRs criticised the 'arbitrary and repressive action' of the Bolsheviks in arresting the Electoral Commission, they went along with a resolution which declined to guarantee that 'both the socialist and bourgeois' sections of the assembly would be summoned.[13]

As the Bolshevik deputies to the Constituent Assembly began to gather in Petrograd, however, it was clear that many of them, while happy to go along with the right of recall, were unimpressed with the idea of excluding the liberals and forming a Revolutionary Convention. The Bolshevik deputies elected a bureau to manage their affairs and the members they chose as their representatives were from the old Central Committee 'minority', those who Lenin had wanted to discipline and who had resigned their posts in protest on 4 November. On 11 December the Central Committee met with only one item on the agenda, 'about the group in the Constituent Assembly' where 'right-wing attitudes had taken hold'. Lenin proposed that the way forward was to 'remove the bureau', appoint a new Central Committee representative and 'remind them of party rules that all representative bodies come under Central Committee authority'. When the new Central Committee representatives addressed the deputies the following day, they were informed for the first time that the Constituent Assembly might have to be dissolved.

In public the Bolshevik Party was still talking about an arrangement whereby the Constituent Assembly and the soviets could be transformed into a Revolutionary Convention. However, as throughout the autumn, two views were emerging about how to proceed. Kamenev saw no need to hurry: the Constituent Assembly needed to be 'tested', it should be allowed to assemble, but if it was clear that it would not endorse the key decrees enacted by the Soviet Government, then moves to establish a Revolutionary Convention should begin. This idea was attacked in *Pravda* on 20 December as fostering 'constitutional illusions'; moves towards a Revolutionary Convention should begin at once. Although it was announced on the 20th that the Constituent Assembly would open on 5 January 1918, it was decided at the same time that the planned Third Congress of Soviets and Third Congress of Peasant Soviets would be brought forward by two weeks 'so that when the Constituent Assembly meets the opinion of the oppressed classes on the most important questions of the day may be represented'. The plan was clear: a Revolutionary Convention would be formed by a simultaneous session of the Constituent Assembly and the two congresses of soviets.[14]

On 21 December the Left SRs had one final meeting with their former colleagues in the Right SRs, but if they had hoped to win them over to the idea of a Revolutionary Convention they were mistaken. So, from the end of December, the Left SRs were committed irrevocably to the idea of a Revolutionary Convention and joined with the Bolsheviks in the Soviet Executive in trying to work out precisely how it could be engineered. When the Soviet Executive debated the issue of the Revolutionary Convention on 3 January 1918, it followed Lenin's hard line and decided to issue the Constituent Assembly with an ultimatum: the Constituent Assembly could join with the Third Congress of Soviets and establish a Revolutionary Convention only if it accepted the Declaration of the Rights of Labouring and Exploited People, a text drawn up by the Left SRs which insisted on the right to recall deputies. When the Constituent Assembly opened on 5 January 1918 it endorsed the major decrees of the Soviet Government, but it would not endorse the Declaration of the Rights of Labouring and Exploited People, even though, as the chairman of the Soviet Executive explained, this would provide 'the basis on which you can enter the coming convention with the Third Soviet Congress'. Riding roughshod over the minority who wanted to allow the Constituent Assembly to continue its debates and to 'confront it with the Third Congress of Soviets', Lenin insisted that the Constituent Assembly had to be dissolved at once.[15] A week later, the Third Congress of Soviets and the Third Congress of Peasant Soviets merged to form a new Soviet Executive.[16]

ARBITRARY RULE

If Bolsheviks and Left SRs were agreed on how to respond to the Constituent Assembly, there was no agreement on the question of arbitrary powers. Under the agreement between the two parties the Commissariat of Justice was given to the Left SR Shteinberg. The use of arbitrary power by the MRC had long been a concern of the Left SRs. When, on 4 November, Lenin had dismissed as 'parliamentary obstructionism' attempts by the Soviet Executive to query his use of the MRC to close newspapers and arrest opponents, the Left SRs announced that they were leaving the MRC. However, under the agreement reached with the Bolsheviks on 14–15 November the Left SRs rejoined the MRC with parity representation. At a meeting of the MRC on 21 November, the Bolsheviks tried to establish a completely new security agency without Left SR representation, but the Left SRs succeeded in preventing this.[17] On 1 December, Shteinberg and the Left SRs again used their position in the Soviet Executive to force Lenin to explain his decision on 28 November to outlaw the Kadets and arrest the party's leading members.[18] The Left SRs were adamant that the Soviet Government should not resort to the sort of police regime so characteristic of the Tsar's rule.

When Lenin dissolved the MRC on 5 December and established the Cheka secret police on 7 December, he was making a pre-emptive strike against Shteinberg, who was quick to challenge Lenin's previous arbitrary actions. On 15 December, Shteinberg published a decree, without consulting his fellow commissars, which ordered that all prisoners detained by the MRC and held outside the normal prison system should be transferred to state prisons, where their cases would be reviewed and they would either be remanded for trial or released. The following day he asserted the right to receive complaints about the activities of the Cheka and asked his fellow commissars for the right to oversee the Cheka, a request that was refused. When on 17 December the Cheka arrested participants in a 'workers' conference' organised by the Mensheviks and Right SRs, Shteinberg visited the scene in person to get the arrested workers released. On 19 December, Lenin's Government rebuked Shteinberg and confirmed that 'directives of the Cheka can only be revised on appeal to the government'. Shteinberg then successfully argued that if this were to be the case, the Left SRs would have to be involved in the Cheka; thus on 4 January 1918, over the objections of its Bolshevik chairman Felix Dzerzhinskii, the Left SRs were allowed to participate in the work of the Cheka.[19]

WORKER UNREST

Part of the reason why Lenin was so determined to shut down discussion at the Constituent Assembly and cut short any further talks about the formation of a Revolutionary Convention was that the 'right of recall' could not always be assumed to work in favour of the Bolsheviks and their Left SR allies. The SR Party held its Fourth Congress from 26 November to 5 December, and this gathering saw the party move smartly to the left, abandoning all mention of cross-class coalitions and plots to overthrow the Bolsheviks. Chernov's policy of 'businesslike' work in the Constituent Assembly was supported wholeheartedly. Chernov argued that the masses would soon tire of the 'unobtainable promises' of the Bolsheviks, and if the SRs drafted serious, well-thought-through legislation to address the key issues of the day, which remained peace, land and the control of production, then the ground could gradually be cut from under the Bolsheviks' feet. So the SRs established 14 commissions to prepare legislation for the opening of the Constituent Assembly, legislative proposals which they hoped would become the dominant agenda as the Constituent Assembly morphed into the Revolutionary Convention. Indeed, on 26–27 December the SRs drafted plans which suggested that they thought it quite feasible that they could play the game of the Revolutionary Convention and win. Their idea was to take part in the Third Congress of Soviets, but also to rally delegates to a parallel Congress of Soviets committed to the Constituent Assembly. There would be a Revolutionary Convention, but one held against the backdrop of rival groups of peasant deputies both claiming legitimacy. It was not the sort of scenario that Lenin could welcome.[20]

In a similar way, as the *Chekist* action against 'workers' conferences' attested, the SRs had had some success in recalling Bolshevik delegates from the soviets. When the Bolsheviks responded by delaying recall elections, the SRs would organise counter 'workers' conferences' to demand that such re-elections took place.[21] This movement, which saw disturbances in some factories in January, would take on a clear organisational form on 13 March when an 'extraordinary meeting' of the Workers' Conference of Factory Representatives was held in Petrograd, a conference which asserted that the soviets 'have ceased to be the political representatives of the proletariat and are little more than judicial or police institutions'. Working-class discontent was easy to understand. Workers had hoped that the formation of a Soviet Government would help support the work of factory committees in maintaining production. William Rosenberg has argued that 'for a few weeks there seemed to be a genuine and widespread belief that the workers themselves could find at least temporary solutions to the problems besetting their plants'. Control of the state would help put an end to the 'sabotage' of the factory owners. However, the widespread, spontaneous nationalisations 'from below' which followed rarely did much more than postpone disaster. At best, work already in the pipeline was completed and a few new orders found in November and December, before work dried up once and for all; by early January any optimism about the future had disappeared. In Rosenberg's words, 'one of the most salient features of revolutionary Russia in the eight months or so after October was that nothing changed for the better'.[22]

Between January and April 1918 nearly 60 per cent of the capital's industrial workforce was forced 'onto the streets'. In the chemical industry the figure was 79 per cent, in the metalworking industry 74 per cent; these two industries had comprised 70 per cent of the capital's workforce and had stood at the core of the factory committee movement. The very groups that had provided the hard core of labour militants since 1912 – the Bolshevik workers at the heart of the factory committee movement – were now those who were suffering most from unemployment. No wonder jaded commentators noted that all that happened at the start of 1918 was that 'factory committees organised commissions to fire workers'; as this happened it was inevitable that a gap opened up between those activists who did the firing and the rank and file. By January and February 1918 there was plenty of talk of factory committee bigwigs enjoying privileges and lording it over the rest.[23]

As the Soviet Government wrestled with priorities, trying to keep a grip on a rapidly collapsing economy, the creative tension between the centre and the factory floor was constantly under pressure. Lozovsky, such a passionate critic of Lenin's desire for discipline, found himself, as Trade Union Secretary, calling for the factory committees to be brought to heal and for limits to be put on their power. For the good of central government, local initiatives had to be controlled. Thus the Triangle Plant sent a factory committee delegation to the south in search of fuel, like so many other factory committees had done in autumn 1917, but when it returned to the capital with 40 rail-tanker trucks of oil, the Soviet Government requisitioned the lot, to the astonishment of the factory committee.[24] This was not as it was supposed to be. Workers' control over production had been promised in a decree passed by the Second Congress of Soviets on 26 October, and on 3 November a further draft decree filling out the detail and making clear that workers' control was to be established in all factories employing more than five people. It would be exercised through the factory committees and all company records would be available to the factory committees whose decisions would be binding. This was then modified in a further decree issued on 14 November, which attempted to introduce an element of centralisation that might enable 'the planned regulation of the economy'; factory committees were to be controlled by local councils of workers' control, which would in turn be subservient to a Russian Council of Workers' Control, which would bring together the Council of Factory Committees, the Central Council of Trade Unions and the Soviet Executive.[25] Under this decree, factory administrations had the power to appeal against any local factory committee decisions by turning to the next level up the committee hierarchy. The existence of the two decrees on how to implement workers' control caused a good deal of confusion, and the right of appeal remained editorially so unclear that it was of little practical assistance to factory managers.[26]

The Russian Council of Workers' Control met only twice, on 25 November and 5 December, and it did very little to develop 'the planned regulation of the economy'; indeed anarchy seemed to reign.[27] From the state's perspective, it was intolerable for 'Bolshevik' railway repair crews to refuse to undertake track maintenance in freezing winter conditions simply because 'bourgeois' white-collar workers sat in warm offices. Nor was it acceptable for factory committee activists to decouple freight cars and seize food supplies.[28] On 16 November the Fifth Conference of Petrograd Factory Committees welcomed the initiatives taken so far by the Bolsheviks, and the Central Council of Petrograd Factory Committees issued yet further instructions on how to implement the workers' control decree. These instructions contradicted the decree of 14 November and spelled out that factory owners were obliged, on pain of state requisitioning, to subordinate themselves to workers' control decisions in finance, purchasing and sales; refusal meant that the workers themselves could declare the firm nationalised.

Not surprisingly, this Petrograd instruction was soon challenged when the Russian Council of Workers' Control issued yet further and much more moderate instructions. These followed the ideas of Lozovsky in arguing that if workers simply took control of existing privately owned firms, they were actually breathing new life into decaying capitalism rather than advancing to a socialist future. It was Milyutin who shortly after this invented the term 'state workers' control' and stressed that such control needed to be exercised through 'one solid state apparatus'. The formation on 1 December 1917 of the Supreme Economic Council was the first step on this road, for it would swallow up the Russian Council of Workers' Control. The Fifth Conference of Factory Committees had spoken of the need for 'friendly joint work' with the trade unions, and at the First Trade Union Congress between 7 and 14 January 1918 both Lozovsky and Ryazanov criticised the Central Council of Petrograd Factory Committees for sliding towards anarcho-syndicalism. By an overwhelming majority the congress decided to bring the factory committees under trade union control by making them the 'primary organs' of the trade unions; the factory committees were to become local union cells and brought under firm control. Workers' control, to all intents and purposes, was abolished as the state took charge of a crumbling economy.[29]

PEACE TALKS

The turning point in this story of disciplining the factory committees and getting to grips with economic decline came when the Soviet Government decreed early in December that all military production, including shell production, should cease entirely, proposing rather lamely as an alternative that the factories affected by this should seek compensatory orders in Siberia. This decision followed on logically from the armistice reached on the Eastern Front on 2 December. As Rosenberg has noted, amongst all the other tasks the factory committees faced, they now had the additional requirement 'to decide what to do with demobilised soldiers who appeared at the gates and demanded their old jobs back'.[30] Demobilisation was an essential feature of the peace process, and industrial demobilisation was part and parcel of that process.

Practical moves towards peace began on 8 November, when Lenin called on the last Supreme Commander-in-Chief of the Russian Army, General N. N. Dukhonin, to begin talks with the aim of establishing a general armistice on all fronts of World War I. Dukhonin had worked closely with the CSRM, and so when he responded on 9 November by requesting more time to discuss this proposal with the Allies, Lenin interpreted this as an act of counter-revolution. Dukhonin was dismissed and at the same time Lenin appealed above his head to the troops at the front to organise their own local armistices. He had reason to hope this would work. In October most of the higher soldiers' committees – at front, army and corps level – were still under Menshevik or SR control and were unwilling to risk submitting to re-election, despite determined pressure from below. However, the Fifth Army had held a congress on 16 October and as a result it had sent a delegation of Bolsheviks and Left SRs to the Second Congress of Soviets. Support for a Soviet Government seemed to be growing at rank-and-file level and the army leadership could change.

After the Soviet Government had been proclaimed, the other armies began to fall into line behind the Fifth Army. Within the first week after the Bolshevik uprising the First, Second and Third Armies all recognised the authority of the MRC. Then the Tenth Army came out in support of the MRC on 7 November, and the Twelfth on 12 November. Several of the votes on these occasions were very close, and always support was expressed for a socialist coalition rather than a purely Bolshevik government; however, by the middle of November every army on the Northern and Western Fronts had voted for new leaderships sympathetic to the Soviet Government.[31] Growing support for the Bolsheviks was also shown by the Constituent Assembly elections: on the Northern Front, the Bolsheviks topped the poll, but their victory was even more convincing on the Western Front where they secured just under 67 per cent of the vote in each army. In those armies on the South Western and Romanian Fronts, the situation was rather different. Here Bolshevik success had to be shared with various Ukrainian parties; on the Romanian Front they failed almost completely, securing scarcely 10 per cent of the vote.[32]

In these circumstances, Lenin felt able to push ahead and enforce the dismissal of Dukhonin. On 11 November the newly appointed Bolshevik Commander-in-Chief, Ensign Nikolai Krylenko, arrived at the headquarters of the Fifth Army in Dvinsk (Daugavpils) and dismissed its commander. With a certain amount of difficulty he then summoned an army congress, on 19 November, which, as well as repeating its support for the Soviet Government, offered Krylenko armed support in arresting Dukhonin. By 19 November, formal armistice talks with the Central Powers had already begun, so time was pressing. Krylenko took a force of 3,000 men to General Headquarters and arrested Dukhonin on 20 November; he was murdered the following day in unexplained circumstances. With the army now fully under Lenin's control, the armistice talks could make progress. Initially, the proposal of the Soviet Government was for an armistice with the Central Powers which would be the precursor for a general armistice on all fronts of World War I. This was put forward when the armistice talks opened, and then adjourned for a week. Kamenev, who attended those first talks, informed the Soviet Executive that 'we can only accept an armistice that is the prelude to a general peace'. However, within days, Lenin had decided that a general peace was quite unrealistic and by 27 November the mandate for the talks spoke only of 'struggling' for a general peace; the agreement reached on 2 December at Brest-Litovsk was for an armistice on the Eastern Front alone.[33]

What complicated the armistice negotiations still further was the fact that on 7 November the Rada Assembly in Ukraine had declared the formation of a People's Republic of Ukraine, which would be a completely autonomous unit within the future democratic and federal Russia to be established by the Constituent Assembly. The Rada then issued a separate general peace call on 10 November, and on 26 November began its own armistice talks with the Central Powers. Up until early December, Lenin was optimistic that the Ukrainian Rada would be a short-lived affair. A Ukrainian Congress of Soviets was due to assemble and would surely support the Soviet Government of Russia. However, when the Ukrainian Congress of Soviets opened in Kiev on 4 December it was dominated by Ukrainian SRs, who, rather than establishing Soviet power, endorsed the Rada as Ukraine's legitimate government. In response, the Bolsheviks walked out of the Ukrainian Congress of Soviets, moved to the industrial city of Kharkov and on 11–12 December transformed the Regional Congress of Soviets of the Donets Basin into the 'legitimate' Ukrainian Congress of Soviets which established a Ukrainian Soviet Republic. Attempts brokered by the Left SRs to defuse this tension proved impossible: the view of the Russian Soviet Executive was that 'self-determination for the Ukrainian people is not, of course, self-determination for counter-revolution'. When the Soviet Government intercepted a coded telegram from the French military mission that the Ukrainians should spin out the peace talks until the spring, and when seemingly as a result of this telegram the Ukrainians demanded on 11 December that their delegation to the peace talks be separate from the Russian delegation, Lenin feared that separate representation for Ukraine would wreck the Brest-Litovsk negotiations and end the prospects for peace.[34]

All these machinations convinced Lenin by the end of December that the only way forward was 'to gain time through a separate peace'. When the talks at Brest-Litovsk resumed on 28 December, it quickly became clear that the Ukrainian delegation had rejected Trotsky's request that they consult with the Russians on all matters; by 1 January 1918 the Ukrainians were holding separate talks with the Central Powers. So, in the last days of December, the Russian Soviet Government supported the Kharkov based Ukrainian Soviet Government when it declared the start of a civil war against the Ukrainian People's Republic, a civil war which seemed very much like a Russian invasion since Moscow provided the troops and the commander for the forces of the Ukrainian Soviet Government. After more than a month of bitter fighting, the Russian-supported forces captured Kiev in early February. But that victory came far too late to help the negotiations at Brest-Litovsk. On 5 January 1918 the Central Powers presented their demands to Trotsky and then called for an adjournment of ten days.

SIGNING THE PEACE TREATY

Trotsky returned from Brest-Litovsk to Petrograd to find Lenin convinced that Soviet Russia had no alternative but to sign a separate peace treaty and accept the terms on offer. His views were not shared by the Central Committee. It met in expanded session on

8 January and favoured war rather than peace. However, when the Central Committee reconvened in narrow session on 11 January, Lenin secured a semi-compromise: it rejected both Lenin's call for an immediate peace and the call for a revolutionary war against the Central Powers; it supported instead Trotsky's proposed formula of 'no peace, no war'. At the same time, Trotsky agreed that he would support Lenin and peace if the Central Powers did not respond to 'no peace, no war' with a compromise. Trotsky's speech to the Third Congress of Soviets on 13 January was quite different, however; here he spoke of 'revolutionary war against world imperialism' and the congress itself resolved never to sign 'an unfortunate and imperialistic peace'.[35] Deputies with long memories could recall that, in the April Theses, Lenin too had seemed to favour revolutionary war, for he had written that if power were transferred to 'the proletariat and poorest sections of the peasantry aligned with the proletariat' then 'the class conscious proletariat can give its consent to revolutionary war'.[36]

The talks at Brest-Litovsk resumed on 17 January. During the adjournment, and partly in response to the dissolution of the Constituent Assembly, Ukraine had declared itself a fully independent state on 9 January and was recognised as such by the Central Powers on the 19th. On 28 January a separate peace treaty was signed with Ukraine. Trotsky had been instructed before returning to Brest-Litovsk to spin out the peace talks for as long as possible in the hope that revolutionary unrest might develop in Germany, but, after securing the treaty with Ukraine, the Central Powers moved on 28 January to issue Trotsky with an ultimatum. He therefore had no choice but to initiate the 'no peace, no war' tactic. He announced that Soviet Russia would not sign a formal peace agreement with the Central Powers but considered that it was no longer in a state of war with the Central Powers and was demobilising its forces. He returned to Petrograd on 30 January. Three days later, on 16 February 1918 – Soviet Russia adopted the Western calendar on 1 February – the Central Powers announced that since no peace treaty had been agreed, the armistice was over and fighting would resume on 18 February, which it did.

Under the terms of the tacit agreement between Lenin and Trotsky, this was the point at which Trotsky should have abandoned the idea of revolutionary war and backed Lenin on the need for an immediate peace. Yet, when Lenin proposed that the Soviet Government contact the Central Powers at once and agree to sign the peace, Trotsky argued that the German offensive should be allowed to begin 'so that the workers of Germany would learn of the offensive as a fact rather than as a threat'. At the Central Committee meeting on 17 February, he had voted for the principle of a peace treaty, but on the 18th he refused to vote for the despatch of the necessary telegram to the Germans. He reported that an aerial bombardment of the town of Dvinsk (Daugavpils) had begun, but argued 'the masses are only just beginning to digest what is happening [...] we have to wait and see what impression all this makes on the German people'. When, later in the day, he reported to the reconvened Central Committee that Dvinsk had fallen, he proposed making a direct appeal to the workers of Berlin and Vienna. Trotsky's behaviour meant that when, on both 17 and 18 February, the Bolshevik Central Committee debated Lenin's proposals that negotiations with the Central Powers be resumed and a peace treaty signed, Lenin had lost by one vote.[37]

The disagreement between Lenin and Trotsky reflected different attitudes towards the peasantry and the prospects for a European revolution. In the April Theses, Lenin had referred to how in the coming socialist revolution the Russian workers would have two allies: the workers of Europe and the poorest peasants of Russia. Trotsky had far less faith in the peasantry. In the aftermath of the 1905 Revolution he had written about the dangers the working class would face from the peasantry if it had succeeded in obtaining power. The peasants would at first support the workers, because the workers would give them land, but thereafter they were increasingly likely to turn against the working-class government.

> The cooling off of the peasantry, its political passivity, and all the more active opposition of its upper sections, cannot but have an influence on the section of intellectuals and the petty-bourgeoisie in the towns. Thus, the more definite and determined the policy of the proletariat in power becomes, the narrower and more shaky does the ground beneath its feet become.[38]

The solution for Trotsky, the way of ensuring that the Russian workers did not clash with their own peasantry, was to make sure that the Russian revolution coincided with a European revolution:

'left to its own resources, the working class of Russia will inevitably be crushed by the counter-revolution the moment the peasantry turns its back on it'.[39] For Lenin there was the back-up of an alliance with the poor peasantry if the European revolution failed; for Trotsky the Russian revolution was probably doomed if the European revolution did not begin soon. And so, the workers of Berlin and Vienna had to be given every opportunity to rise up before the Treaty of Brest-Litovsk was signed.

The Left SR Karelin had been part of the delegation sent to Brest and until the peace terms were known, the Bolsheviks and Left SRs acted pretty much in tandem. It is true that their stances differed on 11 January when the Bolshevik Central Committee opted for 'no peace, no war' and the Left SR Central Committee voted the same day for revolutionary war. However, a couple of days later, after a joint meeting of the two central committees, both parties agreed on the 'no peace, no war' formula. In this way, on 14 January 1918 the Bolsheviks and Left SRs could present the Third Congress of Soviets with an agreed joint resolution on the peace talks. Trotsky's decision to inform the Central Powers of the 'no peace, no war' stance was endorsed by both the Bolshevik and Left SR Central Committees the day after it was issued. Back in Petrograd, both Trotsky and Karelin reported to a joint session of the Bolshevik and Left SR groups in the Soviet Executive on 31 January; the following day they reported to a special session of the full Soviet Executive.[40]

During the evening and night of 18–19 February, Bolshevik and Left SR commissars met in more or less constant session to debate what should be done now that the German offensive had resumed. After bitter and acrimonious debates, first the Bolshevik Central Committee, then the Left SR Central Committee and finally the Soviet Government itself voted in favour of seeking Germany's terms; without consulting the Soviet Executive, Lenin contacted Berlin. Explaining Lenin's hasty decision to the Bolshevik and Left SR members of the Soviet Executive was felt to be so problematic that a plenary session of the Soviet Executive planned for the evening of 19 February was cancelled and a closed meeting of the Bolshevik and Left SR groups was held instead; this met all through the night but came to no conclusion. The following day the Bolshevik Petrograd City Party Conference called for the decision to sign the treaty to be revoked, and the Left SR Central Committee did the same, thus reversing its earlier decision.[41]

When the German terms were received, they were immediately discussed by the Bolshevik Central Committee on the afternoon of 23 February; Lenin made it clear he would resign if they were not accepted and the Central Committee decided to back him; during the course of the 23rd, news came in that the German Army had captured Pskov and military advisers predicted that the fall of Petrograd was inevitable in a few days' time.[42] A joint meeting of the Bolshevik and Left SR groups in the Soviet Executive began late on 23 February at which the Left SRs were united in their opposition to the German terms, while the Bolsheviks heard speeches both for and against; a separate meeting of the Bolshevik group agreed to back Lenin. Thus at 3.00 am on 24 February, the full Soviet Executive met, and Lenin spoke for the Bolsheviks in favour of accepting the terms offered by the Central Powers; Kamkov, speaking for the Left SRs, argued against. Shortly before the deadline set by the Germans expired, Lenin won his mandate. In the final voting, over 20 Left SRs in favour of an immediate peace abstained, while a significant number of Bolsheviks opposed to an immediate peace obeyed party discipline and backed Lenin.

The Treaty of Brest-Litovsk was signed on 3 March 1918, but it still needed to be ratified. Between 5 and 8 March the Seventh Bolshevik Party Congress voted to endorse the treaty, and on 15 March the Fourth Congress of Soviets met to ratify it. Before that congress opened, Bolshevik delegates met on 13 and 14 March and agreed that those Bolsheviks who still opposed the treaty, the so-called Left Communists, would abstain rather than vote against Lenin's peace proposals. Among Left SR delegates arriving for the congress, a clear majority accepted the need to oppose the peace treaty, but there was a great deal of disagreement about how best to do this. At the congress itself, Lenin spoke for ratification and Kamkov again spoke against, rejecting Lenin's idea that he was providing a 'breathing space' for the revolution and insisting that the treaty would in fact suffocate the revolution. Lenin and the ratifiers won the vote, but by the time the Soviet Government met for its first post-congress session, the Left SRs had decided on their response: they would resign as commissars and were joined by four Left Communists.[43] Fearing that Petrograd could yet be occupied by

German troops, Lenin's new purely Bolshevik Soviet Government moved from Petrograd to Moscow on the night of 10–11 March 1918.

A PARITY COALITION GOVERNMENT?

The signing of the Treaty of Brest-Litovsk and the resignation of the Left SR commissars did not end the relationship between the Bolshevik and Left SR parties. Lenin had talked at the Fourth Congress of Soviets of the Treaty of Brest-Litovsk offering a breathing space. During that breathing space it was assumed by most supporters of the treaty that, under the guidance of the new commissar of war, Trotsky, the Russian Army would be rebuilt and, at a suitable moment, the war against the Central Powers would resume. During the fighting of the second half of February the Red Army had briefly retaken Pskov; it had shown some military ability, and the Allied Military Missions were keen to encourage Trotsky in the notion that the breathing space might not last long; indeed Trotsky himself had predicted at the Seventh Congress of the Bolshevik Party that the breathing space would last for only two or three months. When the breathing space ended, massive Allied support would be available to the new Red Army.[44] In the meantime, Trotsky gave tacit support to irregular troops formed by the Left SRs which crossed the demarcation line to harry the German troops in the process of occupying Ukraine. Thus, throughout April, relations of a sort continued between the Bolsheviks and the Left SRs.[45]

Although the Left SRs had withdrawn from the government, they had remained in their posts at every other level of Soviet administration, including the Supreme Military Council and the Cheka. To many Left SRs this was a contradictory decision, one that they wanted to reopen when the party held its Second Congress from 17 to 25 April 1918. Indeed, led by Spridonova, there was much criticism of what seemed to be the rather quixotic decision of half-leaving and half-remaining in the Bolshevik administration. This feeling was so widespread that the party newspaper had to open a special 'discussion' section so the matter could be aired fully on its pages. Many delegates felt that the Bolsheviks and Left SRs had worked pretty well together, especially once Lenin had agreed

Fig. 14: Trotsky, after his appointed as military commissar in March 1918

to include them in his inner 'group of five'. The Second Left SR Congress sought to make clear that although the Left SR commissars had been withdrawn, the party 'had not set out on a path of direct struggle with the Bolsheviks' and would continue to be active within the Soviet administration, especially in 'local regional republics' like the Moscow Regional Government, a base from which they could challenge the authority of Lenin's Government.[46]

It was not until the end of the second week in May that Lenin, after a series of Central Committee meetings lasting several days, finally put an end to Trotsky's flirtation with the Allies and the notion that the Brest-Litovsk 'breathing space' would be a short-lived affair. On 15 May, the newly appointed German ambassador to Soviet Russia was presented with a proposed economic treaty crafted by Lenin; this offered major economic concessions to Germany in return for a commitment not to interfere in the economic affairs of the Soviet state and to recognise the nationalisation of the banks and foreign trade.[47] At the same time as extending the 'breathing space' offered by the Treaty of Brest-Litovsk into the indefinite future, Lenin drafted a new programme for socialist construction, one which his critics felt actually reinstated important aspects of capitalism: out went workers' control and in came one-man management; but more importantly for the Left SRs, out went a free market in grain and in came 'production brigades' empowered to seize grain from the peasants. This policy in particular put the Bolsheviks and Left SRs on a collision course.

On 9 May, Lenin's Government resolved that all grain, beyond the minimum for the coming year's sowing, had to be handed to the state at a fixed price in a valueless currency or else the peasant concerned would be declared an 'enemy of the people' and liable to ten years' imprisonment. When this proposal was discussed in the Soviet Executive, the Left SRs understandably opposed it, but could not prevent its imposition on 13 May.[48] Once it became clear that the production brigades established to forcibly purchase grain would get a hostile reception from the peasants, Lenin launched 'class war' in the countryside. On 8 June the Soviet Government called for the establishment of 'committees of the poor' to help the production brigades seize grain from rich peasant 'kulaks'. When this policy was endorsed by the Soviet Executive on 11 June, the Left SRs made clear that it was a policy which would not be implemented by the Peasant Section of the Soviet Executive and the levels of the Soviet administration which they still controlled.[49] In Lenin's view, he and the Bolsheviks were moving forward with the construction of socialism by rationalising economic management and controlling the supply of grain. Peasant and Left SR opposition was just the sort of 'swamping' of socialist initiatives he had feared. The Left SRs had drifted to the right, had become the mouthpiece of the rich 'kulak' peasant, while true 'poor' peasants had to be found in the new 'committees of the poor'.

Despite this major disagreement, the Left SRs did not break with the Bolsheviks. Indeed, as the country drifted towards civil war, they remained loyal. To the Right SRs and their supporters, May was the moment when dreams of the Treaty of Brest-Litovsk being just a 'breathing space' faded. During the last fortnight of May, the Mensheviks, Right SRs and Kadets all held party conferences which rejected the Treaty of Brest-Litovsk, while an SR appeal of 14 May called for an immediate armed uprising against the Bolsheviks. On 18 May some 400 Constituent Assembly deputies met together and condemned the treaty, declaring that the state of war with the Central Powers continued to be in place. The Allies, no longer in touch with Trotsky, turned instead to Kerensky's former minister of war, Savinkov, who promised to organise an insurrection in Yaroslavl when the British expeditionary force, once promised to Trotsky, arrived at Archangel. Early in June, the SR insurgents in Samara turned to another military unit which had once been destined for Trotsky's reconstituted and pro-Ally Red Army: the Czechoslovak Legion. Formed from Austro-Hungarian prisoners of war, it had been stationed on the South West Front near Kiev. With the signing of the Treaty of Brest-Litovsk, they had slowed the advance of the German forces into Ukraine, and then decided to leave Russia via the Trans-Siberian railway for France. As this massive regroupment began, the Allies had suggested that some at least of the Legion could remain in Russia to support Trotsky when he brought 'the breathing space' with Germany to an end. When Lenin put an end to Trotsky's talks with the Allies, Trotsky had no choice but to honour the request of the new German ambassador and disarm the departing Czechoslovaks; they refused to disarm, rebelled and in rebelling helped the Right SRs not only capture Samara but much of the Volga river basin. By early June the Soviet Government was mobilising to fight a civil war.[50]

Yet the Left SRs did not take up arms against the Bolsheviks in early June. Indeed, the man sent to lead the forces confronting the Czechoslovaks and Right SRs on the Volga was Muraviev, the Left SR commander who had defeated Krasnov at Pulkovo Hill at the end of October 1917. It was only at the end of June that the Left SRs' patience with their erstwhile Bolshevik allies ran out. One incident which prompted this change was the Bolshevik decision on 9 June to close down the Moscow Regional Government, which the Left SRs controlled and used to resist the 'committees of the poor'; the Left SRs protested at this arbitrary move at the Fifth Congress of Soviets of the Moscow Region on 27 June, but to no avail – for Lenin it was a classic example of pro-peasant attempts to 'swamp' his socialist programme.[51] However, the main reason why the Left SRs lost patience with Lenin at the end of June was what the Left SRs perceived as the ever-growing control of Germany over the life of Soviet Russia once the German ambassador had arrived in Moscow. On 24 June, the Left SR Central Committee met to decide how to respond and passed a resolution calling for an end to Lenin's 'breathing space' and the start of a campaign of terror against 'representatives of German imperialism'. The party recognised that this would lead to clashes with the Bolsheviks, but drew a distinction between Lenin's policy, which it opposed, and the policies of the Bolshevik Party, which it was willing to support. As Kamkov explained a few days later to the Third Left SR Congress, held from 29 June to 1 July, Lenin's desire for an economic treaty with Germany had turned Soviet Russia into 'a servant of German capitalism'.[52] The Left SRs argued at this congress that 'our aim is not to overthrow the Bolsheviks but the correct implementation of Soviet power'. However, the method they chose to 'correct' Soviet power – tearing up the Treaty of Brest-Litovsk and instigating a popular peasant uprising – was clearly targeted at the Bolsheviks. Confusingly and naively, the congress resolution hoped that the planned popular uprising against Lenin would result in the formation of a new Left SR–Bolshevik Coalition Government based on the principle of parity.[53]

At the time they took this decision, the Left SRs were still confident that they would win over 40 per cent of the delegates to the Fifth Congress of Soviets, which was scheduled to assemble at the beginning of July in order to adopt a new constitution. From such a base, the party hoped to win a vote overturning the Treaty of Brest-Litovsk, after which they would rejoin the Bolsheviks in government as an equal partner. For Lenin, parity of representation was anathema; the Bolsheviks had to lead socialist construction, so the elections to the Fifth Congress of Soviets had to be rigged. As its opening on 4 July approached, so the scale of Lenin's gerrymandering became clear: official figures gave the Bolsheviks 678 delegates and the Left SRs 269; the historian Alexander Rabinowitch has carefully recalculated these figures to reach the conclusion that the actual results were Bolsheviks 378, Left SRs 379, with 30 delegates going to the SR Maximalists, a small SR splinter group in the process of merging with the Left SRs.[54] As more and more Left SR delegates were ruled ineligible, and more and more representatives of the 'committees of the poor' were allowed to attend, the Left SRs realised that the Bolsheviks had deprived them of a slim congress majority and allocated them less than a third of the seats.[55] Opening the congress, with characteristic bravado, Trotsky led the attack on the Left SRs. He now declared that any group which opposed German actions on the Russia–Ukraine border without government authorisation would in future be shot on sight, a far cry from his attitude in April. When the Left SR Central Committee met on the night of 4–5 July, it decided that a dramatic response to Trotsky's speech was essential and voted in favour of assassinating the German ambassador. When, on 5 July, Lenin also used his congress speech to attack the Left SRs, the party put down a resolution asserting that Lenin's Russia had become 'a colony of German imperialism', then, declaring the need for 'an uprising of all labourers', they walked out of the congress and staged a protest rally carrying slogans like 'Down with the imperialists and conciliators!'. The next day, two Left SR assassins succeeded in killing the German ambassador.[56] Lenin felt he had ample grounds to exclude the Left SRs from the soviets and end their political influence once and for all.

THE DRIFT TO CIVIL WAR

The Left SR uprising had no real planning, and the attempt to seize control of Moscow was put down within 24 hours. Although the Left SR sailors of the so-called Popov Brigade had 200 men with 8 heavy guns, 48 machine guns and 4 armoured cars and outnumbered the forces loyal to Lenin, ultimately they were no match for the heavy artillery deployed against them.[57] On the River Volga, Muraviev supported the Left SR action, abandoned the Bolsheviks and declared the formation of a Volga Soviet Republic which was at war with Germany. Although loyal Bolsheviks soon gunned him down, this dislocation of the Volga front led to the fall of Kazan on 7 August to forces loyal to the Right SRs.[58] As Trotsky put it, in August 1918 Bolshevik power hung by a thread.[59] Lenin's Government survived with German support. The US ambassador described Moscow in August as 'a German occupied zone' and denounced the secret agreement to allow un-uniformed German soldiers to guard their embassy.[60] The trade treaty signed with Germany on 27 August allowed troops on the demarcation line to be stood down and transferred to the Volga; Trotsky's counter-offensive retook Kazan on 7 September and the Bolsheviks lived to fight another day.[61]

German support was not the only explanation for the survival of Lenin's Government through August 1918. During the bitter debates in November 1917 about the formation of a purely Bolshevik Government, Lenin's critics, the Bolshevik 'minority', made clear that when the Bolsheviks ruled alone they had no choice but to resort to terror. And terror began in earnest once the Left SRs had broken with the Bolsheviks. As soon as Kazan fell, Lenin feared that a counter-revolutionary insurrection might be about to break out in Nizhnii Novgorod; if that Volga city fell so quickly after the loss of Kazan, the road to Moscow would be open. So Lenin made it clear on 9 August that '[in Nizhnii Novgorod] it is necessary to use all force, to set up a troika of dictatorship, to institute mass terror, to shoot and deport hundreds of prostitutes who get the soldiers drunk, former officers etc. There is not a minute to waste.' Determined action was required, 'mass searches' were needed, it was necessary to 'shoot for the holding of weapons'; in addition the 'mass deportations of Mensheviks and unreliables' should begin.[62] Terror and civil war formed the crucible in which the Soviet Union was forged over the subsequent two years, and arbitrary rule would characterise the Soviet state for the next 70 years.

CONCLUSION

If in October 1905 the Tsar had responded to the popular unrest he faced by offering a genuine constitution, the fate of Russia might have been very different. That the Tsar responded with a half-constitution, conceding the bare minimum to retain his authority and excluding the great mass of workers and peasants from genuine representation in the affairs of state, meant that a second revolution in 1917 was inevitable. This Short History of the Russian Revolution has shown that it was equally inevitable that the revolutionary wing of the Russian Social Democrats, the Bolsheviks, would play a crucial role in that second revolution. The years 1905–17 did not see a flowering of constitutional Russia. At the time of the October general strike in 1905, liberals rushed to accept whatever the Tsar offered them, and right up to the very eve of the Tsar's overthrow, reaching an understanding with the Tsar seemed more important to most liberals than taking determined action to end his reign. In these circumstances, there was no flowering of reformist trade unionism among Russian workers as historians once suggested; the years between 1905 and 1917 were in fact a period of intense labour confrontation in which the revolutionary tradition of Russian labour became firmly established. When the Tsar was overthrown by working-class action in February 1917, the potential for Bolshevik power was already there.

That did not mean that a second Bolshevik-led revolution was inevitable in 1917. In the days immediately after the overthrow of the Tsar a system of 'dual power' was unavoidable. The Provisional Government, with its origins in the Provisional Committee of the State Duma, had no serious working-class representation to call on and had to look outside the Duma if the working-class masses who had overthrown the Tsar were to be controlled. The Petrograd Soviet offered just such an opening to the masses, and its reformist leaders were only too willing to co-operate. As the Liaison Committee and then the First Coalition Government showed, when liberals and reformist socialists were determined to work together, they could; dual power did not inevitably mean going in separate directions. The First Coalition Government nearly worked. It was based on the principle of mutual concessions, a process made easier by the reformist socialists accepting that it was the historic mission of the liberals to rule as a new democratic Russia emerged from the old autocracy; the reformist socialists just had to moderate any capitalist extremes, so their interventions in government could be modest. More importantly, however, the First Coalition was held together by a shared commitment to victory in World War I. Tsereteli got a grip on the Soviet, Kerensky wooed the rank-and-file soldier, and a successful offensive looked to be in the Coalition's grasp – if that offensive had resulted in the defeat of the Central Powers within two months, as its planners hoped, the Bolsheviks would have remained a troublesome force, but a minority one as the July Days showed.

When explaining his April Theses to a sometimes sceptical Bolshevik Party, Lenin called for its members to undertake 'systematic and patient explanation' in the soviets in order to win a majority for the party's point of view. This his comrades did. They worked in the factory committees, they worked among women, they worked among Red Guards, they worked among soldiers, and by the time the First Coalition Government collapsed at the beginning of July, they had already won the support of the Workers' Section of the Petrograd Soviet. What the July Days showed was that, despite the efforts of the Bolshevik Military Organisation among garrison troops and at the Kronstadt naval base, not enough 'systematic and patient explanation' had been done among the soldiers. Had the Bolsheviks made a determined attempt to seize power in July, they would have been crushed by Tsereteli and Kerensky. Lenin realised this and at the last minute reined in those calling for immediate action.

What enabled the Bolshevik work of 'systematic and patient explanation' among the soldiers to succeed was the attempted military coup by Kornilov. By establishing the Second Coalition Government as his personal regime, Kerensky had distanced himself from the Soviet and those like Tsereteli who insisted the Soviet should still be represented in government. Kerensky without Tsereteli was only half the show. Kerensky was distancing himself from the Soviet, but how far from the Soviet would he go? Did his desire for more authoritative government mean looking to the support of the army? In the shadow boxing which developed between Kerensky and Kornilov, both seemed to think they could manipulate each other. Kerensky wanted Kornilov's support in a definitive crackdown on the Bolsheviks, while Kornilov wanted, despite much hesitation, to follow up such action with the establishment of a military dictatorship. Kornilov's coup was prevented by mobilising the same masses who had overthrown the Tsar in February, and soldiers played a key role in this process. Immediately after Kornilov's defeat, the Soldiers' Section of the Petrograd Soviet voted for a Soviet Government, enabling the full Petrograd Soviet to do the same.

By September, 'systematic and patient explanation' had worked: the Bolsheviks had the support of the Soviet, and power was theirs for the taking. But how should the transfer of power be achieved? For Lenin it was essential for the Bolshevik Party to seize power at once. Not all his Bolshevik comrades agreed. Some, like Trotsky, argued that a Bolshevik assumption of power had to be linked to the Second Congress of Soviets when it met in October; others, like Kamenev and Zinoviev, argued that a seizure of power was unnecessary and dangerous since the Second Congress of Soviets would anyway establish a Soviet Government by democratic means. It was Kerensky who ended this Bolshevik disagreement on tactics when he tried to enforce the redeployment of troops from the Petrograd garrison to the front. This provided a crisis of authority between the government and the Soviet which enabled the Bolsheviks to assume power on the back of popular action as Trotsky had hoped. When Kerensky closed the Bolshevik press and arrested Soviet commissars on the morning of 24 October, insurrection began of its own momentum as the traditions of the Russian Revolution reasserted themselves.

In his April Theses, Lenin had explained that he saw revolutionary Russia starting out on a new socialist path and for this to happen a government had to be formed which represented the 'democratic dictatorship of the proletariat and poorest peasantry'. Here the key word was 'poorest'. The SRs, not even the emerging Left SRs, did not divide the peasantry into rich and poor; in their view, with a very few exceptions, all peasants faced the same issue of land shortage and so could not be divided on class lines. Lenin, like all Marxists, feared the 'petty bourgeois mentality' of the peasant, and felt the Bolsheviks had to control who would represent the peasant in the new Soviet Government. So, for the first ten days of the existence of the Soviet Government, the Bolsheviks were torn apart by a second row: whether or not to agree to take part in a coalition socialist government, a Soviet Government comprised of all the parties in the Soviet. Lenin used the Bolshevik tradition of party discipline, and the exercise of its supposed leading role over the working class, to ensure that a Soviet Government was only formed on his terms.

When a 'democratic dictatorship of the proletariat and poor peasantry' was finally formed in the shape of a Bolshevik–Left SR Coalition Government, the Left SRs had hoped that it would be based on the principle of parity, but the way the elections transpired, the Bolsheviks controlled a majority of the commissariats. This coalition worked well enough. It could do little about the collapse of the industrial economy, but it came up with agreed policies on land reform and how to respond to the election results from the Constituent Assembly. Where it did disagree – on the use of arbitrary powers – the Left SRs felt they were able to moderate the Bolsheviks' more extreme actions. What wrecked the Bolshevik–Left SR Coalition was the question of peace with the Central Powers. The Left SRs could not accept Lenin's decision to sign the Treaty of Brest-Litovsk in March 1918.

Even after the Left SRs had left government, however, they were able to limit Lenin's ambitions by remaining involved in every other level of soviet administration. Although Lenin could pass decrees establishing 'production brigades' and 'committees of the poor' to implement 'class war in the countryside', the impact of these decrees was not felt in the many parts of the country where the soviets were in Left SR hands, or where, like the Moscow Region, they had a strong presence. The Left SRs hoped to outmanoeuvre Lenin by winning a majority at the Fifth Congress of Soviets at the start of July 1918, after which they would tear up the Treaty of Brest-Litovsk and establish a new Left SR–Bolshevik Coalition based on the principle of parity, with or without Lenin. For Lenin, parity meant swamping, and so a massive campaign of gerrymandering was undertaken to deprive the Left SRs of their electoral victory. Lenin preferred to define the interests of the 'poorest' peasantry himself, rather than to let the Left SRs do it for him. When the Left SRs responded to Lenin's electoral fraud with ill-thought-through calls for a popular uprising, Lenin had the justification he needed to exclude them from the soviets so that the Bolsheviks could rule alone.

Concluding the introduction to this Short History, mention was made of Gorbachev's view that the February Revolution should have been allowed to 'continue its course'. The efforts to derail the revolution from its course were all associated with Lenin. The first attempt came when Lenin argued for the Bolsheviks to seize power before the Second Congress of Soviets. His second attempt was made when he used the concept of party discipline to wreck the attempt to establish the Soviet Government as a coalition of socialist parties. Despite these interventions, it was a socialist coalition of Bolsheviks and Left SRs which set about implementing the revolutionary slogans of 'Bread, Peace and Land'. It was when Lenin decided in May 1918 that the Brest-Litovsk 'breathing space' was not a forced and temporary step backwards but a permanent feature of Soviet policy that the Left SRs deserted him. So what finally prevented the February Revolution from 'continuing its course' was Lenin's electoral fraud of July 1918.

Counter-factual history is an imprecise art, but if Lenin had been defeated at the Fifth Congress of Soviets, the future can be surmised. The Left SRs assumed that there would be sufficient Bolsheviks, mostly Left Communists, who would join them in a parity based coalition without Lenin. When in 1938 Stalin staged a show trial of the former Left Communist Nikolai Bukharin, surviving Left SRs leaders like Kamkov were brought from their prison cells to give detailed 'evidence' of how this government was to be established. How would the Left SR–Bolshevik Government have faired? Fighting would have resumed on the Eastern Front of World War I, and in the course of it the German Army might well have succeeded in seizing control of Moscow. In the short term the prospects for this Soviet Government would certainly have been difficult, yet, it is arguable at least that as the fighting of World War I resumed, so Russia's nascent civil war would have been called off, with the Right SRs ending their insurrection and the Czechoslovak Legion resuming talks with the Soviet authorities. Resuming the fighting on the Eastern Front was bound to be a gamble, but the position of the Allies on the

Western Front was stronger in summer 1918 than it had been in the spring. Indeed, less than a fortnight after the assassination of the German ambassador, the final 'one hundred day' offensive began on the Western Front which was to lead to Allied victory. The Left SR–Bolshevik coalition might not have lost control of Moscow for long since, as General Haig launched the final onslaught in the West, German troops were pulled out of the East and engaging them would not have been the challenge which Lenin feared. A Left SR–Bolshevik Government just might have survived and spared Russia its civil war.

Lenin, however, was not sad to see the back of the Left SRs, even if civil war and terror were the way forward. He did not like the risks offered by democratic politics. He wanted to boycott the Pre-parliament, he wanted to seize power before the Second Congress of Soviets, he insisted on curtailing the activities of the Constituent Assembly and ended moves to turn it into a Revolutionary Convention. For all his theoretical conviction that Russia needed a government of 'the proletariat and poorest peasantry' to advance towards socialism, his true conviction came out during the Vikzhel talks when he asserted on 2 November that 'there can be no repudiation of the purely Bolshevik Government without betraying the slogan of Soviet Power'. Under Lenin, the Bolsheviks were determined to continue to rule alone and would do so until Gorbachev introduced an element of democracy to the soviet electoral system in 1989, prompting the collapse of the Soviet Union two years later. Russia's popular masses wanted a socialist revolution, but because of what Lozovsky described as 'incomprehensible manoeuvres' by Lenin, ended up with a Bolshevik dictatorship.

Further Reading

A CLASSIC STUDY

Keep, J. L. H., *The Russian Revolution: A Study in Mass Mobilisation* (London: Weidenfeld and Nicolson, 1976).

OTHER SHORT HISTORIES

Read, C. J., *From Tsar to Soviets: The Russian People and their Revolution, 1917–21* (London: UCL Press, 1996).
Smith, S. A., *The Russian Revolution: A Very Short Introduction* (Oxford: Oxford University Press, 2002).
Wade, R. A., *The Russian Revolution, 1917* (Cambridge: Cambridge University Press, 2000).

THE 1905 REVOLUTION

Ascher, A., *The Revolution of 1905* (Stanford, CA: Stanford University Press, 1988 & 1992).
Surh, G. D., *1905 in St. Petersburg: Labor, Society and Revolution* (Stanford, CA: Stanford University Press, 1989).

BETWEEN THE REVOLUTIONS

Levin, A., *The Second Duma* (New Haven, CT: Yale University Press, 1940).
McKean, R. B., *St. Petersburg between the Revolutions* (New Haven, CT: Yale University Press, 1990).

Melancon, M., *The Socialist Revolutionaries and the Russian Anti-War Movement 1914–1917* (Columbus: Ohio State University Press, 1990).

Siegelbaum, L. H., *The Politics of Industrial Mobilisation in Russia, 1914–17* (Basingstoke: Macmillan, 1983).

Swain, G. R., *Russian Social Democracy and the Legal Labour Movement, 1906–14* (Basingstoke: Macmillan, 1983).

THE FEBRUARY REVOLUTION TO APRIL DAYS

Hasegawa, T., *The February Revolution: Petrograd 1917* (Seattle: University of Washington Press, 1981).

Pearson, R., *The Russian Moderates and the Crisis of Tsardom, 1914–1917* (Basingstoke: Macmillan, 1977).

Rosenberg, W. G., *Liberals in the Russian Revolution: The Constitutional Democratic Party, 1917–1921* (Princeton, NJ: Princeton University Press, 1974).

Swain, G. R., *The Origins of the Russian Civil War* (Harlow: Longman, 1996).

JULY TO OCTOBER

Gill, G. J., *Peasants and Government in the Russian Revolution* (Basingstoke: Macmillan, 1979).

Rabinowitch, A., *Prelude to Revolution: The Petrograd Bolsheviks and the July 1917 Uprising* (Bloomington: Indiana University Press, 1968).

—— *The Bolsheviks Come to Power: The Revolution of 1917 in Petrograd* (New York: Norton and Co., 1976).

Smith, S. A., *Red Petrograd: Revolution in the Factories, 1917–18* (Cambridge: Cambridge University Press, 1983).

Swain, G. R., *The Origins of the Russian Civil War* (Harlow: Longman, 1996).

Wade, R. A., *Red Guards and Workers' Militias in the Russian Revolution* (Stanford, CA: Stanford University Press, 1984).

Wildman, A. K., *The End of the Imperial Russian Army* (Princeton, NJ: Princeton University Press, 1980 & 1987).

AFTER OCTOBER

Brovkin, V. N., *The Mensheviks after October: Socialist Opposition and the Rise of the Bolshevik Dictatorship* (Ithaca, NY: Cornell University Press, 1987).

Rabinowitch, A., *The Bolsheviks in Power: The First Year of Soviet Rule in Petrograd* (Bloomington: Indiana University Press, 2007).

Radkey, O. H., *Russia Goes to the Polls* (Ithaca, NY: Cornell University Press, 1977).

Swain, G. R., *The Origins of the Russian Civil War* (Harlow: Longman, 1996).

BIOGRAPHIES AND AUTOBIOGRAPHIES

Abraham, R., *Alexander Kerensky: The First Love of the Revolution* (London: Sidgwick and Jackson, 1987).

Allen, B. C., *Alexander Shlyapnikov, 1885–1937: Life of an Old Bolshevik* (Leiden: Brill, 2015).

Mstislavskii, S., *Five Days Which Transformed Russia* (London: Hutchinson, 1988).

Poole, D-W. C., *An American Diplomat in Bolshevik Russia* (Madison: University of Wisconsin Press, 2014).

Price, M. P., *Dispatches from the Revolution: Russia 1916–18* (London: Pluto Press, 1997).

Read, C. J., *Lenin: A Revolutionary Life* (London: Routledge, 2005).

Roobol, W. H., *Tsereteli – a Democrat in the Russian Revolution* (The Hague: Martinus Nijhoff, 1976).

Sukhanov, N. N., *The Russian Revolution, 1917: A Personal Record* (Princeton, NJ: Princeton University Press, 1984).

Swain, G. R., *Trotsky* (Harlow: Pearson-Longman, 2006).

DOCUMENTS

The Bolsheviks and the October Revolution: Central Committee Minutes of the Russian Social Democratic Labour Party (Bolsheviks), August 1917–February 1918 (London: Pluto Press, 1974).

Browder, R. P. and A. F. Kerensky, *The Russian Provisional Government, 1917: Documents*, 3 vols (Stanford, CA: Stanford University Press, 1961).

Bunyan, J. and H. H. Fisher, *The Bolshevik Revolution: Documents and Materials* (Stanford, CA: Stanford University Press, 1961).

Keep, J. L. H., *The Debate on Soviet Power: Minutes of the All-Russian Central Executive Committee of Soviets* (Oxford: Oxford University Press, 1979).

Notes

Introduction

1   The dates referred to in this book use the old Russian calendar, which was 13 days behind the calendar used in the rest of Europe, until 14 February 1918 when the two calendars were aligned.

2   *Times Literary Supplement*, 6 November 1992.

3   S. A. Smith, *Red Petrograd: Revolution in the Factories 1917–18* (Cambridge: Cambridge University Press, 1983); W. G. Rosenberg, 'Russian Labor and Bolshevik Power after October', *Slavic Review* 44/2 (1985), pp. 213–38; R. A. Wade, *Red Guards and Workers' Militias in the Russian Revolution* (Stanford, CA: Stanford University Press, 1984); A. K. Wildman, *The End of the Russian Imperial Army*, 2 vols (Princeton, NJ: Princeton University Press, 1980, 1987); G. J. Gill, *Peasants and Government in the Russian Revolution* (Basingstoke: Macmillan, 1979); M. Donald, 'Bolshevik Activity amongst the Working Women of Petrograd in 1917', *International Review of Social History* 27 (1982), pp. 129–60; and S. Badcock, 'Women, Protest, and Revolution: Soldiers' Wives in Russia During 1917', *International Review of Social History* 49 (2004), pp. 47–70.

4   L. Schapiro, *The Communist Party of the Soviet Union* (Oxford: Oxford University Press, 1963).

5   *Clive Anderson Talks Back*, BBC 1, 3 November 1996.

Chapter 1: The Revolutionary Tradition of Russian Labour

1   S. Harcave, *The Russian Revolution of 1905* (London: Collier-Macmillan, 1964), pp. 93, 285.

2   G. D. Surh, *1905 in St. Petersburg: Labor, Society and Revolution* (Stanford, CA: Stanford University Press, 1989), pp. 139, 167.

3   Ibid., p. 214.
4   U. A. Shuster, *Peterburgskie rabochie v 1905–1907 gg.* (Leningrad: Nauka, 1976), p. 117.
5   Surh, *1905*, p. 300.
6   Shuster, *Peterburgskie*, p. 153.
7   *Polnoe sobranie zakonov Rossiiskoi Imperii*, 3rd series, XXV/I, no. 26803 (2010).
8   G. Swain, *Trotsky* (Harlow: Longman, 2006), pp. 24–6.
9   G. Swain, *Russian Social Democracy and the Legal Labour Movement, 1906–14* (Basingstoke: Macmillan, 1983), p. 3.
10   A. Levin, *The Second Duma* (New Haven, CT: Yale University Press, 1940), pp. 74–9.
11   Ibid., p. 227.
12   M. Pavlov, *Dumskaya taktika Bolshevikov v revolyutsii 1905–07 gg.* (Moscow: Gosizdat, 1940), p. 222.
13   Ibid., p. 217; Levin, *Second*, p. 188.
14   Levin, *Second*, pp. 106, 144–7, 178, 188.
15   Ibid., p. 230.
16   Ibid., p. 340.
17   Swain, *Legal*, p. 31.
18   Ibid., p. 25.
19   Ibid., p. 67.
20   Ibid., p. 122.
21   L. Haimson, 'The Problem of Social Stability in Urban Russia, 1905–1917', in C. Emsley (ed.), *Conflict and Stability in Europe* (London: Croom Helm, 1979), p. 245.
22   Swain, *Legal*, pp. 151, 172–3.
23   Haimson, 'The Problem', pp. 238–9.
24   Swain, *Legal*, pp. 173–6.
25   M. Melancon, *The Socialist Revolutionaries and the Russian Anti-War Movement 1914–1917* (Columbus: Ohio State University Press, 1990), p. 89.
26   L. H. Siegelbaum, *The Politics of Industrial Mobilisation in Russia, 1914–17* (Basingstoke: Macmillan, 1983), p. 163.
27   Melancon, *Socialist Revolutionaries*, p. 93.
28   Siegelbaum, *Politics*, p. 164.
29   Melancon, *Socialist Revolutionaries*, pp. 93–5; Siegelbaum, *Politics*, p. 166. For Bagdatiev's past career, see Swain, *Legal*.
30   Melancon, *Socialist Revolutionaries*, p. 96.
31   Siegelbaum, *Politics*, p. 167.
32   R. B. McKean, *St. Petersburg between the Revolutions* (New Haven, CT: Yale University Press, 1990), p. 402, p. 558 (note 134).
33   Derived from Table 10 in S. A. Smith, *Red Petrograd: Revolution in the Factories 1917–1918* (Cambridge: Cambridge University Press, 1983), p. 50.

Chapter 2: The Provisional Government

1   M. Hughes, '"Revolution was in the Air": British Officials in Russia during the First World War', *Journal of Contemporary History* 31 (1996), p. 93.
2   R. Pearson, *The Russian Moderates and the Crisis of Tsardom, 1914–1917* (Basingstoke: Macmillan, 1977), p. 44.
3   Ibid., pp. 60, 91, 94.
4   Ibid., pp. 105, 108, 112.
5   Ibid., p. 117.
6   T. Fallows, 'Politics and the War Effort in Russia: The Union of Zemstvos and the Organisation of the Food Supply, 1914–16', *Slavic Review* 37 (1978), p. 85.
7   G. Katkov, *Russia 1917: The February Revolution* (London: Collins, 1969), p. 115.
8   Pearson, *Russian Moderates* p. 125.
9   Katkov, *1917*, pp. 11, 39, 173–5, 181.
10 Pearson, *Russian Moderates*, pp. 128, 136–40.
11 For 'bread and herring', see M. Donald, 'Bolshevik Activity amongst the Working Women of Petrograd in 1917', *International Review of Social History* 27 (1982), p. 132. For discussion of the food supply, see R. P. Browder and A. F. Kerensky, *The Russian Provisional Government, 1917: Documents* (Stanford, CA: Stanford University Press, 1961), vol. 1, pp. 27–9.
12 Pearson, *Russian Moderates*, pp. 109, 124.
13 Browder and Kerensky, *Provisional Government*, vol. 1, p. 26.
14 S. A. Smith, *Red Petrograd: Revolution in the Factories 1917–1918* (Cambridge: Cambridge University Press, 1983), p. 52.
15 N. N. Sukhanov, *The Russian Revolution, 1917: A Personal Record* (Princeton, NJ: Princeton University Press, 1984), p. 5.
16 Browder and Kerensky, *Provisional Government*, vol. 1, p. 27.
17 Sukhanov, *1917*, p. 6.
18 Ibid., pp. 16, 25, 28.
19 Ibid., pp. 34, 45.
20 For the arrests, see Sukhanov, *1917*, pp. 51 and 57; otherwise this summary is from Pearson, *Russian Moderates*, pp. 154–73.
21 T. Hasegawa, 'The Bolsheviks and the Formation of the Petrograd Soviet in the February Revolution', *Soviet Studies* 29/1 (1977), pp. 89, 94, 99.
22 Ibid., p. 104.
23 T. Hasegawa, 'The Problem of Power in the February Revolution of 1917 in Russia', *Canadian Slavonic Papers* 14 (1972), pp. 614–15, 621.
24 D. A. Longley, 'The Divisions in the Bolshevik Party in March 1917', *Soviet Studies* 24 (1972), p. 63.
25 Sukhanov, *1917*, pp. 68, 71.
26 Hasegawa, 'Power', p. 625.
27 Ibid., pp. 620–1.
28 Sukhanov, *1917*, p. 8.
29 Hasegawa, 'Power', p. 615.

30 E. Acton and T. Stableford (eds), *The Soviet Union: A Documentary History*, vol. 1 (Exeter: University of Exeter Press, 2005), pp. 10–11.

31 Hasegawa, 'Power', p. 626.

32 Sukhanov, *1917*, pp. 84, 86.

33 For the Imperial coats of arms, see the extracts from the diary of M. M. Prishvin in Acton and Stableford, *The Soviet Union: A Documentary History*, p. 6. For the readings in schools, I am grateful to Elizabeth White for this information; she has consulted the recorded memories of émigré children cared for by the *Zemgor* organisation in the 1920s.

34 L. H. Edmondson, *Feminism in Russia, 1900–17* (Stanford, CA: Stanford University Press, 1984), pp. 165–6; L. Schapiro, *1917: The Russian Revolutions and the Origins of Present Day Communism* (Hounslow: Maurice Temple Smith, 1984), p. 61; L. Schapiro, 'The Political Thought of the First Provisional Government', in R. Pipes (ed.), *Revolutionary Russia* (Oxford: Oxford University Press, 1968), p. 108.

35 I. D. Thatcher, 'Scripting the Russian Revolution', in K. Baker and D. Edelstein (eds), *Scripting the Revolution: A Historical approach to the Comparative Study of Revolutions* (Stanford, CA: Stanford University Press, 2015), p. 216.

36 Ibid.

37 Ibid.

38 W. G. Rosenberg, *Liberals in the Russian Revolution: The Constitutional Democratic Party, 1917–1921* (Princeton, NJ: Princeton University Press, 1974), p. 90.

39 Sukhanov, *1917*, pp. 44, 165, 191, 200.

40 Ibid., p. 211.

41 Browder and Kerensky, *Provisional Government*, vol. 2, pp. 878–80.

42 Sukhanov, *1917*, pp. 204, 223, 227.

43 Ibid., pp. 216–17, 220.

44 Ibid., pp. 233–4, 239, 294.

45 Ibid.

46 F. King, *The Narodniks in the Russian Revolution* (London: Socialist History Society, 2007), p. 27.

47 Sukhanov, *1917*, p. 245.

48 Ibid., pp. 246–53.

49 W. H. Roobol, *Tsereteli: A Democrat in the Russian Revolution* (The Hague: Martinus Nijhoff, 1976), p. 99.

50 Sukhanov, *1917*, pp. 253, 264.

51 Ibid., p. 294, 299, 310, 314.

52 Browder and Kerensky, *Provisional Government*, vol. 2, p. 1098.

53 G. R. Swain, *The Origins of the Russian Civil War* (Harlow: Longman, 1996), p. 16.

54 Rosenberg, *Liberals*, p. 108.

55 Swain, *Origins*, pp. 17–18.

56 Browder and Kerensky, *Provisional Government*, vol. 2, pp. 1069–70.

57 Schapiro, 'Political Thought', pp. 98, 101.

58 Roobol, *Tsereteli*, p. 117.

Chapter 3: The Success of Coalition

1   W. H. Roobol, *Tsereteli: A Democrat in the Russian Revolution* (The Hague: Martinus Nijhoff, 1976), p. 120.
2   W. G. Rosenberg, *Liberals in the Russian Revolution: The Constitutional Democratic Party, 1917–1921* (Princeton, NJ: Princeton University Press, 1974), pp. 122, 154.
3   Roobol, *Tsereteli*, p. 103.
4   J. L. H. Keep, *The Russian Revolution: A Study in Mass Mobilisation* (London: Weidenfeld and Nicolson, 1976), p. 144.
5   Roobol, *Tsereteli*, p. 127.
6   Rosenberg, *Liberals*, p. 152.
7   Roobol, *Tsereteli*, pp. 132ff.
8   N. N. Sukhanov, *The Russian Revolution, 1917: A Personal Record* (Princeton, NJ: Princeton University Press, 1984), p. 361.
9   Roobol, *Tsereteli*, p. 138.
10 R. P. Browder and A. F. Kerensky, *The Russian Provisional Government, 1917: Documents* (Stanford, CA: Stanford University Press, 1961), vol. 2, p. 876.
11 R. Abraham, *Alexander Kerensky: The First Love of the Revolution* (London: Sidgwick and Jackson, 1987), p. 196.
12 B. I. Kolonitskii, 'Nastuplenie Kerenskogo', paper given to the Conference of the Study Group on the Russian Revolution, 7–9 January 2016.
13 Abraham, *Kerensky*, p. 200.
14 Kolonitskii, 'Nastuplenie'.
15 Abraham, *Kerensky*, pp. 196, 199, 203, 215.
16 Ibid., pp. 208–9.
17 Kolonitskii, 'Nastuplenie'.
18 Abraham, *Kerensky*, pp. 217–18.
19 Kolonitskii, 'Nastuplenie'.
20 D. A. Longley, 'The Divisions in the Bolshevik Party in March 1917', *Soviet Studies* 24 (1972), p. 63.
21 Ibid., pp. 66–8.
22 Ibid., pp. 69–75.
23 J. Frankel, 'Lenin's Doctrinal Revolution of April 1917', *Journal of Contemporary History* 4/2 (1969), p. 122.
24 Ibid., pp. 129–30.
25 V. I. Lenin, *Selected Works in Three Volumes*, vol. 2 (Moscow: Progress, 1970), p. 44.
26 Frankel, 'Doctrinal Revolution', p. 131.
27 Longley, 'Divisions', p. 66.
28 C. J. Read, *Lenin: A Revolutionary Life* (London: Routledge, 2005), p. 154.
29 G. Sokolnikov, 'How Should the History of October be Treated?', *International Press Correspondence*, 11 December 1924.
30 Sukhanov, *1917*, p. 324.
31 Browder and Kerensky, *Provisional Government*, vol. 2, p. 721.

32   Sukhanov, *1917*, p. 372.
33   Read, *Lenin*, p. 154.
34   A. Rabinowitch, *Prelude to Revolution: The Petrograd Bolsheviks and the July 1917 Uprising* (Bloomington: Indiana University Press, 1968), p. 231.
35   Sukhanov, *1917*, p. 372.
36   Personal communication from Professor Vitalijs Šalda of Daugavpils University, Latvia, 28 January 2016.
37   Rabinowitch, *Prelude*, p. 53.
38   Ibid.
39   Sukhanov, *1917*, pp. 359, 372.
40   Rabinowitch, *Prelude*, pp. 56–60, 67–72.
41   Read, *Lenin*, p. 156; Rabinowitch, *Prelude*, pp. 76–80, 232.
42   Read, *Lenin*, p. 156.
43   Rabinowitch, *Prelude*, p. 147; Roobol, *Tsereteli*, pp. 142ff.
44   Sukhanov, *1917*, p. 416.
45   Rabinowitch, *Prelude*, p. 131.
46   Ibid., p. 139.
47   Abraham, *Kerensky*, p. 207.

Chapter 4: The Failure of Coalition

1   A. Rabinowitch, *Prelude to Revolution: The Petrograd Bolsheviks and the July 1917 Uprising* (Bloomington: Indiana University Press, 1968), p. 151.
2   N. N. Sukhanov, *The Russian Revolution, 1917: A Personal Record* (Princeton, NJ: Princeton University Press, 1984), pp. 429–31.
3   I. Deutscher, *Stalin* (London: Penguin Books, 1966), p. 156.
4   Rabinowitch, *Prelude*, pp. 162–4, 172–5; the appeal of 4 July is reproduced in E. Acton and T. Stableford (eds), *The Soviet Union: A Documentary History*, vol. 1 (Exeter: University of Exeter Press, 2005), p. 24.
5   Rabinowitch, *Prelude*, pp. 182–6. For the casualties, see Sukhanov, *1917*, p. 452.
6   G. Swain, *Trotsky* (Harlow: Pearson Education, 2006), p. 63.
7   Rabinowitch, *Prelude*, p. 184.
8   R. Abraham, *Alexander Kerensky: The First Love of the Revolution* (London: Sidgwick and Jackson, 1987), p. 220.
9   Sukhanov, *1917*, pp. 454, 463.
10   W. H. Roobol, *Tsereteli – a Democrat in the Russian Revolution* (The Hague: Martinus Nijhoff, 1976), p. 154.
11   R. P. Browder and A. F. Kerensky, *The Russian Provisional Government, 1917: Documents* (Stanford, CA: Stanford University Press, 1961), vol. 3, p. 1259.
12   J. White, 'The Kornilov Affair: A Study in Counter-revolution', *Soviet Studies* 20 (1968), p. 196.

13 Abraham, *Kerensky*, p. 239.
14 Roobol, *Tsereteli*, p. 160.
15 W. G. Rosenberg, *Liberals in the Russian Revolution: The Constitutional Democratic Party, 1917–1921* (Princeton, NJ: Princeton University Press, 1974), pp. 185–90.
16 White, 'Kornilov', pp. 189–97.
17 Ibid., pp. 187–8, 194.
18 Browder and Kerensky, *Provisional Government*, vol. 3, pp. 1550, 1546.
19 White, 'Korniov', p. 189.
20 Ibid., p. 199.
21 G. R. Swain, *The Origins of the Russian Civil War* (Harlow: Longman, 1996), p. 25.
22 Browder and Kerensky, *Provisional Government*, vol. 3, pp. 1547–8.
23 Ibid., pp. 1220, 1451.
24 Abraham, *Kerensky*, p. 260.
25 Swain, *Origins*, pp. 27, 31; White, 'Kornilov', p. 201.
26 Browder and Kerensky, *Provisional Government*, vol. 3, pp. 1551–68.
27 Ibid., pp. 1571–2.
28 Sukhanov, *1917*, p. 511.
29 Swain, *Origins*, p. 37.
30 Browder and Kerensky, *Provisional Government*, vol. 3, p. 1571.
31 Sukhanov, *1917*, pp. 508–9.
32 Ibid., p. 486.
33 R. A. Wade, *Red Guards and Workers' Militias in the Russian Revolution* (Stanford, CA: Stanford University Press, 1984), p. 37.
34 Ibid., p. 43.
35 Ibid., pp. 79, 95–6.
36 Ibid., pp. 96, 105, 110.
37 Ibid., p. 112.
38 Rabinowitch, *Prelude*, p. 108.
39 R. A. Wade, 'The Rajonnye Sovety of Petrograd: The Role of Local Political Bodies in the Russian Revolution', *Jahrbücher für die Geschichte Osteuropas* 20 (1972), p. 235.
40 C. J. Read, *Lenin: A Revolutionary Life* (London: Routledge, 2005), p. 163.
41 Sukhanov, *1917*, p. 491.
42 Wade, 'Rajonnye Sovety', p. 236.
43 Ibid., pp. 237–9.
44 Sukhanov, *1917*, p. 492.
45 Rosenberg, *Liberals*, p. 220.
46 Sukhanov, *1917*, pp. 505–8, 513.
47 Ibid., pp. 522–3.

Chapter 5: Six Months of Social Revolution

1 Derived from chapter 1 of S. A. Smith, *Red Petrograd: Revolution in*

the *Factories 1917–1918* (Cambridge: Cambridge University Press, 1983).

2   Ibid., p. 55.
3   Ibid., p. 61.
4   Ibid., p. 66.
5   J. L. H. Keep, *The Russian Revolution: A Study in Mass Mobilisation* (London: Weidenfeld and Nicolson, 1976), p. 69.
6   Smith, *Red Petrograd*, pp. 76–7.
7   Ibid., p. 62.
8   Ibid., p. 170.
9   P. Flenley, 'Industrial Relations and the Economic Crisis of 1917', paper given to the Conference of the Study Group on the Russian Revolution, 8–10 January 1988.
10 Smith, *Red Petrograd*, p. 170.
11 R. P. Browder and A. F. Kerensky, *The Russian Provisional Government, 1917: Documents* (Stanford, CA: Stanford University Press, 1961), vol. 2, p. 731.
12 Ibid., p. 722.
13 Smith, *Red Petrograd*, pp. 180–1.
14 Ibid., p. 168.
15 Keep, *Russian Revolution*, p. 73.
16 Smith, *Red Petrograd*, p. 176.
17 Ibid., pp. 177, 184.
18 Ibid., p. 179.
19 Browder and Kerensky, *Provisional Government*, vol. 2, p. 723.
20 E. Acton and T. Stableford (eds), *The Soviet Union: A Documentary History*, vol. 1 (Exeter: University of Exeter Press, 2005), p. 34.
21 Smith, *Red Petrograd*, pp. 171–4.
22 Ibid., p. 176.
23 M. Donald, 'Bolshevik Activity amongst the Working Women of Petrograd in 1917', *International Review of Social History* 27 (1982), pp. 134, 139–41.
24 S. Badcock, 'Women, Protest, and Revolution: Soldiers Wives in Russia During 1917', *International Review of Social History* 49/1 (2004), p. 52.
25 Donald, 'Bolshevik Activity', p. 141.
26 Badcock, 'Women', p. 53.
27 Donald, 'Bolshevik Activity', pp. 144, 146.
28 Ibid., pp. 149–52.
29 G. J. Gill, 'The Mainsprings of Peasant Action in 1917', *Soviet Studies* 30 (1978), pp. 66, 80.
30 G. J. Gill, 'The Failure of Rural Policy in Russia, February–October 1917', *Slavic Review* 37 (1978), p. 242.
31 Ibid., pp. 242–3.
32 G. J. Gill, *Peasants and Government in the Russian Revolution* (Basingstoke: Macmillan, 1979), pp. 22, 25, 29.
33 Gill, 'Failure', p. 249.
34 Keep, *Russian Revolution*, p. 163.

35 Gill, 'Failure', p. 252.
36 Keep, *Russian Revolution*, p. 230.
37 R. Kowalski, *The Russian Revolution, 1917–1921* (London: Routledge, 1997), p. 132.
38 Keep, *Russian Revolution*, p. 166.
39 Gill, 'Failure', p. 255.
40 Ibid., *Peasant*, p. 92.
41 Keep, *Russian Revolution*, p. 166; Gill, 'Failure', p. 255.
42 Gill, *Peasant*, p. 87.
43 Ibid., 'Failure', p. 256.
44 Ibid., *Peasant*, pp. 58, 155.
45 Ibid., 'Failure', p. 250.
46 Ibid., *Peasant*, pp. 135, 143; H. White, '1917 in the Rear Garrisons', paper given to the Conference of the Study Group on the Russian Revolution, 5–7 January 1990.
47 Keep, *Russian Revolution*, pp. 209–10.
48 M. P. Price, *Dispatches from the Revolution: Russia 1916–18* (London: Pluto Press, 1997), p. 62.
49 White, 'Rear Garrisons'.
50 A. K. Wildman, 'The February Revolution in the Russian Army', *Soviet Studies* 22 (1970), pp. 14–15.
51 Ibid., pp. 16, 19–22.
52 Ibid., p. 17.
53 White, 'Rear Garrisons'.
54 Ibid.
55 This is the argument of T. F. Kuzmina in *Revolyutsionnoe dvizhenie soldatskikh mass Tsentra Rossii nakanune Oktyabrya: po materialam Moskovskgo voennogo okruga* (Moscow: Nauka, 1978).
56 Browder and Kerensky, *Provisional Government*, vol. 2, p. 1036.
57 White, 'Rear Garrisons'.

Chapter 6: Insurrection

1 R. P. Browder and A. F. Kerensky, *The Russian Provisional Government, 1917: Documents* (Stanford, CA: Stanford University Press, 1961), vol. 3, p. 1656.
2 V. I. Lenin, *Between the Two Revolutions: Articles and Speeches of 1917* (Moscow: Progress Publishers, 1971), p. 367.
3 R. A. Wade, *The Russian Revolution, 1917* (Cambridge: Cambridge University Press, 2005), p. 214.
4 Browder and Kerensky, *Provisional Government*, vol. 3, p. 1224.
5 G. R. Swain, *The Origins of the Russian Civil War* (Harlow: Longman, 1996), p. 44.
6 Lenin, *Between the Two Revolutions*, pp. 391, 394–5.
7 G. R. Swain, 'Before the Fighting Started: A Discussion on the Theme of a Third Way', *Revolutionary Russia* 4 (1991), p. 212.

8   G. R. Swain, *Trotsky* (Harlow: Pearson Education, 2006), p. 67.
9   Wade, *Russian Revolution*, pp. 221–2.
10 Lenin, *Between the Two Revolutions*, pp. 412–15.
11 Ibid., pp. 475–6, 482. See also J. White, 'Lenin, Trotsky and the Arts of Insurrection: The Congress of Soviets of the Northern Region, 11–13 October 1917', *Slavonic and East European Review* 77 (1999), p. 123.
12 Swain, *Trotsky*, p. 67.
13 *The Bolsheviks and the October Revolution: Central Committee Minutes of the Russian Social Democratic Labour Party (Bolsheviks), August 1917–February 1918* (London: Pluto Press, 1974), pp. 89–95.
14 Ibid., p. 88.
15 Wade, *Russian Revolution*, p. 225.
16 Swain, *Trotsky*, p. 68.
17 *Minutes*, p. 109.
18 Swain, *Trotsky*, p. 68.
19 Wade, *Russian Revolution*, p. 226.
20 *Minutes*, pp. 97–101.
21 Ibid., pp. 101–2, 109.
22 Ibid., p. 121.
23 Swain, *Trotsky*, pp. 69–70.
24 *Minutes*, pp. 111, 123; *Lenin Between Two Revolutions*, p. 488.
25 Wade, *Russian Revolution*, p. 231.
26 Ibid., p. 229.
27 Swain, *Trotsky*, pp. 71–2; Wade, *Russian Revolution*, p. 231.
28 Wade, *Russian Revolution*, p. 231.
29 Swain, 'Before', p. 213.
30 Swain, *Origins*, p. 46.
31 Swain, 'Before', p. 214.
32 Swain, *Origins*, p. 46.
33 Ibid., p. 47.
34 Browder and Kerensky, *Provisional Government*, vol. 3, pp. 1774–7.
35 N. N. Sukhanov, *The Russian Revolution, 1917: A Personal Record* (Princeton, NJ: Princeton University Press, 1984), p. 611.
36 Swain, *Origins*, p. 48.
37 Swain, 'Before', p. 215.
38 Swain, *Trotsky*, p. 73.
39 Ibid., p. 73.
40 *Minutes*, pp. 124–5.
41 Swain, *Trotsky*, p. 72.
42 Lenin, *Between the Revolutions*, p. 505.
43 Ibid.
44 C. J. Read, *Lenin: A Revolutionary Life* (London: Routledge, 2005), p. 182.

Chapter 7: A Soviet Government

1   G. R. Swain, *Trotsky* (Harlow: Pearson Education, 2006), pp. 74–5.

2   N. N. Sukhanov, *The Russian Revolution, 1917: A Personal Record* (Princeton, NJ: Princeton University Press, 1984), p. 643.

3   G. R. Swain, *The Origins of the Russian Civil War* (Harlow: Longman, 1996), p. 54.

4   Swain, *Trotsky*, p. 76.

5   Ibid.

6   *The Bolsheviks and the October Revolution: Central Committee Minutes of the Russian Social Democratic Labour Party (Bolsheviks), August 1917–February 1918* (London: Pluto Press, 1974), p. 126.

7   G. R. Swain, *Russian Social Democracy and the Legal Labour Movement, 1906–14* (Basingstoke: Macmillan, 1983), p. 13.

8   M. Melancon, '"Stormy Petrels": The SRs in Russia's Labor Organisations, 1905–14', *The Carl Beck Papers No. 703* (Pittsburgh: University of Pittsburgh Press, 1988), pp. 22, 40.

9   M. Melancon, '"Marching Together!": Left Bloc Activities in the Russian Revolutionary Movment, 1900–February 1917', *Slavic Review* 49 (1990), p. 249.

10 M. Melancon, *The Socialist Revolutionaries and the Russian Anti-War Movement 1914–1917* (Columbus: Ohio State University Press, 1990), pp. 53, 62, 88, 202–4.

11 M. Melancon, 'The Left SRs and the Bolshevik Uprising', in V. N. Brovkin, *The Bolsheviks in Russian Society: The Revolution and Civil Wars* (New Haven, CT: Yale University Press, 1997), p. 61.

12 Ibid., pp. 61–2.

13 I. Shteinberg, *Ot Fevralya po oktyabr' 1917g.* (Berlin: Problemy russkoi revolyutsii, 1919), pp. 63, 90. For the Spiridonova incident, see A. Rabinowitch, *Prelude to Revolution: The Petrograd Bolsheviks and the July 1917 Uprising* (Bloomington: Indiana University Press, 1968), p. 182.

14 Melancon, 'Left SRs', pp. 64, 69. For the Democratic Conference, see R. A. Wade, *The Russian Revolution, 1917* (Cambridge: Cambridge University Press, 2005), p. 214.

15 Melancon, 'Left SRs', p. 70.

16 Sukhanov, *1917*, p. 610.

17 S. Mstislavskii, *Five Days Which Transformed Russia* (London: Hutchinson, 1988), p. 112.

18 Melancon, 'Left SRs', p. 70.

19 A. Rabinowitch, *The Bolsheviks in Power: The First Year of Soviet Rule in Petrograd* (Bloomington: Indiana University Press, 2008), pp. 18–19.

20 Ibid., p. 20.

21 G. R. Swain, 'Before the Fighting Started: A Discussion on the Theme of a Third Way', *Revolutionary Russia* 4 (1991), pp. 216–17.

22 Swain, *Origins*, p. 56.

23 Rabinowitch, *Bolsheviks*, pp. 23–4.

24 Ibid., p. 27; Swain, 'Before', pp. 218–19.

25 Swain, *Origins*, p. 60.

26 Swain, 'Before', p. 219.

27   Ibid., pp. 220–2.
28   Rabinowitch, *Bolsheviks*, p. 31.
29   *Minutes*, p. 143.
30   Rabinowitch, *Bolsheviks*, p. 33.
31   *Minutes*, pp. 132–5.
32   Rabinowitch, *Bolsheviks*, p. 37.
33   Ibid., p. 39.
34   *Minutes*, p. 141.
35   Swain, 'Before', p. 227; Rabinowitch, *Bolsheviks*, p. 40.
36   *Minutes*, pp. 136–9. For Lenin's request for signed statements of support, see Rabinowitch, *Bolsheviks*, p. 41.
37   Swain, 'Before', p. 227.
38   *Minutes*, 140–2.
39   J. L. H. Keep, *The Debate on Soviet Power* (Oxford: Clarendon Press, 1979), pp. 85–6.
40   *Minutes*, p. 143.
41   Rabinowitch, *Bolsheviks*, p. 49.
42   J. Bunyan and H. H. Fisher, *The Bolshevik Revolution: Documents and Materials* (Stanford, CA: Stanford University Press, 1934), p. 206.
43   A. Ascher (ed.), *The Mensheviks in the Russian Revolution* (London: Thames and Hudson, 1976), pp. 44–5.
44   G. D. Surh, *1905 in St. Petersburg: Labor, Society and Revolution* (Stanford, CA: Stanford University Press, 1989), p. 330.
45   Swain, *Legal*, pp. 13–20.
46   Ibid., p. 40.
47   Ibid., p. 46.
48   Ibid., p. 141.
49   Ibid., pp. 181–2.
50   I. Thatcher, 'The St. Petersburg/Petrograd *Mezhraionka*, 1913–17: The Rise and Fall of a Movement for Social Democratic Unity', *Slavonic and East European Review* 87 (2009), p. 286.
51   R. B. McKean, *St. Petersburg between the Revolutions* (New Haven, CT: Yale University Press, 1990), pp. 402, 558 n.134.
52   B. C. Allen, *Alexander Shlyapnikov, 1885–1937: Life of an Old Bolshevik* (Leiden: Brill, 2015), pp. 49–51.
53   Ibid., p. 65.

Chapter 8: The Bolshevik–Left SR Coalition

1   J. L. H. Keep, *The Debate on Soviet Power* (Oxford: Clarendon Press, 1979), pp. 86, 89.
2   A. Rabinowitch, *The Bolsheviks in Power: The First Year of Soviet Rule in Petrograd* (Bloomington: Indiana University Press, 2008), p. 50.
3   Ibid., p. 52.
4   *Partiya Levykh Sotsialistov Revolyutsionerov: Dokumenty i Materialy*, 2 vols (Moscow: Rosspen, 2000), vol. 1, p. 107. Hereafter *LSR*.

5   T. A. Sivokhina, *Krakh melkoburzhuaznoi oppozitsii* (Moscow: Politizdat, 1973), p. 74.

6   Rabinowitch, *Bolsheviks*, pp. 83–4.

7   This summary is derived from J. Channon, 'Peasant Revolution and Land Reform: Land Redistribution in European Russia, October 1917–1920', PhD thesis, University of Birmingham, 1983.

8   G. R. Swain, *The Origins of the Russian Civil War* (Harlow: Longman, 1996), p. 76.

9   Ibid., pp. 76–7.

10   *LSR*, vol. 1, pp. 124, 133.

11   Keep, *Debate*, p. 144.

12   Swain, *Origins*, p. 80.

13   Keep, *Debate*, p. 264.

14   Swain, *Origins*, p. 81.

15   Ibid., p. 82.

16   Rabinowitch, *Bolsheviks*, p. 126.

17   Ibid., pp. 47, 81.

18   Keep, *Debate*, p. 173.

19   Rabinowitch, *Bolsheviks*, pp. 84–7.

20   Swain, *Origins*, pp. 89–90.

21   Ibid., p. 91.

22   William G. Rosenberg, 'Russian Labor and Bolshevik Power after October', *Slavic Review* 44/2 (1985), pp. 220, 230.

23   Ibid., pp. 223–4, 226, 230.

24   Ibid., p. 227.

25   P. H. Avrich, 'The Bolshevik Revolution and Workers' Control in Russian Industry', *Slavic Review* 22 (1963), pp. 43, 49.

26   W. Rosenberg, 'Workers and Workers' Control in the Russian Revolution', *History Workshop* 5 (1978), p. 92.

27   Avrich, 'Workers' Control', p. 49 n.11.

28   Rosenberg, 'Workers' Control', p. 95.

29   Avrich, 'Workers' Control', pp. 51, 56, 61.

30   Rosenberg, 'Labor', p. 224.

31   A. K. Wildman, *The End of the Imperial Russian Army: the Road to Soviet Power and Peace* (Princeton, NJ: Princeton University Press, 1987), pp. 318–49.

32   O. H. Radkey, *Russia Goes to the Polls* (Ithaca, NY: Cornell University Press, 1977), p. 38.

33   Swain, *Origins*, pp. 92–4.

34   Ibid., p. 95.

35   Ibid., p. 99.

36   V. I. Lenin, *Selected Works in Three Volumes* (Moscow: Progress, 1970), vol. 2, p. 43.

37   G. R. Swain, *Trotsky* (Harlow: Pearson Education, 2006), p. 82.

38   Ibid., p. 29.

39   Ibid.

40   Rabinowitch, *Bolsheviks*, pp. 146–6, 152–3, 155, 157.

41 Ibid., pp. 161–6.
42 Swain, *Trotsky*, p. 83.
43 Rabinowitch, *Bolsheviks*, pp. 175–8, 197, 205.
44 Swain, *Trotsky*, p. 84.
45 Swain, *Origins*, p. 131.
46 *LSR*, vol. 1, pp. 217, 295, 315, 548.
47 Swain, *Origins*, p. 131.
48 *LSR*, vol. 2, pp. 70–1.
49 Ibid., pp. 91, 95.
50 Swain, *Origins*, pp. 157–9, 164–72.
51 *LSR*, vol. 2, pp. 72, 100, 144.
52 Ibid., p. 139.
53 Ibid., pp. 161–3, 167, 169, 178.
54 Rabinowitch, *Bolsheviks*, pp. 288, 442 n. 26.
55 *LSR*, vol. 2, pp. 304–5.
56 Rabinowitch, *Bolsheviks*, p. 289.
57 G. R. Swain, 'Vacietis: The Enigma of the Red Army's First Commander', *Revolutionary Russia* 16 (2003), p. 75.
58 Swain, 'Russia's Garibaldi: The Revolutionary Life of Mikhail Artemevich Muraviev', *Revolutionary Russia* 11 (1998), pp. 70–5; Swain, *Origins*, p. 177.
59 Swain, *Trotsky*, p. 94.
60 D-W. C. Poole, *An American Diplomat in Bolshevik Russia* (Madison: University of Wisconsin Press, 2014), p. 134.
61 Swain, *Trotsky*, p. 99.
62 V. I. Lenin, *Polnoe sobranie sochinenii*, 5th edn (Moscow: Politizdat, 1963), vol. 50, pp. 142–3.

Index

The letter *f* following an entry indicates a page that includes a figure.